VGM Professional Careers Series

W9-DHO-169

CAREERS
IN GOVERNMENT

MARY ELIZABETH PITZ

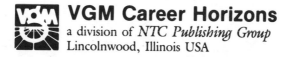

VGM Career Horizons
a division of *NTC Publishing Group*
Lincolnwood, Illinois USA

Cover Photo Credit:
Architect of the Capitol

Library of Congress Cataloging-in-Publication Data

Pitz, Mary Elizabeth.
    Careers in government / Mary Elizabeth Pitz.
        p.   cm.
    ISBN 0-8442-4194-6 (hard) ISBN 0-8442-4195-4 (soft)
    1. Civil service positions—United States   I. Title.
JK716.P58   1994
350'.00023'73—dc20   93-47955
                                               CIP

Published by VGM Career Horizons, a division of NTC Publishing Group
4255 West Touhy Avenue
Lincolnwood (Chicago), Illinois 60646-1975, U.S.A.
© 1994 by NTC Publishing Group. All rights reserved.
No part of this book may be reproduced, stored in a retrieval system,
or transmitted in any form or by any means,
electronic, mechanical, photocopying, recording or otherwise,
without the prior permission of NTC Publishing Group.
Manufactured in the United States of America.

4 5 6 7 8 9 0 VP 9 8 7 6 5 4 3 2 1

CONTENTS

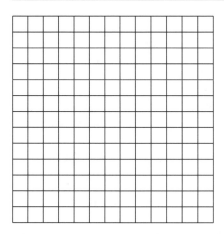

INTRODUCTION: GOVERNMENT CAREERS

Choosing a career in government, whether at the federal, state, county, or municipal level, is choosing a way of life. It involves a different mind-set than going to work at the local manufacturing plant or for a law firm. This book is designed to help make the decision that is right for you and to aid you in your search for a job in government.

The information and recommended actions in this book are for nonelective positions. Obviously elected offices represent a highly visible career in government. Many elected positions offer reasonable pay, wield considerable power, and give the elected official the opportunity to serve the voters. Since the voters evaluate the performance of elected officials every time they vote, the elected official operates with the pressure of the next election always in mind.

Included with electees are those administrators, commissioners, and functionaries who are appointed by elected officials. Both elected and appointed officials serve at the discretion of the voter. In fact, the careers of many highly placed nonelected professionals in government are also influenced directly and indirectly by elected officials and the decisions they make. Deciding on an elected office, running a campaign, campaigning, and the other considerations involved in choosing an elected position are a subject for another book.

This book focuses on the nonelective positions available in government. Since elected officials and the decisions they make have a definite impact on the institutions, agencies, and bureaucracies that administer programs, govern society, and enforce laws, they can not be disregarded in planning a career in government. Generally speaking, the higher a nonelected position is, the more that position will be affected by the outcome of elections. People working in the beginning to middle levels of government are normally not influenced by which party or person is in power. The major exception, of course, is when the decision is made to downsize or eliminate a department or agency; then everyone is touched by the power of elected officials.

Whether you are changing careers or simply looking for a job, exploring the opportunities available in government will help you decide if a career there is for you. Government offers excellent career choices in many different fields. One of the first realities you will encounter is the enormity of government. The sheer size of government can be mind-boggling.

Government employs millions of people with widely divergent backgrounds, credentials, and experience. More than 3 million civilians work for the federal government alone. Millions more are employed by state, county, and municipal governments. In reality, government hires more than 1,000 people a day in jobs ranging from mail clerk to nuclear physicist. Sometimes, government is the only employer (e.g., law enforcement); in other cases, government is the largest employer (e.g., of engineers).

Traditionally, government has been a highly desirable career choice because it pays good starting salaries, has attractive benefits, offers continued training, ensures promotion through the middle ranks, and provides job security. Today, the situation is in transition because our country is in transition. Changes in the White House, in Congress, in the Supreme Court, in state legislatures, in local governing bodies, and in the economy will profoundly affect the availability of jobs in government in the nineties.

For this reason, the material in this book is best utilized as a guide in helping you determine what type of government career you would like to pursue and then counseling you in the ways and means of a successful job search. It is not meant to be the definitive word on careers in government. With the rapid changes occurring in government today, definitive advice is out-dated before it can be published.

Government eventually mirrors the economic health and societal priorities of its citizens. The changes occurring in the economy and in social issues are eventually reflected in all levels of government. Although they tend to happen more slowly than in the private sector, they do occur and are occurring more rapidly than in the past.

Cutbacks and technology are the two major issues forcing federal agencies and other government offices to downsize their staff as well as revise their procedures and practices. This is more than a trend, this is the reality of the nineties. Even with these permanent new developments, working for the government still offers many advantages. The decision is yours.

To help you in your decision-making process, the information in this book is divided into three main sections. The first section discusses the advantages of working for the government and relates the real-life experiences of men and women who have opted for careers in government. The purpose of this section is to present the benefits and the considerations involved in deciding to work for the government as well as the personality that seems to do well in pursuing a career in government. The brief case histories of individuals from different backgrounds who are pursuing various careers help you see how others live and why their choices work successfully for them.

The second section concentrates on the rudiments of job hunting. Because it describes the step-by-step process involved in developing a proper worksheet, filling out applications, preparing a resume, writing letters, and having a successful interview, it is the most detailed portion of the book. The advice presented will benefit you, regardless of the career you choose. As you learn to use the recommended communication tools, you will begin adapting certain techniques of your own that will help you throughout your career.

The third section provides an overview of jobs at all levels of government and is divided into two subsections—the federal government and other government (state, county, and municipal). It is probably the most helpful in giving a clearer idea of the numerous classifications of jobs at the federal level and a better perspective of the federal agencies as well as the great diversity of positions available in local, county, and state government.

Jobs are broadly divided into two major groupings. The first covers administrative, professional, and scientific positions and the second includes clerical, blue-collar, and technical positions. Following the federal description of these two groupings, there is a lengthy chapter describing 39 of the federal agencies. This will give you an awareness of the vast differences and corresponding opportunities available in the federal system. Since these agencies hire according to GS ratings and standards, they have no real counterpart at the local level. The state, county, and municipal descriptions of jobs available in the two major groupings follow the federal material.

The three appendices contain lists of resources and other useful information that will help point you in additional directions. Job hunting is an ongoing exercise. Some people continue it long past retirement age. It can be enjoyable if you decide to use it as one of the more practical learning experiences you will have. You can be your best friend or your worst enemy. The choice is yours; it is one you will have to make every day as you go about the process of finding a job.

When you get discouraged, remember everyone does. This is a normal feeling. Then do something practical—look up additional announcements, contact another agency, revise your resume, et cetera. Specific action dispels discouragement and depression. It also has the added bonus of encouraging you to keep trying. You can make your own luck by being proactive every day. The more people you contact, the more applications you correctly fill out, the more letters you write, the better your chances are of being in the right place at the right time. Done effectively, job hunting is a full-time job.

Once you are hired, actually write down you what you have learned, what you would do differently, how you feel about the process, and the individuals and resources that were the most helpful to you during your search. Then put it in your files, along with your resume, worksheet, and correspondence. Sooner or later, you will be able to use this information to your advantage.

Good luck and happy hunting!

Section I
Government, Yes or No

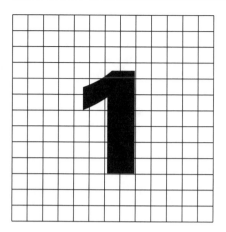

WHAT TO DO

Before you can decide whether you want to work for the government, you have to know what you would like to do. For some occupations—e.g., law making, law enforcement—the answer is simple because they are possible only with the government. For others—e.g., fire fighters, paramedics, or lawyers, which exist in the private sector as well—the answer is still fairly easy since government, by far, is the larger employer. For occupations that exist in both the public and private sector, you will have to weigh the pros and cons of working for the government and then make your decision. This chapter is designed to help you determine what your qualifications are and to acquaint you with the rewards and benefits government employment offers.

Determining what you would like to do is perhaps the most challenging aspect of the job-hunt process. It is a little more complicated that simply choosing to be an astronaut, a forest ranger, or an accountant. An essential part of the process is to know what best suits you, your abilities, your personality, and your lifestyle.

DECIDING ON A PROFESSION

There are numerous books written on this topic alone. However, a relatively easy way of helping you understand what will work for you is to answer the following questions.

What really motivates you?

What is the most important to you—prestige, money, or service?
It is helpful to prioritize these three basics and know if they are short-term concerns or part of your lifelong ambition. For example, if you have pressing financial problems, money may be a prime concern in

the short term. However, once you are in a position to alleviate some of the financial pressure, you may discover that helping others is more important to you than money. Knowing that about yourself at the start of a job search will benefit you in the short and long terms.

How flexible are you in your living conditions?

Some considerations are geographic (the South, Northwest, Midwest), some are locational (cities, small towns, rural areas), and others—available school systems, church groups, and similar issues—will pertain more to your family members. You may find that while you might prefer certain conditions you are willing to be more flexible if it will benefit your career or you may discover you are not. There is no right or wrong answer. Whatever you learn about yourself will benefit you in your career planning.

Under what conditions do you like to work?

This includes knowing if you prefer indoors to outdoors, working autonomously or on a team, in a large institution or in a more intimate environment, as well as a number of related concerns.

What are your skills?

What are your interests?

What are your active and latent talents?

Are you interested in continuing training and learning on a formal or informal basis?

What is your physical condition?

What is your education?

What is your work history?

As you answer these questions, you will learn more about what you really want to do as well as what you are currently capable of handling. That is why this first step is the proverbial giant one.

MATCHING YOUR ABILITIES WITH AVAILABILITIES

The second step is exploring what best fits your short- and long-term capabilities, talents, and desires. As you read the following sections, you will become more aware of the extensive range of employment opportunities government offers. Your task is to decipher which ones are a match for you.

After you determine which occupations appeal to you, you will need to find out what the specific qualifications are for those fields. Then you will start your search for available jobs. Government jobs generally require a lengthy application process, except for the lower-end clerical and unskilled jobs where there is continual turnover. For this reason, it is better to determine if you need to acquire additional skills or education to qualify for a particular occupation before you begin applying for it.

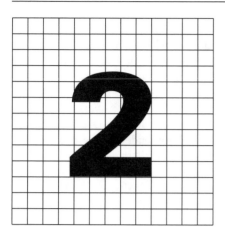

THE NEXT STEP

ACQUIRING ADDITIONAL QUALIFICATIONS

More often than not, you may find you will have to prepare for an occupation by taking extra courses, receiving further training, or even acquiring a degree or certificate. This can be very expensive. More importantly, it is no guarantee that you will be hired for the position you desire, which is why you want to be certain that you are making the correct decision for you.

Next you need to evaluate how much energy and time you are willing to devote to improving your skills. You also need to be aware of your flexibility concerning relocation, adjusting your financial requirements, and similar issues. To do that requires research on your part.

Research is both internal and external. Internal research is the time and energy you devote to deciding what you want to do and preparing for a job search. External research refers to locating job opportunities.

Since the employment situation in government is changing dramatically, it is strongly recommended to have a second choice for an occupation. Selecting two occupations makes sense. Given the length of time it takes to obtain a government job plus the current cutbacks and freezes on hiring, your chances of being hired are increased twofold if you have a backup plan. Plus, it gives you added flexibility.

If your first choice requires substantial training, you may want to pursue another career while preparing for what you really want to do. You may decide to take a job that is more in line with your second choice, simply because it is available, rather than being unemployed. Or, you may take a job that puts you in a position to transfer to a department where you would really like to work. Most career counselors believe the majority of people will change careers at least twice during their working life.

In fact, that may be the reason you are currently considering a career in government. Government offers tremendous flexibility in career switching. It is far easier to transfer in government than in the private sector, because government personnel are more comfortable hiring someone who has proven he or she can work within the system, rather than an outsider.

To have an overview of what changes are occurring in various occupations, you may want to consult various short- and long-range forecasts for rising or declining professions, which are recommended at the back of this book. But remember these are only predictions. While they may be accurate, you must remember there are exceptions to every rule. The most important criterion for job satisfaction is liking what you are doing. In study after study, researchers have observed that when people like what they are doing, they do a good job, make consistently positive contributions, and are rarely ill.

As you begin investigating what is open to you, you will want to consider what is actually available in your immediate area or relatively close to you. You also will want to explore your own private network of friends, family, and coworkers to learn of any job openings. Sometimes government positions are available locally, although the hiring may be done through a central or regional office. This is more true of federal and state positions than county or municipal jobs.

There are several government offices whose sole purpose is to help citizens find employment within the government. In addition to the federal government, many large states and counties have their own offices for assisting people in obtaining jobs.

OFFICE OF PERSONNEL MANAGEMENT

The Office of Personnel Management (OPM) in the past served as the federal government's personnel agency, which is quite different than an employment agency. Now that the federal hiring process is considerably more decentralized, OPM has become less involved. Individual agencies are taking more responsibility for announcing vacancies and rating, interviewing, and selecting applicants. OPM still provides overall support and ensures compliance with federal hiring procedures, but the wave of the future is for prospective employees to take a far more active role in contacting individual agencies to identify openings.

FEDERAL JOB INFORMATION CENTERS

The regional and local offices of OPM are the Federal Job Information Centers (FJICs). (For a complete listing of FJICs see the end of this chapter.) Their primary responsibility is to provide assistance to anyone looking for a federal job, which means they have all the job announcements and requisite application forms. FJICs are also charged with the responsibility of explaining where and how to apply for jobs as well as referring you to testing locations and employment agencies. In reality, the system does not work quite that easily.

Many of these centers do not have attendants. All the information is simply posted on bulletin boards. An interested applicant is required to address a mailing label noting the information he or she desires and then insert it into a mail slot. Within 10 days, the person will receive the job information and an application form. Even the phone numbers prominently displayed only offer prerecorded information. It is difficult and often very frustrating to find an authorized person to answer questions you may have. This is also true of many agencies.

The job you apply for may or may not be in your immediate area. Most job descriptions will tell you where the job is. In other instances, hiring for certain federal positions, e.g., an FBI agent, is done in Washington, D.C. If this is true for the occupation you select, then you will begin the process from your own home, but you should recognize that you will probably be relocated once you are hired.

JOB SERVICE OFFICES

To learn where jobs are available at all levels of government will require some legwork on your part. The state equivalent of the FJIC is the Job Service Office, the address for which will be in the state government section of your telephone book. State Job Service Offices are run by the state government and have the most up-to-date material about open jobs. Counselors in their offices give aptitude tests, suggest training programs, and assist you in finding a job.

If you live in a remote area, you may want to phone the nearest Job Service Office and make an appointment or write for information before going. The Job Service Office is a state agency whose main purpose is to help citizens find employment with the state. That is its job. Do not feel as if you are imposing.

OTHER RESOURCES

In addition to the FJIC and the Job Service Offices, there are school counselors or placement services. The amount of help a counselor will provide to someone who has not attended the school varies widely. As a minimum, however, you should be able to use some of the printed material. You will also be able to scan the bulletin boards for information about local job possibilities.

Books

There are several categories of books that will help you in pursuing a government career: books about your chosen occupation, books about the government, and books about job hunting.

Books have been written about almost every occupation in which you could possibly be interested. Your librarian can help you find them. In addition, there are some very large books that describe hundreds of occupations. Two are published by the government, but they are not restricted to government occupations. They are the *Dictionary of Occupational Titles* and the *Occupational Outlook Handbook.* Most people only want to read a few pages in these books, so, instead of buying them, look for them in a library.

Several books and pamphlets deal only with the government. Most are published by the government, and some are no more trustworthy than other recruiting literature. Some are free, some are not. Before buying a government book or pamphlet, contact the agency that published it; you can often get a single copy free. Sometimes, members of Congress obtain free copies of government publications for their constituents.

Here are some useful books published by the government. The first two are *not* free.

U.S. Government Manual is published each year by the General Services Administration, Office of the Federal Register. It contains almost 900 pages of names, addresses, telephone numbers, and descriptions for every federal agency. Sources of information about employment are usually given.

Qualification Standards for White-Collar Positions Under the General Schedule is published by the Office of Personnel Management. It fills two fat loose-leaf binders, and there is a companion volume for blue-collar work. They are supplemented by position descriptions for all the government occupations. The position descriptions are small booklets, but their number makes up for their size. Also, there are comparable loose-leaf books for the qualification standards for occupations with the U.S. Postal Service.

The descriptions of jobs in this book are distilled from all these volumes. These books are not readily available, and they are written in a language peculiar to personnel offices. However, it is this last feature that makes them worth searching out; their language is the language you want to use on your application form. The books—sometimes on microfiche—can be found in their true home: the personnel offices of government agencies. They are also at the Federal Job Information Centers. Incidentally, the fat book for white-collar jobs is always called X-118; the blue-collar manual is X-118A. Occupations are listed by their GS or WG number.

Among the timely books not published by the government is the *College Placement Annual.* It gives current information each year about government and nongovernment hiring plans. Published by the College Placement Council, it is available through college placement offices.

In addition to the *U.S. Government Manual* described above, there are several commercially published directories to government offices. You can use them to find the names of more people to contact. Two of the most complete are the *Washington Information Directory* published by Congressional Quarterly and the *Federal Yellow Book* published by the Washington Monitor Inc. The first is arranged by subject; the second is by agency. Telephone books are the easiest way to find agencies in nearby cities and towns; the library should have them.

Job-hunting manuals have proliferated in recent years. Two good ones are *What Color Is Your Parachute?* by Richard N. Bolles (Berkeley, California: Ten Speed Press, 1993) and *Joyce Lain Kennedy's Career Book* by Joyce Lain Kennedy and Dr. Darryl Laramore (Lincolnwood, Illinois: VGM Career Horizons, 1992).

Besides books, magazines—especially those aimed at young people— often have articles on jobs and job hunting. Some magazines, such as *Career World* and the *Occupational Outlook Quarterly,* are devoted exclusively to these subjects.

You can also contact potential employers and people now working in a field to determine what is open at present and to evaluate how the future looks.

FURTHER SCHOOLING

If you are considering additional formal education or training, you have to know what is required. There are some private schools that offer civil service courses for passing certain exams. As these schools are run for profit, be sure you know exactly what will be taught and exactly how much you will have to pay.

Unethical schools may say the government requires a civil service course or that they can guarantee you a government job. Both statements are totally untrue. No course is required for any civil service exam. OPM has never approved any. There is no single civil service test that is given for all federal jobs. Many positions do not even require a written test. And no one can promise you a civil service job.

Checking References   ·   It is important to know what the school's reputation is. There are several ways of doing this. Begin by asking the school how many of their graduates are successfully employed and where they are working. Contact several graduates and ask them how beneficial the school or institution was in obtaining their job. You may also ask them if their extra training makes a difference in how they perform in their job. The purpose is to evaluate whether the investment you are considering making in additional schooling will truly be worthwhile.

You may also consider asking the employers of various graduates what their opinion of the school is. Any school that refuses to give references should be treated with caution and suspicion. Another way to obtain essential information is to contact people already working in the field as well as possible future employers. This will give you a better perspective on your job potential. The Better Business Bureau will be able to tell you if any complaints have been lodged against the school.

If you do not know where to go to obtain information on additional training or education, contact your local librarian. The public library has many reference materials whose sole purpose is to provide information on education and training programs.

FEDERAL JOB INFORMATION CENTERS

Current federal job opportunities information is available by push-button telephone. You may call the Federal Job Information Center 7 days a week, 24 hours a day for a variety of topics on federal employment, including such subjects as jobs for which applications are being accepted, student programs, and summer employment. Of course, job announcements and the all-important SF-171 are also available at Federal Job Information Centers.

Alabama
Building 600, Suite 341
3322 Memorial Parkway S.
Huntsville, AL 35801-5311

Alaska
222 W. Seventh Ave., #22
Anchorage, AK 99513-7572

Arizona
Century Plaza Building, Room 1415
3225 N. Central Ave.
Phoenix, AZ 85012

Arkansas
(See Oklahoma Listing)

California
9650 Flair Drive, Suite 100A
El Monte, CA 91731

4695 Watt Ave., North Entrance
Sacramento, CA 95660-5592

Federal Building, Room 4-S-9
880 Front St.
San Diego, CA 92188

P.O. Box 7405
211 Main St., Second Floor, Room 235)
San Francisco, CA 94120

Colorado
P.O. Box 25167
(Located at 12345 W. Alameda
    Parkway, Lakewood)
Denver, CO 80225

Connecticut
Federal Building, Room 613
450 Main St.
Hartford, CT 06103

Delaware
(See Phildelphia Listing)

District of Columbia
1900 E St. N.W., Room 1416
Washington, D.C. 20415

Florida
Commodore Building, Suite 150
3444 McCrory Place
Orlando, FL 32803-3701

Georgia
Richard B. Russell Federal Building
Room 940A, 75 Spring St. S.W.
Atlanta, GA 30303

Hawaii
(Hawaiian Islands and overseas)
Federal Building, Room 5316
300 Ala Moana Blvd.
Honolulu, HI 96850

Idaho
(See Washington Listing)

Illinois
175 W. Jackson Blvd., Room 530
Chicago, IL 60604

Indiana
Minton-Capehart Federal Building
575 N. Pennsylvania St.
Indianapolis, IN 46204
(For Clark, Dearborn, and Floyd
    counties see Ohio listing)

Iowa
(For Scott County see Illinois
    listing; for Pottawatamie County
    see Kansas listing)

Kansas
One-Twenty Building, Room 101
120 S. Market St.
Wichita, KS 67202

Kentucky
(See Ohio listing; for Henderson
    County see Indiana listing)

Louisiana
1515 Poydras St., Suite 608
New Orleans, LA 70112

Maine
(See New Hampshire Listing)

Maryland
Garmatz Federal Building
101 W. Lombard St.
Baltimore, MD 21201

Massachusetts
Thos. P. O'Neill, Jr. Federal
    Building
10 Causeway St.
Boston, MA 02222-1031

Michigan
477 Michigan Ave., Room 565
Detroit, MI 48226

Minnesota
Federal Building, Room 501
Ft. Snelling
St. Paul, MN 55111

Mississippi
(See Alabama Listing)

Missouri
Federal Building, Room 134
601 E. 12th St.
Kansas City, MO 64106
(For counties west of and including
    Mercer, Grundy, Livingston,
    Carroll, Saline, Pettis, Benton,
    Hickory, Dallas, Webster,
    Douglas, and Ozark)

400 Old Post Office Building
815 Olive St.
St. Louis, MO 63101
(For all other Missouri counties not
    listed under Kansas City above)

Montana
(See Colorado listing)

Nebraska
(See Kansas listing)

Nevada
(See Sacramento, CA, listing)

New Hampshire
Thomas J. McIntyre Federal
    Building
Room 104
80 Daniel St.
Portsmouth, NH 03801-3879

New Jersey
Peter W. Rodino, Jr., Federal
    Building
970 Broad St.
Newark, NJ 07102

New Mexico
Federal Building
421 Gold Ave. S.W.
Albuquerque, NM 87102

New York
Jacob K. Javits Federal Building
26 Federal Plaza
New York, NY 10278

James H. Hanley Federal Building
100 S. Clinton St.
Syracuse, NY 13260

North Carolina
P.O. Box 25069
4505 Falls of the Neuse Road
Suite 450
Raleigh, NC 27611-5069

North Dakota
(See Minnesota Listing)

Ohio
Federal Building, Room 506
200 W. Second St.
Dayton, OH 45402
(For Van Wert, Auglaize, Hardin,
Marion, Crawford, Richland,
Ashland, Wayne, Stark, Caroll,
Columbiana counties and all
counties north of these see
Michigan listing)

Oklahoma
(Mail only)
200 N.W. Fifth St., Second Floor
Oklahoma City, OK 73102

Oregon
Federal Building, Room 376
1220 S.W. Third Ave.
Portland, OR 97204

Pennsylvania
Federal Building, Room 168
P.O. Box 761
Harrisburg, PA 17108

Wm. J. Green, Jr., Federal Building
600 Arch St.
Philadelphia, PA 19106

Federal Building
1000 Liberty Ave., Room 119
Pittsburgh, PA 15222

Puerto Rico
Frederico Degetau Federal Building
Carlos E. Chardon Street
Hato Rey, PR 00918

Rhode Island
Pastore Federal Building
Room 310, Kennedy Plaza
Providence, RI 02903

South Carolina
(See Raleigh, NC, listing)

South Dakota
(See Minnesota Listing)

Tennessee
200 Jefferson Ave.
Suite 1312
Memphis, TN 38103-2335

Texas
(Mail or phone only)
1100 Commerce St., Room 6B12,
Dallas, TX 75242

8610 Broadway, Room 305
San Antonio, TX 78217

Utah
(See Colorado listing)

Vermont
(See New Hampshire listing)

Virginia
Federal Building, Room 500
200 Granby St.
Norfolk, VA 23510-1886

Washington
Federal Building
915 Second Ave.
Seattle, WA 98174

Wyoming
(See Colorado listing)

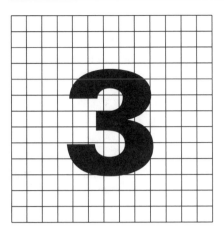

FINDING A JOB

If you want to work for government, you will have to do more than send out a letter or two. The federal government is the largest government employer. What is true of the federal government is generally true for local governments, although to a lesser degree. No one person, office, or agency can direct you to all the openings available at any given time.

Although the largest concentration of federal jobs is in Washington, D.C., 85% of federal employees work in other regions of the country. Only 5% live and work outside the country. With the increasing decentralization in hiring, individual agencies and their local offices, as pointed out in Chapter 2, are excellent places to begin your search. Despite cutbacks and freezes, openings are being filled every day.

THE MERIT SYSTEM

Most states and large local governments use some form of merit system for job openings. The larger the government is, the more likely it is to have a merit system.

Under a merit system, the duties and responsibilities of a particular job are clearly defined. All applicants for a position must be ranked according to their skills and training; the position must then be offered to one of the most highly ranked applicants.

Note that the job need not go to the highest-ranked individual, but it must be awarded to one of the highest. The person doing the hiring has some leeway in the actual hiring. A school principal, for example, often has the last word in employing a new teacher.

For this reason, it is important to conduct a job search to the best of your ability and not wait for your name to come to the top of the list. People are more likely to hire someone they have spoken with or who has contacted them than a name on a paper.

The specifics of merit systems differ from one government to another. But in all of them, when a position opens up and someone needs to be hired, an announcement of some kind is normally issued.

ANNOUNCEMENTS

Announcements can be a single page or a small booklet. Announcements almost always indicate the occupations being filled, their salary range, the qualifications required, the duties performed in the job, application procedures, and sources of more information.

Three kinds of announcements are common.

- *Open announcement.* Applications are always accepted. Typically, this procedure is followed only for occupations with steady turnover, especially in the clerical field.
- *Announcement of an examination.* Applications are being accepted for evaluation or for a test; only after the evaluation will people be considered for actual job openings as they arise.
- *Position announcement.* Applications are being accepted for a job that is currently available. In many cases, the people doing the hiring only consider applicants who have already been evaluated as a result of an announcement of an examination.

Note that you must often answer two announcements to find one job: first, an announcement of an examination, and second, a position announcement. This means that *you cannot look for a job on Friday and start work on Monday.* Even for clerical positions, where the need is constant and the evaluation process streamlined, you can easily spend 3 to 6 months between the day you decide to look for a job and the day you start work. In many other occupations—such as police officer, fire fighter, and teacher—hiring takes place only once a year. If you miss the date on which applications to take a test are being accepted, you may have to wait an entire year before you can apply. The test itself may be some months later than the cutoff date for applications, and actual hiring may not take place for several months more. As a consequence, *three years* can pass between your decision to seek a job and your first paycheck. If you do miss the filing date, you'll at least have plenty of time to prepare for the test.

GENERAL REQUIREMENTS AND TYPES OF TESTS

Besides the specific qualifications for the job, applicants must usually meet some general requirements. United States citizenship is often required. Many state and local governments also prefer to hire residents as much as possible, but as a practical matter, they will hire otherwise qualified people for hard-to-fill jobs. For example, when librarians were hard to find during the 1960s, residency requirements were often ignored; now they are more often adhered to. According to John Zehrig in *Careers in State and Local Government,* only about half of all governments require residency.

Governments often—but not always—have a standard procedure to evaluate job applicants. The procedure is often called an examination, although no test might be given. The most frequently used evaluation procedures are the following:

- *Written tests.* Often multiple choice, samples of the tests are usually available from the government. Commercial publishers also sell books of sample tests for many occupations.
- *Performance tests.* Applicants for clerical and craft jobs must often show that they can operate the equipment or use the tools needed on the job.
- *Physical agility.* Applicants for police, fire fighter, sanitation, or other positions that require specific levels of strength or agility must take tests designed to show that they can perform the same type of tasks as workers in the occupation.
- *Medical examinations.* Generally, applicants should be in good health. For some jobs, such as fire fighter and police officer, standards are more rigorous than usual.
- *Ratings of education, training, and experience.* For many jobs, especially at the professional entry level, candidates are judged on the basis of the appropriateness of their education and experience to the occupation. An announcement that a government is accepting applications for such an evaluation should indicate the kind of education and experience sought. If you fill out such an application, it is your responsibility to make sure that your forms have all the needed information, even to the point of using the very words of the job description where appropriate. *Your rating depends exclusively on the evaluator's ability to find the required qualifications on your application.*
- *Interviews.* These are similar to the rating of education and experience described above. Interviews are used for occupations in which workers have frequent contact with the public, including police officer, fire fighter, and claims examiner.
- *All of the above.* For some jobs—police and fire fighter recruits, for example—all these evaluation procedures are used.

In addition, many employers, both private and public, are requiring job applicants to sign affidavits that attest to the applicants' marital status, citizenship, and criminal record, if any. It is a mistake to attempt to conceal any facts about yourself. You will spend a lot of time and money and suffer the loss of your hopes and dreams if you are found out.

If you lie, the chances are excellent that you *will* be found out. Your signature on a false affidavit is all the grounds needed to terminate your employment. You will be better off if you are truthful, even if you must ask permission to explain the circumstances behind some of your responses. Section II explains this aspect of your job search in detail.

In most cases, after you take a test or submit evidence of your education and experience, the personnel department rates you and notifies you of your rating. If you score highly enough, you are eligible for employment. Even a high rating is no guarantee of a job, however, and—as said above—your chances of employment are almost always improved if you go out and look for a position rather than wait for the personnel department to send your name to someone with a vacancy.

FINDING THE ANNOUNCEMENT

Governments publicize their announcements several ways. The following are the most common.

- *Bulletin boards* in government buildings are almost always used. The obvious place is near the personnel office, but announcements are also found elsewhere. The state of Connecticut lists 70 places where it posts announcements, including courthouses and hospitals.
- *Public libraries,* perhaps because branches are often located throughout a government's area, often receive copies of all announcements.
- *Local newspapers* print brief notices of job openings in the help-wanted section.
- *Job Banks,* which are run by the Job Service, a state agency, usually list both state and local position announcements as well as other jobs. The locations of Job Service Offices are given in the state government section of telephone books. The Job Bank, or listing, is also sometimes available at libraries and schools.
- *Community organizations,* such as the YMCA, NAACP, and churches, receive announcements; Baltimore sends such notices to more than 100 organizations.
- *College placement offices* often post job announcements; you can usually check the bulletin board even if you are not enrolled.
- *Newspapers and other periodicals* aimed at government workers—federal, state, or local—carry position announcements. Examples of such newspapers are *The Chief* in New York City and the *Federal Times* in Washington, D.C. Besides the announcements, the articles in such newspapers can point you toward agencies that are likely to begin hiring even before an official announcement is issued.
- *Publications of associations of government workers* carry both job notices and pertinent articles on trends. Titles of such publications appear throughout this book.

- *Publications of associations in fields with many government workers,* such as civil engineering and nursing, also carry both help-wanted ads and informative articles. These publications, too, are listed throughout this book.
- *Commercial publications* also collect and print the job vacancy announcements for several agencies or governments; some publications are limited to a single level of government, such as federal, state, city, or county; others focus on all governments within a region. Titles of some of these publications are given in Appendix A. Check with a librarian to learn which would be most useful to you.
- *Recorded telephone messages.* Many governments, especially the larger ones, have regularly updated recorded messages concerning openings and announcements. The number will usually be listed in the government section of the telephone book under the agency's name.

When you find an announcement, make careful note of the following information:

- The date by which you must apply.
- If the announcement is for an examination, the titles of the occupations covered.
- If the announcement is for positions, the titles of the jobs and where they are.
- The minimum education and experience required.
- The job duties.
- Where to send your application.
- Whom to contact for more information, if stated.

If you are going to be evaluated on the basis of your education and experience rather than by a test, the announcement's description of the job's duties can help you use the terms the personnel office will recognize when you write about your qualifications. This is explained in greater detail in Section II.

PRIVATE EMPLOYMENT AGENCIES

Private employment agencies listed under employment services in the yellow pages may also have information about government jobs. If you use such an agency, make sure you know whether you are going to have to pay any fees, and if so, how much. In most cases, the person who hires you will pay the fee, not you. In others, you will pay the fee. Most agencies are reputable and will give you fair service for your money, but some are not. If you do have to pay, you should grill the agency to learn exactly what it can do for you before you make a final decision or sign any papers. Ask for the names of other clients and contact them to learn if they feel the agency's fees were worth paying; contact their supervisors, too, to learn if they use the agency very often. You can also check with the Better Business Bureau to ask whether or not the private employment agency has a good business history.

NETWORKING

The public sector, like the private sector, is influenced by networking. While in the public sector the prospective employee must satisfactorily complete the more formal application requirements for a job, other factors do affect who gets the position. Remember the person hiring wants an employee who has a good character with solid work habits and a stable life-style that will fit in well with the other people in the workplace.

In his excellent book, *The Complete Guide to Public Employment,* Dr. Ronald L. Krannich suggests that as many as 70 percent of high-level government vacancies may be somewhat less than fully open and competitive. He terms the widespread use of an unfair tactic in filing vacancies "wiring." This is a system of preselecting candidates on an informal basis and then writing a job description that is guaranteed to make them the best qualified for the job. He suggests that the practice may be unethical or unfair, but it is not illegal.

Dr. Krannich says entry-level positions are less likely to be affected by such practices. But even at that level, you will want to do your best to make yourself stand out as a strong candidate rather than remain another properly filled out application form. A sincere recommendation from a friend already employed by a unit of state or local government will always benefit you. Your responsibility is to see that your formal application is completed skillfully.

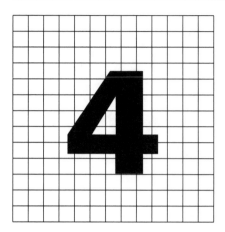

CONSIDER THE REWARDS

For millions of government employees, the meaningful reward they receive from their job is the people they help. The rewards they experience are in the good that is accomplished, the ignorance that is corrected, the sickness that is healed, and the fears that are comforted.

The major benefits of government—having the opportunity to serve the public good and have a direct impact on other people—are intangible. As a government official, social worker, teacher, police officer, or fire fighter, you will be able to see how your work benefits individuals and the community at large.

EARNINGS

Generalizing about the pay practices of thousands of different employers is risky. Studies show that one government pays its clerical positions relatively well while its electricians would do better with a private company. Another government does the opposite, paying electricians considerably better than average and clerical workers less than the going rate.

After studying many surveys of government vs. private sector wages, Shawna Grosskopf concludes, "Roughly speaking, high-skill occupations are relatively underpaid in the public sector, and low-skill occupations are over-paid relative to the private sector." That does not mean you can assume a particular government job pays better or worse than one with a private firm.

SALARY OVERVIEW

When asking about salaries, people often request a figure, but they really want to know how one occupation's salary compares with another's. Here are some occupations and average 1990 salaries.

Civil Engineer	$35,200
Computer Programmer	30,600
Accountant	29,500
Police Officer	26,700
Fire Fighter	25,500
Teacher (secondary level)	30,300
Registered Nurse	32,100
Teacher (elementary level)	28,900
Administrative Assistant	21,700
Typist/Word Processor	18,100
Nursing Aide	12,000
Physician Assistant	29,600

In 1990 the median income for all workers was $28,000. Besides putting salary information into a context, comparisons have the advantage of remaining accurate for a longer period. Changes in economic conditions quickly make salary figures out of date, but the relative salaries for different occupations remain more constant. You can use this information when you are offered a salary to help you evaluate the proposal.

THE FEDERAL GOVERNMENT

The salary of government workers compares favorably with that offered by private companies, especially at the lower grades. Other benefits enjoyed by federal jobholders include paid vacations and sick leave, life and health insurance plans, training opportunities, transfer privileges between agencies, considerable job security, and retirement pensions.

SALARY

Step Increases

Several different salary schedules are used by the federal government. They can be divided among *General Schedule (GS), Wage Board Schedule (WG), Postal Service,* and all others. Since government salaries are adjusted annually to keep them aligned with the salaries of workers in the private sector, salary data are subject to change. In 1993, however, the starting salary for clerk-typists (GS-2) was $13,382, and for college graduates (GS-5), $18,340. Up-to-date salary information is available from any government personnel office.

The GS pay system is used for most professional, administrative, clerical, technical, and scientific workers. About 45 percent of all federal employees are paid under the system.

In the GS system, you can receive two kinds of raises: step increases within the same grade and promotions from one grade to another. The first three step increases are scheduled at 1-year intervals; the next three at 2-year intervals; and the last four at 3-year intervals. People are usually hired at the first step of a grade.

For clerical positions, most career ladders start at GS-1; high school graduates are hired at GS-2, however, so that is where most people start. The rungs of the ladder are one grade apart. Very few clerical positions have ladders reaching higher than GS-6, although some positions have ladders all the way up to GS-11.

For professional occupations, the bottom grade is often GS-5; the rungs are two grades apart. Promotions are rare after GS-12.

The *Wage Board Schedule (WG)* governs the pay of most blue-collar workers. The pay rate varies from place to place, so government blue-collar workers are paid about the same amount as workers for private companies in the same area.

Promotions

Promotions to higher grades carry much larger raises than do the step increases. For most occupations, promotions are arranged in a career ladder. New employees are hired on the first or second rung of the ladder and promoted if they perform their jobs satisfactorily. The first two promotions may come only 1 year apart. Thereafter, the wait is longer, varying from employee to employee. Once employees reach the top rung of the career ladder for their position, they cannot be promoted—though they do receive step increases—unless they find a new position.

Postal Service Employees

Postal Service employees are paid according to yet another system. In fact, they are paid under several different schedules, depending on their occupations. For example, there are separate pay schedules for city mail carriers and rural ones. Employees receive periodic raises, which, because the workers are unionized, and the unions—unlike most unions in the government—are strong, tend to keep salaries relatively high. You can learn current pay rates for specific occupations from any local post office.

Finally, there are special salary plans for some agencies and employees. The Tennessee Valley Authority, the Federal Reserve Board, the Foreign Service section of the State Department, and doctors and nurses employed by the Department of Veterans Affairs all have different salary systems.

THE BENEFITS

Paid Vacations and Sick Leave

Government employees earn annual leave at rates based on the number of years they have been in government service. For the first 3 years, they earn 4 hours of leave every 2 weeks (13 vacation days a year); from their 4th to 15th years, 6 hours every 2 weeks (rounded to 20 days a year); and after 15 years, they earn 8 hours every 2 weeks (26 days a year).

All full-time employees earn sick leave at the same rate: 4 hours every 2 weeks, or 13 days a year. Unused sick leave accumulates from year to year, making it an excellent form of insurance against lost income during long illnesses. Accumulated sick leave can also be credited toward retirement benefits.

Life and Health Insurance

Federal employees are offered several levels of group life insurance for themselves plus optional coverage for their spouses and children. The government contributes to part of the cost of the premium for basic insurance, and the employee pays the balance through payroll deductions.

Many different health plans are available. Some are offered nationwide, some are restricted to certain parts of the country, and some are reserved for employees of a particular union or association. New employees are given booklets describing the benefits offered under each plan they are eligible to join. Whenever the cost of the plans rises (which is just about every year), people can change plans.

Training

Most large companies now give their employees vacations and health plans similar to those offered government employees. But few companies can match the range of opportunities for training found in the government. Training of some sort is provided for most new government employees. For some workers, such as FBI special agents and air traffic controllers, the training takes many weeks. For an apprentice in the blue-collar trades, it takes years. For most workers, however, training takes only a short period and may be informal.

Optional Training

Employees can choose to attend special training programs during work. Clerical employees, for example, can attend classes in typing, English, or statistics. Employees at higher levels are offered seminars in managerial techniques, budgeting, and public speaking, among other subjects.

Employees can also attend college and graduate school classes at the government's expense—either during work hours or at other times—if they can show that the courses will help them improve their performance on the job. The amount of training employees can take at any time depends on the funds available, but all employees can take some training fairly regularly. Of course, all this training will do you little good if you still have the same job after you complete your training. That is where the next benefit comes in.

Transfer Privileges

Once you are hired, the sheer size of the federal government will not make much difference to you. You will work with a small group of people, just as you would with any company. But if you tire of your job, the size and scope of the government's employment opportunities will once more become important. As a federal employee, you will enjoy distinct advantages over people who do not work for the government when you transfer from job to job. You are a preferred candidate for many jobs, because the procedures another agency must follow to hire government workers are a little simpler than the ones followed to hire outsiders. Your accumulated leave, pension rights, and health insurance benefits are also transferable, something rarely allowed when you change jobs in the private sector.

JOB SECURITY

Incompetent government workers do get fired, and unneeded workers do get laid off. But they are not fired at the whim of a supervisor or laid off because of a short-term reduction in their work load. Before people can be fired, they must be given a written explanation of *why* they should be fired and allowed time to respond to the charges against them. If a decision is made to fire them, they can appeal to the head of their agency, the Merit Systems Protection Board, and, ultimately, the courts.

Layoffs are called "reductions in force." They occur when an agency's budget is slashed, when projects are completed, or when reorganizations make certain jobs unnecessary. Large-scale reductions in force are rare. More common are reductions that affect only a few people. Agencies do, however, make an effort to find new jobs for people laid off.

RETIREMENT

The government offers a retirement program called the Federal Employees Retirement System (FERS). FERS provides workers with benefits from three sources: a Basic Benefit Plan, Social Security, and a Thrift Saving Plan. Each pay period, the government and the employee make contributions to the Basic Benefit and Social Security portions of the plan. The government puts a contribution equal to 1 percent of the employee's pay each pay period in the Thrift Savings Plan account, which is set up automatically when the worker is hired. One of the strongest aspects of this retirement program is that many of the features are portable, so employees are still eligible for many of the benefits even if they leave federal employment.

STATE GOVERNMENT

Despite the great number of employers and the many different occupations involved, many government and private-sector employees enjoy comparable fringe benefits. The most common are paid vacation and sick leave, paid holidays, medical insurance, retirement plans, and tuition assistance. Comprehensive data are not available for local governments. However, the practices of the states generally offer the usual benefits.

New workers typically get 2 weeks of vacation and 12 to 18 days of sick leave. Almost all the states give additional vacation time to workers with more service; 25 or more days a year is the maximum in several states. Most states grant at least 8 paid holidays a year, and many have as many as 12 or 13; Hawaii gives 15. The entire cost of medical insurance is paid in 14 states; 21 pay for life insurance. The rest of the states pay at least part of the cost of medical insurance and offer some kind of life insurance plan.

Government pensions are often considered generous. Florida, Mississippi, and Oklahoma pay the entire cost of the pension. In the rest of the states, the employer contributes to a pension fund, and the worker pays the balance.

Almost all the states provide tuition assistance for college. The amount provided and the kinds of courses that may be taken vary widely.

Other frequently mentioned benefits of government jobs are job security and advancement opportunities. Government employment is not guaranteed in bad times, as the teachers in many a shrinking school district can attest. Still, a government is less likely to be affected by temporary economic setbacks than is a private company. This side effect of government employment is especially beneficial in occupations that are prone to high unemployment, such as the construction crafts.

As for advancement, government positions often have clearly defined career ladders. Furthermore, in many government agencies, managerial positions are usually held by people who once worked at lower levels of the organization. For example, school administrators are often former teachers in the system; police sergeants and officers almost always come from the patrol ranks.

CONSIDERATIONS

While government service offers some solid advantages, it also has certain unique characteristics. The degree to which they bother you is likely to depend on your own personality. One frustration of government work for some is the inability to measure achievement in terms of profit and loss. When a private company offers goods or services to the public, it can use sales to measure its success. Governments do not sell products on the open market, and government programs rarely have a clear-cut success.

No matter how good the schools, no matter how safe the community, no matter how well kept the roads, some citizens will always be found to say that the service should be better or cheaper or both.

Politics and Promotion The promotion system in the federal service is a mixed blessing. Promotions are almost automatic, at least at the start of a career, leaving little room for individual recognition. When everyone is treated as average, people stop trying to be superior and lose the satisfaction of believing themselves among the best. As a result, a job that began as a challenge becomes a bore. The situation is worst, according to many government workers, when a bored employee is promoted into a supervisory position. Such supervisors have built their careers on doing no more than the minimum. An employee who wants to push a program to the maximum soon finds such supervisors immovable barriers to achieving excellence.

Politics and the world of the career civil servant are unrelated to each other in civics textbooks and the promotional literature published by government agencies. In reality, the two have an uneasy marriage. Some agencies and some programs are relatively isolated from political concerns. Most are not. Every new president has his own priorities. Slowly but surely, these priorities are reflected in the federal budget. When they are, programs wither away from lack of interest.

Politics also has a major effect on government workers, since politicians control the budget and make the final decisions. This can be a disadvantage to those who always want to have the last word on their own work. The same organization controls that provide job security can protect the job of someone you feel you should replace, leading to a stalemate and frustration.

The Prestige Issue

Prestige contributes a great deal to job satisfaction. The prestige of a job cannot be measured very easily. Government jobs, except for those at the very top, tend to be low in prestige. Tell people you work for the government, and they seem forced to say, "I guess you don't work too hard, then. You government workers have it made." Usually remarks like that mean little, but they are so common that one is bound to hit you on a day when you started work early, skipped lunch, and had to put in some overtime, so that four different projects—all set up by people elected by the person making the remark, in order to serve the person making the remark—could move forward.

The Earnings Issue

The GS pay system is fairly rigid. It is the same throughout the country, and when cost-of-living adjustments are given—as they are most years—they are usually a flat percentage increase for all grades and steps. For these reasons, and because of the way occupations are grouped together, some government employees would be better paid by private firms. For example, writer-editors fresh out of college receive relatively high wages in government jobs, but experienced lawyers do not. And federal employees in the South are better paid in relation to their cost of living than employees in the North and Far West. Furthermore, no one who is honest becomes rich in a government job. Government workers do not command the incomes of very successful doctors, lawyers, sales representatives, or executives.

None of these issues are very important in themselves, but taken together they can be formidable. You should think about them before you go looking for a government job. Like a small pebble in your shoe, they seem unimportant at first, but they can make you awfully sore.

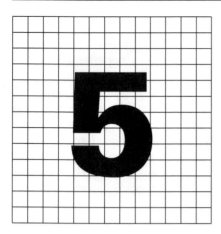

CASE HISTORIES

To give you a better idea of what it is like to have a career in government, the following three case histories illustrate why these people chose to work for the government and how their careers evolved. The first two have jobs that are typical of government work, but you may not think of these positions when beginning a career in government. The last person, David Welsh, has a job that exists only in the federal government, one that he consciously trained to be able to do.

Martin Wilson built a successful career with the government through a series of transfers and interesting assignments. Anna Hill benefited from government training programs and David Welsh channeled his desire to make a difference into an area where he can substantially affect the lives of industrial workers.

MARTIN WILSON

Martin graduated from college during the Depression. Like many others, he was well trained, but still could not find a job. He resolved to do what he could, so that people—especially young people—would be better prepared to make informed choices about careers. This would require that they know which educational and training programs to pursue, so that when the programs were completed, the graduates would have a fair chance of employment. But first, he needed a job for himself. He took a test, something like the college entrance exams today's high school students take. Martin's test led to a job as a clerk.

Martin passed the test and worked as a clerk for several years. He became familiar with the first computers, studied for his master's degree, and kept on the lookout for a better job. One day, he heard that the War Manpower

Commission was revising the *Dictionary of Occupational Titles,* a basic tool for career counselors both then and now. Martin knew that by improving the *Dictionary,* he would improve the career counseling received by high school and college students. He applied for a job as an occupational analyst in the division that prepared the *Dictionary.* He got the job.

As an occupational analyst, Martin visited factories and other places of business and watched the workers. He saw what tasks they performed, learned the names of their jobs, and asked about the job titles of other employees with whom they worked. Back at the office, he wrote descriptions of the jobs he had studied.

Martin moved up while an analyst and was soon responsible for a complete section of the *Dictionary.* His division was moved to the Department of Labor, and things progressed smoothly until the early 1950s. At that time, the federal government laid off thousands of employees, including Martin.

His next position was with the Bureau of Labor Statistics. The new job had nothing to do with the analysis of occupations, and meant moving to New York, but it was better than unemployment. Martin did his work, which involved the collection of information about employment and earnings, bided his time, and waited for something better to turn up. After his division moved back to Washington, Martin heard that the *Dictionary* was hiring again. He returned to occupational analysis.

About this time, the International Labor Office, a specialized agency of the United Nations, decided that an *International Standard Classification of Occupations* was needed, so that people from different countries would have a common reference when they talked about jobs. Martin was the representative from the United States. He went to Geneva, Switzerland, where, with representatives from six other countries, he contributed to the new book.

During the year Martin spent in Geneva, he learned of many different ways to organize occupational material and became friends with experts on occupational analysis from all over the world. He was especially friendly with the Canadian representatives to various committees, who would soon incorporate the new methods into the Canadian occupational guide. In the 1970s, when the fourth edition of the *Dictionary* was prepared, Martin would use some of the ideas himself. But before the fourth came the third; and, after his stint with the United Nations, Martin returned to the United States to work on it.

While working again in the Division of Occupational Analysis, Martin heard about a new program in the Office of Education's Bureau of Vocational Training and Adult Education. Vocational training helps students most when it is closely related to particular occupations, and when students can get jobs related to their training. Martin worked to improve the coordination of training with specific occupations. He was doing what he wanted most to do and knew most about. During the time he spent with the Office of Education, he supervised the preparation of *Vocational Education and Occupations,* a book that can be used to organize data and guide students and counselors.

Martin next returned to the Bureau of Labor Statistics. While with the bureau, he worked closely with the Office of Management and the Budget, which operates under the White House. The office was developing a *Standard Occupational Classification Manual* to deal with a frequent problem in government, making sure that everyone is talking the same language. The government needs information in order to manage the economy. When the information is gathered, everybody must use the same set of definitions. Books like the *Manual* provide those definitions. Preparing such books might not be as glamorous as writing new laws, but it is important if the laws are to make any sense.

After helping with the *Manual,* Martin went back to work on the *Dictionary of Occupational Titles.* Now he had the knowledge and experience needed to make real changes in it. The fourth edition was being prepared, and he incorporated many improvements that he had thought of while with the United Nations, the Office of Education, and the Bureau of Labor Statistics.

When Martin left his house on his way to his retirement luncheon, the fourth edition of the *Dictionary* had just been published. He thought his job was done. But a few days later, Martin heard from an old friend, a member of a special committee that had been formed to coordinate the work of all the government agencies that gather and distribute information about occupations. His friend wanted Martin to join in the task. Martin thought it over, took a deep breath, and agreed.

Martin went to work on a new book, something like the one he had done for the Office of Education. It would consolidate the information now found in many different volumes. Indeed, the book would bring together material from several stages of Martin's own career.

Since the above paragraph was written, the new book has been finished. Called *Vocational Preparation and Occupations,* it serves as a fitting capstone to the work of a dedicated public servant who accomplished what he set out to do: improve the public knowledge of occupations so young people can receive better guidance when choosing a career.

ANNA HILL

Anna Hill's face shines with the contented, confident expression of a woman who knows that she beat the odds. She has worked her way up from secretary to editor on one of the most distinguished journals published by the government, the *Monthly Labor Review.* Her climb was challenging and not clearly marked.

Anna worked as a receptionist for a lawyer and a doctor when she first came to Washington. The job was varied and provided good experience. After a while, Anna moved on to a clerical job with the government.

She was working as a secretary when her agency announced a new training program that prepared participants for positions as economists. The agency stressed that the training would take a long time and that new jobs were not guaranteed. Still, Anna signed up, seeing it as her chance to get the college-level training she wanted.

At the end of the training period, Anna's supervisor helped her get placed in her current position. Anna says she was lucky. Her supervisor supported her, and she worked for an agency that offered just the kind of training she could use. Perhaps she *was* lucky, at least in part. To benefit from government training, you often do need to be in the right place at the right time. But others might say that Anna made her own luck. After all, her supervisor helped her because she showed interest and promise. Moreover, the training would have been wasted, had she not had the ability to apply it.

Anna's current job as an editor makes full use of the training she received. She evaluates articles on labor economics that have been written by some of the most notable people in the field. She must be constantly alert to the originality of an author's theory and the validity of the statements made. Anna recommends that an article be accepted for publication or rejected.

Once accepted, the article still needs to be edited. Anna determines what the author's main points are and makes sure that they are clear to the reader and supported by the article. Sections of the article may need minor revisions or major rewriting. When satisfied that the article is ready for publication, Anna confers with the author to ensure that the changes she has made are acceptable. That ends the most challenging part of her job.

Before the public reads the article, Anna will read it several more times at various stages, from manuscript to magazine, to see that no errors appear in the finished product. Within two months, the article will be on the desks of the magazine's readers. By that time, Anna will have turned her attention to new articles.

DAVID WELSH

David Welsh is an industrial hygienist with the Occupational Safety and Health Administration, but he did not grow up wanting to be one. In fact, when he was growing up, industrial hygiene was almost unheard of and the Occupational Safety and Health Administration did not exist. Since then, our awareness of how we have poisoned our environment has grown, and the need for people like David has increased.

When the shortage of industrial hygienists first became evident, David was preparing for a career in medicine. But instead of going to medical school right after college, he decided to enter a graduate program in industrial hygiene. He liked it, and a year later felt that he could make as great a contribution to people's health by working as an industrial hygienist as he could as a doctor.

The cast-iron dome of the nation's Capitol looms over the building in which David now works. This is only right, after all, for David's work is an extension of the lawmaking power of Congress. The major laws passed by

Congress are not intended to cover particulars. They might be thought of as general statements of the will of the people, rather than as detailed lists of prohibited or required acts. To clarify how the general law applies in a particular situation, regulations must be written.

The regulations David writes clarify the *Occupational Health and Safety Act.* According to the act, workers have the right to a safe environment. David helps determine what a safe environment is. Some of his regulations restrict the use of poisons that cause lung disease. Others deal with the use of special equipment, the safety of the places people work, or the control of poisons, such as arsenic. Jobs like his, involving the preparation of legally binding regulations, are found only with the government.

David does not decide to write regulations in a vacuum. Although he makes recommendations, the normal process is for officials to decide what regulations or standards are needed according to the Occupational Safety and Health Administration.

For example, if David is asked to write a regulation on a dangerous substance used widely in industry and government, he begins by gathering information, a process that does not end until the regulation is actually signed. He consults with experts, searches out scientific papers, and along with the lawyers assigned to the case consults with additional experts and conducts hearings until he knows as much about the substance as possible.

When he is ready, he drafts the regulation and publishes it in the *Federal Register,* where all regulations are first printed. In effect, this invites comment from all interested parties—unions, industry representatives, consumer groups, Congress, other government agencies, and individual citizens.

The process of writing drafts and inviting comments is repeated until there is some agreement on how the regulation should read and what it means. This can mean more than a year of hearings, revisions, and reviews.

Finally, the standard is ready to be signed by the head of the Occupational Safety and Health Administration. Once signed, it has the same weight as the law passed by Congress that made the regulation necessary.

After a regulation is signed, the task of ensuring the safety of the United States' workers passes to the inspectors employed by the agency. Meanwhile, David starts to research another dangerous substance.

The experiences of Martin Wilson, Anna Hill, and David Welsh demonstrate why some people work for the government. Their careers gave them a chance to make a decent salary, advance in their profession, and contribute to the good of society. Perhaps the last reason is the most important, the one that outweighs some of the disadvantages of government work described in the previous chapter.

Section II
The Basics
of Job Searching

City, county, state, and federal governments, like other employers, want to hire people who can do the job. To learn who these people are, they use application forms, written tests, performance tests, medical examinations, and interviews, and ask for a resume. If the thought of any of these makes you queasy, remember they are only tools, ones you can learn to use well. Essentially they are communication skills. Mastering them will benefit you throughout your career.

This section is designed to help you acquire and refine the skills you need to obtain the position you desire. The following chapters will review and discuss each aspect or skill. The emphasis is on how to accomplish the task—getting a job and launching your career in government.

The governmental hiring process can be less personalized, be more detailed, and take longer than the private sector. This may raise your anxiety level. But if you remind yourself it is simply a process, a means to an end, and above all, you are doing this because you want to want to work for the government, then a sense of direction replaces those misgivings.

In fact, you may not have a choice if the government is the only employer for the career you have chosen, e.g., air traffic controller, law enforcement, et cetera. Nevertheless, knowing you are consciously choosing a career in government will help offset the difficulties you may encounter in the hiring process. The hiring system is a rite of passage, one which you will eventually find yourself sharing and laughing about with your fellow employees. Everyone who will be working with you has gone through it.

THE MIND-SET THAT MAKES A POSITIVE DIFFERENCE

Hunting for a job can be stressful, depressing, and rewarding. Since emotions and events are influenced enormously by your mental attitude, it is important to stay positive. You will improve your chances of being hired if you apply the information given to you in the following pages.

ADVICE FOR A SUCCESSFUL JOB SEARCH

The three basic tips for successfully obtaining a governmental position are doable and practical. When applied, they will increase your chances of obtaining the position you desire by keeping you action-oriented and focused.

1. Know that application forms, tests, and resumes are opportunities to show how good you really are.
2. Identify what is causing your anxiety and take action.
3. Learning new skills and using certain tools transform worry and tensions into positive performance.

JOB SEARCHING IS A GOLDEN OPPORTUNITY

Enjoy it. Use it to learn more about yourself and to improve your communication skills. Remember, you will get a job; it is simply a question of which one. This knowledge starts inside you and builds the more you affirm it. Since your goal is to obtain the position you want, reminding yourself daily of this keeps you focused and reinforces your level of self-confidence.

If you start to panic or feel a vague sense of fear overwhelming you when you think about filling out forms and taking tests, take a deep breath and remind yourself this is what you do to get to a job. If you want to go to a movie, you buy a ticket. That is the price of admission. The same is true of getting a job. You have to apply for it—that is the price of admission.

But with this price of admission, you have an added advantage—the opportunity to present yourself in your best light. You are in control. After all, you are the one who determines what your abilities and potential areas are as well as when and how you demonstrate them. Part of mastering the job search process is learning to be your own best friend.

IDENTIFY ANXIETIES

Applying for a governmental position is easier when you remove the fear of the unknown. The first step is identifying exactly what part of the process is causing you the most anxiety. Some questions that may help you recognize the source or causes are:

Do the questions and lines on application forms all seem to run together?

Is it difficult to read forms?

Is it hard to understand what the form is asking?

Do tests or even the thought of a test make you nervous?

Does your mouth go dry talking to someone you do not know?

Does meeting new people make you feel uncomfortable?

Do you dread putting in writing your work and educational experience?

Answering yes to one or more of these questions will tell you what aspect of the job search makes you anxious. For example, if the words on forms all blend together, then you know that forms are your yellow flag. You need to proceed with caution and set up a plan that will allay your fears. If none of these questions help identify the cause of your discomfort, then ask yourself which questions stimulate a reaction, even a minor one. Once you are able to pinpoint your anxiety, then you have taken the first step to removing its power over you.

Knowing the root of your anxiety is the first step to correcting it. You know where to direct your attention and efforts. The second step is taking the necessary action. If more than one type of question causes butterflies, arrange them in chronological order (forms, resume, interviews, and tests) and begin at the top of your list.

You will start to feel better when you tackle the first item. You may also find the other areas on your list may cause less and less anxiety. Conquering one anxiety or transforming it into concrete activity gives you the confidence to transform all of them. Knowledge and self-directed action are powerful tools in eradicating fears associated with finding a position.

LEARN NEW SKILLS

The best way to transform worry and fear is taking specific action, formulating a plan and putting it into effect. When it involves looking for a position in government, there are definite skills you can learn and tools you can use that will increase your chance of being hired. Some of these are developing and using a worksheet, practicing completing forms, preparing cover letters, rehearsing interviews, polishing thank-you notes, et cetera.

You can correct whatever bothers you if you want to make the effort. For example, if forms tend to unnerve you, preparing in advance the information they most likely will request will make you feel more comfortable. Being prepared increases your self-confidence because you know that you have the information they will undoubtedly ask for at your fingertips.

Self-confidence makes the difference between panic and being able to perform. Even if a question is asked that you are not prepared for, self-confidence gives you the security of knowing you can give a correct answer. It is simply a question of taking a minute to think about the information they want, remembering your facts, deciding what best fits, then writing it in the appropriate space. This is easiest to do if you have prepared a worksheet. In the next chapter, we will discuss how to put a worksheet together and the many ways it can benefit the job seeker.

The skills you acquire while looking for a job will continue to benefit you once you are employed. The most important gift you can give yourself is keeping a positive attitude. This will serve you well professionally and personally.

In the following chapters, we will describe other tools and skills that will help you obtain the job you want. Since they are communication methods, they will serve you well throughout your career. Each is discussed along with suggestions and illustrations. In learning how to complete forms, prepare resumes, take tests, and have a successful interview, you will find yourself adapting the techniques we present to suit your own situation. This is a normal part of the learning curve. As you master the ability to select what best benefits you, you are honing your communication skills, which will be of enormous value to you throughout your career.

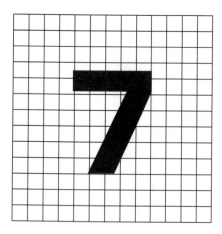

THE WORKSHEET

A worksheet is the single most important item you will use during your job search. A master worksheet is the original paper you prepare, listing pertinent information on your background in an easy-to-use format. It is indispensable. You will find yourself constantly referring to it. A worksheet is a practical tool that saves you time and lessens anxiety. You will find it extremely helpful in preparing resumes, filling out forms, especially the SF-171, and in preparing for interviews.

If you photocopy the master sheet, then you can carry at least one copy with you when you go on a job interview. Putting the original or master sheet in a safe place is a good idea so you will not have to start all over again if you misplace the copy. As you interview and fill out forms, you may want to add additional information to your master worksheet.

Since application forms generally ask for standard information, having a worksheet enables you to complete a form quickly, easily, and accurately. You are not burdened with having to remember names, addresses, years, and other facts frequently demanded. Each time you are given a form, you can breathe a sigh of relief knowing you have the information the form requires. Even if forms do not make you apprehensive, it is extremely helpful to prepare a worksheet as it organizes you and enables you to complete an application quicker, and to write a resume and prepare for an interview with greater efficiency.

It is relatively easy to prepare your own worksheet. Some of the information that should be included on your worksheet is listed under the following categories.

Personal.   Include your name, current address, phone number, Social Security number, previous addresses, length of habitation, dependents, hobbies, interests, professional organizations, civic and religious activities, charitable organizations, volunteer work, and nonacademic honors and recognitions you have received.

If you are difficult to reach during the day, you can include a phone number and the name of a reliable person who is able to take a message for you. If you have a phone machine, record a message asking that callers leave their name, phone number, and the most opportune times to return the call. Then be sure to contact them at the time they have stated. When you speak with them, introduce yourself and thank them for their phone call.

It is a good idea to list your previous domiciles if you have been at your current address less than three years. Unless your school address was your legal address, it is advisable to put your parents' home as your address since it is normally considered to be your legal residence during your school years.

Education.   List the name and location of your grade school, high school, and college, degrees received, major course of study, graduate schooling, technical schooling, technical skills, specialty training or courses, adult education courses, job-related seminars and workshops, professional certificates, language skills, computer software programs, office equipment (duplicators, calculators, audio visual equipment), laboratory equipment, machines, and tools you are able to use, clubs, associations, and groups you belong to, and honors and awards you have received.

Be sure to include special summer and home study sessions you took as well as all seminars, workshops, and conventions you attended while going to school or when you were employed. It is helpful to identify the brand names and model numbers of all the equipment and machines you are capable of using.

Experience.   Specify paid and unpaid work, stating the name and address of all prior employers (paid and volunteer), length of employment, job title (beginning and ending), salary earned (beginning and ending), tasks performed, job responsibilities, and reasons for leaving.

Some of the common reasons for leaving are moving, returning to school, finding a better position, the company went out of business, downsized, or merged, or your department was eliminated. If you were fired because you were asked to perform an unethical task, then this becomes a plus. Even if you were fired, remember that everyone makes mistakes.

Learning from your mistake is what makes the positive difference. How you present or explain your reason is what is important. You want to state the facts in a positive light. For example, if you were fired because you were constantly late, the reason could have been that your baby sitter or day-care situation was not reliable. If your personal situation has changed, you could state that your child is now in school full time and that you have also arranged to have a nonworking neighbor on call. You would say that at the time, you had to put your child's welfare first. But now you are in a position to concentrate on your career, which will also benefit the welfare of your child. If there was not a strong reason for your lateness, simply admit that you learned a tough lesson and that being on time is now a definite plus in your life, professionally and personally. This and similar statements have validity only if they are true.

This is also where you write out all the offices you held or were elected to during your schooling or any you held as a result of your religious, community, charitable, or social involvements. Include the dates you served as well as the titles you held.

Special Qualifications. Put down all skills and talents, even emerging ones (e.g., photography) if you have recently enrolled in a course. Although these abilities are generally considered to be part of your experience, it is advantageous to separate them from your paid and unpaid work to be able to choose more easily which of your accomplishments you may want to include when applying for a particular position. Some of the skills, talents, and other attributes that belong here are your training or knowledge of public speaking (list dates and titles of speeches, lectures, and readings), publishing (give the names, dates, and brief recaps of the articles, books, columns, et cetera, you have produced), writing (ads, brochures, newsletters, letters, commercials you wrote), design (describe what you do—visual graphics, interiors, landscapes, et cetera), photography, organizing conferences, hobbies, working with the physically challenged, disadvantaged youth, or the elderly, distributing food and clothing to the needy, serving in a hospice or in a hospital volunteer program, and so on. It is as important to list your unpaid achievements (articles, designs, photos) as it is your compensated work.

You want to be able to pick and choose from this category. In certain circumstances, you will want to put down all your abilities. At other times, it may be more to your advantage to mention them in an interview or in a follow-up letter where you can present them in relation to a topic or aspect of the job you want to be hired to do.

Goals. Prepare two versions of your career goals. The first should be an abbreviated version, about the length of a sentence, as space on application forms is generally limited. In the event you have more room, you can use your second version, which can be as long as a paragraph. In both instances, it is important that your career goals be carefully thought out and well written.

Goals serve an important function by telling the person reviewing your application or resume what you are directing your efforts toward and what you want to achieve. Throughout the hiring process, you need to remember that employers, especially governments, want to hire people they know will do well in a particular position. They also are looking for individuals who are willing to make a long-term commitment. Having a defined goal enables a potential employer to see how you will best fit into the organization over a long period by explaining your motivations and desires.

The government's structure is step-oriented. Promotion and pay increases are based on experience, length of service, and performance. At times, government is criticized for promoting individuals slower than the private sector. However, there are definite compensations—flexibility to transfer, job security, and so on. Your commitment to your goal will be questioned during the interview process. Giving careful consideration to your goal will benefit you.

Salary Requirements.   Remain flexible in attitude and in your written response. Stating a specific amount, level, or rating is risky as it may eliminate you from consideration for a position. For this reason, it is better to give a salary range, especially if you are committed to a career in government. In fact, you may be willing to accept less money or a slightly lower position for geographical location, opportunities for advancement, travel privileges, or similar benefits.

It is critical to know where you can compromise or adjust your expectations to achieve your goal. For example, you may decide to accept an administrative position with the fire department which offers less money than you are currently making since your goal is to become a paramedic. Working with the fire department allows you to network among the fire department staff and become familiar with the paramedics and the work they do. You may also qualify for free training to become a paramedic. In evaluating these factors, you decide that it is to your ultimate advantage to accept the administrative position because it will constructively help you become a paramedic.

Sensitive Areas

Disabilities.   Since disabilities are protected by federal law, be open about them. At the same time, focus on your abilities. Being physically challenged illustrates your determination and commitment among other positive qualities that will make you a good choice.

All aspects of the job search can be used to show your capabilities and steadfastness of character. The tone in your voice and writing will speak loudly. Careful preparation will keep the focus positive and show clearly what your level of performance is.

Convictions.   If you have ever been convicted of a crime, admit it. If you were acquitted of any charges, it is not necessary to mention them.

References.   You will need to have three business and three personal references. If this is your first job, you can select for your business references teachers, advisers, school administrators, or others with whom you have worked on specific projects who know your abilities and potential. For personal references, it is advisable to select adults recognized in the business community or those who hold positions of respect—ministers, doctors, teachers, elected officials—who are familiar with your volunteer, charity, religious, or community service. In their recommendations, they need to be able to cite specific examples of the skills they have observed in you. A good rule of thumb is to choose individuals who have known you for a minimum of five years.

Generally, it is not suggested to use the name of someone who has known you for less than three years. It is also not appropriate to use family members for references.

Once you have decided whom you would like to use for references, it is essential to obtain their permission to do so and to ask them whether they prefer being contacted during business hours or in the evenings. Clearly specify the times they can be reached when you give their names and phone numbers on forms or in interviews.

For convenience, list your three business and three personal references separately. You will want to include their titles, places of business, addresses (business and home), and their business and home phone numbers. Be certain to note any requests or qualifying information that your references have mentioned; for example, that they will be on vacation for three weeks in August.

You may think you will easily remember your references when you are interviewing and filling out application forms. And you may. However, the Chinese saying that the faintest pencil is better than the strongest memory definitely applies.

Applying for work can be very stressful. It is to your advantage to eliminate potentially tense situations by recording relevant information on the worksheet.

Many counselors suggest putting references down on forms and resumes. However, if you want to have some control over the process, then it is considered acceptable to write that you will supply references upon request. This allows you to alert your references and give them the name of the person who will be checking with them. Most importantly, you will need to write each reference you use a thank-you note for their willingness to recommend you. A prompt, handwritten note thanking each reference is as essential to your job search as properly completing an application form is.

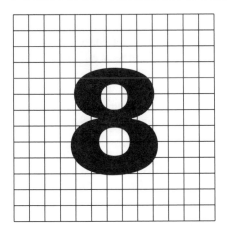

STANDARD FORM 171

The 171, as is it commonly called (most people think it takes that many hours to complete!), is a four-page form which functions as a resume for the majority of federal jobs. It is the personal qualifications statement of the federal government. See the form at the end of this chapter.

To receive one you normally have to go to a Federal Job Information Center and complete a request form, which is a mailing label. Then you drop it in a slot. The center is generally a very small room filled with notices of available job opportunities. It can be a sobering experience since you will not be able to speak to anyone in authority. You may meet other job seekers and see an announcement for a toll-free phone number that you can call 7 days a week for a recorded message, but that is it.

Approximately 1 week after you have deposited the mailing label in the slot, you will receive the SF-171 in the mail. As soon as you receive your SF-171, make several blank copies to use for drafts. This will permit you to practice. When you are ready for a final version, you will find it easier and more efficient to prepare if you have had several trial attempts.

Since this form is the first description of your qualifications that anyone will see, it is worth every effort you make to type it neatly and fill it with information that accurately describes you. Frequently, your complete SF-171 will determine whether or not you are even asked for an interview. Most federal agencies, excluding the post office, require it.

Although the instructions on the SF-171 are clear and most items are standard, there are certain items that may cause you concern. The following section identifies items that are difficult to complete but can, with some preparation, be used to your advantage.

Item 1—What kind of job you are applying for? Since you probably will be applying for a variety of positions with different agencies, it is a good idea to leave this particular item blank on your master copy. When you have completed your master, make several copies of it. As you apply for various positions, you can fill in the information for this item as well as the other items that need to be adapted for a particular position.

Item 12—What is the lowest pay [or grade] that you will accept? Since pay rates change annually, it is simpler to put down a grade. Besides, supervisors think of openings in terms of grades rather than salaries. So it is better to speak their language and use the grading system.

Deciding which grade to put down is the dilemma. You may well be qualified for a grade higher than the position for which you are applying. For example, if you are a college graduate with two full years of experience, you are qualified for a GS-9 salary for many federal positions. Since there is more hiring at the GS-7 and GS-5 levels, if you demand a GS-9, you will be screened out at the first run.

On the other hand, if you put down a GS-7, you will probably not be hired as a GS-9 regardless of your qualifications and interview skills. But you may be offered the job at a GS-7 level, which, depending upon your circumstances, may be a first step in attaining your career goal. You will weigh accepting a lower grade with the near certainty of being promoted after a year against holding out for a higher-graded position, which may or may not become available.

Items 14 through 17—Willingness to work part-time, to accept temporary appointments, and to travel. Government officials have an easier time of hiring someone who already has a job with them as opposed to someone who has to be hired. For this reason, accepting temporary or part-time positions often pays in two ways. First, if you impress your supervisor and work well with your coworkers, you have a better chance of being offered a permanent position. Second, you are in a good position to learn of other job openings as you have access to the grapevine.

If you decide to accept part-time or temporary work, be sure to tell your supervisors and coworkers that your goal is to obtain a permanent position. People remember good workers and government supervisors prefer hiring someone who knows the system and has a track record of working in government, however short it may be.

Items 18 through 22—Military and veteran service. Do not leave this blank. If you have not served in the military, place an "X" in the box next to "No Preference." You can receive a 5- to 10-point advantage in your eligibility rating if you have military experience or are the spouse, widow, or mother of a veteran. If you claim veteran preference, you will have to meet specific criteria and supply documentation as proof. A large percentage of male federal employees are former veterans.

To qualify for the 10-point advantage, you will have to complete the SF-15, which is the official application form for anyone seeking the 10-point preference. There are four categories of people who are eligible to qualify for the 10-point preference: non-compensably disabled or Purple Heart recipient; compensably disabled (less than 30%); compensably disabled (30% or more); and spouse, widow(er), or mother of a deceased or disabled veteran.

Item 24—Experience. This is your Mount Everest. You will need to leave this item blank on your master copy, since you will want to tailor your response to each position you apply for. This is one of the instances where you will appreciate having a comprehensive worksheet. Your worksheet will have summarized all your experience so it will simpler for you to pick and choose the emphasis you want when applying for a particular position.

The seven basic steps to follow in completing this item successfully are:

1. Type your single-spaced response on a separate sheet of paper. The only way to put down the appropriate information on these narrow, lined spaces is to type it onto a separate sheet of paper, glue or adhere it to the original, then photocopy it. The result will be a much cleaner-looking SF-171. Work on drafting your response until you have the wording you want.

2. Read very carefully the language used in the qualifications statement and in the job description. You want to use the same or similar words in your response. Certain verbs, e.g., *coordinate, organize,* and *direct,* occur over and over in the announcements. Repeat them in describing your experience. For example, you would write "coordinated interdepartmental communication, organized the master file system, and directed the summer internship program" instead of "talked staff into cooperating, filed all correspondence, and worked with the summer help."

3. Demonstrate you have the ability asked for in the "Evaluation Factors" at the end of the announcement. Repeating the language used in the "Evaluation Factors" is critical. If it asks that the applicant be able to "evaluate and analyze financial material," your response must show you have that capability. An example would be "Reviewed invoices and statements to verify they accurately reflected the charges authorized."

4. Make your descriptions as complete and exact as possible. Add figures, percentages, and concrete examples wherever possible. Instead of "checked applications for completeness," your response will be better received if you write "checked seven different kinds of insurance applications for completeness; forms were six to 12 pages in length." Show what percentage of your time was allocated to different job functions. For example:

   Received visitors (10%); answered correspondence or routed it to the appropriate staff person (25%); received bulk orders for 60 different publications, organized storage, and kept inventory (30%); made travel arrangements for the staff (5%); maintained files (15%); prepared monthly report of inquiries received, biweekly time cards, and records of time spent on duty for eight employees (10%); kept supplies on hand (5%).

5. Describe each major job change with the same employer as a separate job. A major job change is described as one in which you received a promotion, new responsibilities, and an increase in pay. Transferring to a lateral position in another section, department, or agency for more pay does not qualify as a major job change.

6. List all unpaid work, volunteering, and other work you have done in a family business. For the salary block, insert "volunteer." Use the same descriptive language that you did for your paying jobs and begin with the title you held or the equivalent title for your responsibilities.

7. Ask an experienced person to proof your answer. It is very difficult to proof and edit your own writing. Ask someone you trust who is in a position of hiring others, teaches, trains, or supervises one or more people, or has similar credentials to read your description. Because of her or his hands-on experience, she or he generally will offer a suggestion that will improve your definition.

Items 25 through 31—Education and training. This is another opportunity for you to emphasize your abilities and to benefit from your current worksheet. For your formal education include the name and location of the school, college, or university, the degrees earned, the year you received them, and what your major or area of expertise was.

You have the option of attaching copies of the transcripts of your grades to your SF-171. If you are applying for your first job or your actual work experience is light and your academic performance is strong, you may want to consider adding copies of your transcripts. This can have a positive influence, particularly if your grades are impressive in subjects that relate to the position you would like to obtain.

For your informal education, list in chronological order all the courses, seminars, workshops, conferences, adult education programs, vocational training, and special educational sessions you attended. Also include those you attended that were sponsored by your employer, church, civic associations, professional organizations, and social clubs. The title of each informal education course or session should be listed along with where you took it and how long it lasted. If the title is vague, give a brief description of the subject material covered.

Items 32 through 36—Special skills, accomplishments, and awards. This is another opportunity for you to save considerable time by using the worksheet you prepared. Depending upon the position you are applying for, you will select which of your experiences in public speaking, publishing, writing, design, photography, organizing conferences, and similar activities will be to your advantage to mention. You also need to include the names and, where appropriate, model numbers of machines, equipment (audio, calculators, laboratory, et cetera), and computer software programs that will give added weight to your application.

Awards carry special weight. List all awards you have received in school, at work, from the community, or from other civic, social, and religious organizations that have honored you and recognized your contribution. This is another golden opportunity. Use it to your full advantage by including every award, even if you do not consider the award very significant.

Item 37—References. You are required to name three people, other than relatives and supervisors, who know about your abilities. Select three references from your worksheet. Since you will have listed six references (three personal and three business) on the worksheet, you will want to record in your private files which three references you use for each position you apply for requiring the SF-171.

Generally, it is preferable to use three business references who know you personally. However, the form requires that only one of your business references needs to know you personally. If that is the case, indicate the reference who knows you personally on the form.

Also, remember to inform your references where you have included their names, what the position is, and who may be calling them. You should immediately write thank-you notes or letters to your references.

Items 38 through 47—"Citizenship, Convictions, Termination, Retirement Benefits, and Relatives." These are self-explanatory and easy to complete. You may want to review the advice we gave on convictions and termination in Chapter 2.

Items 48 through 49—Signature and date. Sign and date each photocopied SF-171 *only* when you are ready to mail it. As there will often be lapses of time between the positions you apply for, they should never be signed and dated in advance.

As the SF-171 replaces the resume for many federal jobs, it is important to remember that personalizing each SF-171 for the specific position you are applying for will increase your chances of being selected for the next step in the hiring process. Sometimes the next step is an interview. Sometimes it is a request for you to take certain tests. Your goal is to be chosen to proceed to the next round.

Once you have signed and dated a completed SF-171 and are ready to mail it, photocopy it and file one copy in a folder marked *Active Applications.* When you are notified the position is no longer available, attach a note to the application with any pertinent information about who was hired and why, then transfer it to a file marked *Inactive Applications.* Often the reasons someone else was hired may help you obtain a different position. Being organized about your job search is a psychological plus. It gives you a sense of control and accomplishment when you are experiencing varying degrees of insecurity.

Extra Space

You may find that you need additional space to answer one or more items on your SF-171 application. You have two options. You can use the SF-171-A application form, which is attached to the back of the SF-171. Make several photocopies of it before you write on it. This will give you the opportunity to draft your answers before finalizing them as well as give you additional sheets of the SF-171-A for your answers.

Another option is to use a sheet of plain, white paper the same size as the SF-171 and put your name, Social Security number, the announcement number or job title, and the item number on each sheet. Each additional sheet of paper must contain this information. All supplementary sheets must be attached to the SF-171 application at the top of page 3. *Each additional copy you attach must be signed and dated in ink.* This is mandatory. Failure to do so will delay the review of your application and result in losing a job opportunity.

To ensure clarity, it is advisable to transfer the headings from the SF-171 onto the paper, photocopy it, type in your response, then photocopy it again. This will result in a cleaner, more professional appearance.

SUMMARY

The SF-171 is the first and most important form you will complete for a federal position. The requirements offer little leeway in presentation. Several key points are:

1. All items must be answered on the SF-171 fully and correctly.
2. The application must be typed or printed clearly in dark (black or dark blue) ink.
3. Do not attach additional support material such as performance evaluations, training certificates, copies of diplomas, official position descriptions, letters of recommendations, or samples of printed material. Any material of this nature will be removed from your application and will not be returned to you. (This does not refer to the SF-171-A or the plain sheets of white paper you have used to complete various items.)
4. Have a reliable third party proof your completed form for errors and content.
5. Have another person proof your completed form for errors and content.
6. Proof your completed application yourself one more time for errors and content.
7. Make at least four copies of the final form. Mail one, file one in your *Active* file, file another in your chronological file, and save one to work on for your application.

Application for Federal Employment — SF 171

Application for Federal Employment—SF 171

Read the instructions before you complete this application. *Type or print clearly in dark ink.*

Form Approved
OMB No. 3206-0012

GENERAL INFORMATION

1 What kind of job are you applying for? Give title and announcement no. (if any)

2 Social Security Number

3 Sex
☐ Male   ☐ Female

4 Birth date (Month, Day, Year)

5 Birthplace (City and State or Country)

6 Name (Last, First, Middle)

Mailing address (include apartment number, if any)

City   State   ZIP Code

7 Other names ever used (e.g., maiden name, nickname, etc.)

8 Home Phone
Area Code | Number

9 Work Phone
Area Code | Number   Extension

10 Were you ever employed as a civilian by the Federal Government? If "NO", go to Item 11. If "YES", mark each type of job you held with an "X".

☐ Temporary   ☐ Career-Conditional   ☐ Career   ☐ Excepted

What is your highest grade, classification series and job title?

Dates at highest grade: FROM   TO

FOR USE OF EXAMINING OFFICE ONLY

Date entered register

Form reviewed:
Form approved:

Option	Grade	Earned Rating	Veteran Preference	Augmented Rating
			☐ No Preference Claimed	
			☐ 5 Points (Tentative)	
			☐ 10 Pts. (30% Or More Comp. Dis.)	
			☐ 10 Pts. (Less Than 30% Comp. Dis.)	
			☐ Other 10 Points	

Initials and Date

☐ Disallowed   ☐ Being Investigated

FOR USE OF APPOINTING OFFICE ONLY

Preference has been verified through proof that the separation was under honorable conditions, and other proof as required.

☐ 5-Point   ☐ 10-Point—30% or More Compensable Disability   ☐ 10-Point—Less Than 30% Compensable Disability   ☐ 10-Point—Other

Signature and Title

Agency   Date

AVAILABILITY

11 When can you start work? (Month and Year)

12 What is the lowest pay you will accept? (You will not be considered for jobs which pay less than you indicate.)

Pay $ _____ per _____ OR Grade _____

13 In what geographic area(s) are you willing to work?

14 Are you willing to work:

	YES	NO
A. 40 hours per week (full-time)?		
B. 25-32 hours per week (part-time)?		
C. 17-24 hours per week (part-time)?		
D. 16 or lower hours per week (part-time)?		
E. An intermittent job (on-call/seasonal)?		
F. Weekends, shifts, or rotating shifts?		

15 Are you willing to take a temporary job lasting:

A. 5 to 12 months (sometimes longer)?		
B. 1 to 4 months?		
C. Less than 1 month?		

16 Are you willing to travel away from home for:

A. 1 to 5 nights each month?		
B. 6 to 10 nights each month?		
C. 11 or more nights each month?		

MILITARY SERVICE AND VETERAN PREFERENCE

17 Have you served in the United States Military Service? If your only active duty was training in the Reserves or National Guard, answer "NO". If "NO", go to item 22.

YES | NO

18 Did you or will you retire at or above the rank of major or lieutenant commander?

MILITARY SERVICE AND VETERAN PREFERENCE (Cont.)

19 Were you discharged from the military service under honorable conditions? (If your discharge was changed to "honorable" or "general" by a Discharge Review Board, answer "YES". If you received a clemency discharge, answer "NO".) If "NO", provide below the date and type of discharge you received.

YES | NO

Discharge Date (Month, Day, Year)   Type of Discharge

20 List the dates (Month, Day, Year), and branch for all active duty military service.

From	To	Branch of Service

21 If all your active military duty was after October 14, 1976, list the full names and dates of all campaign badges or expeditionary medals you received or were entitled to receive.

22 Read the instructions that came with this form before completing this item. When you have determined your eligibility for veteran preference from the instructions, place an "X" in the box next to your veteran preference claim.

☐ NO PREFERENCE

☐ 5-POINT PREFERENCE -- You must show proof when you are hired.

☐ 10-POINT PREFERENCE -- If you claim 10-point preference, place an "X" in the box next to the basis for your claim. To receive 10-point preference you must also complete a Standard Form 15, Application for 10-Point Veteran Preference, which is available from any Federal Job Information Center. ATTACH THE COMPLETED SF 15 AND REQUESTED PROOF TO THIS APPLICATION.

☐ Non-compensably disabled or Purple Heart recipient.

☐ Compensably disabled, less than 30 percent.

☐ Spouse, widow(er), or mother of a deceased or disabled veteran.

☐ Compensably disabled, 30 percent or more.

THE FEDERAL GOVERNMENT IS AN EQUAL OPPORTUNITY EMPLOYER
PREVIOUS EDITION USABLE UNTIL 12-31-90

NSN 7540-00-935-7150   171-110   Standard Form 171 (Rev. 6-88)
U.S. Office of Personnel Management
FPM Chapter 295

Page 1

WORK EXPERIENCE *If you have no work experience, write "NONE" in A below and go to 25 on page 3.*

23 May we ask your present employer about your character, qualifications, and work record? *A "NO" will not affect our review of your qualifications. If you answer "NO" and we need to contact your present employer before we can offer you a job, we will contact you first. . . . . .* | YES | NO |

24 READ WORK EXPERIENCE IN THE INSTRUCTIONS BEFORE YOU BEGIN.

- Describe your current or most recent job in Block A and work backwards, describing each job you held during the past 10 years. If you were unemployed for longer than 3 months within the past 10 years, list the dates and your address(es) in an experience block.

- You may sum up in one block work that you did more than 10 years ago. But if that work is related to the type of job you are applying for, describe each related job in a separate block.

- INCLUDE VOLUNTEER WORK *(non-paid work)*--If the work *(or a part of the work)* is like the job you are applying for, complete all parts of the experience block just as you would for a paying job. You may receive credit for work experience with religious, community, welfare, service, and other organizations.

- INCLUDE MILITARY SERVICE--You should complete all parts of the experience block just as you would for a non-military job, including all supervisory experience. Describe each major change of duties or responsibilities in a separate experience block.

- IF YOU NEED MORE SPACE TO DESCRIBE A JOB--Use sheets of paper the same size as this page (be sure to include all information we ask for in A and B below). On each sheet show your name, Social Security Number, and the announcement number or job title.

- IF YOU NEED MORE EXPERIENCE BLOCKS, use the SF 171-A or a sheet of paper.

- IF YOU NEED TO UPDATE (ADD MORE RECENT JOBS), use the SF 172 or a sheet of paper as described above.

A | Name and address of employer's organization *(include ZIP Code, if known)* | Dates employed *(give month, day and year)* | Average number of hours per week | Number of employees you supervise |

From: ___ To: ___

Salary or earnings | Your reason for wanting to leave
Starting $ ___ per
Ending $ ___ per

Your immediate supervisor | Exact title of your job | If Federal employment *(civilian or military)* list series, grade or rank, and, if promoted in this job, the date of your last promotion
Name ___ | Area Code | Telephone No. ___

Description of work: Describe your specific duties, responsibilities and accomplishments in this job, including the job title(s) of any employees you supervise. *If you describe more than one type of work (for example, carpentry and painting, or personnel and budget), write the approximate percentage of time you spent doing each.*

For Agency Use (skill codes, etc.)

B | Name and address of employer's organization *(include ZIP Code, if known)* | Dates employed *(give month, day and year)* | Average number of hours per week | Number of employees you supervised |

From: ___ To: ___

Salary or earnings | Your reason for leaving
Starting $ ___ per
Ending $ ___ per

Your immediate supervisor | Exact title of your job | If Federal employment *(civilian or military)* list series, grade or rank, and, if promoted in this job, the date of your last promotion
Name ___ | Area Code | Telephone No. ___

Description of work: Describe your specific duties, responsibilities and accomplishments in this job, including the job title(s) of any employees you supervised. *If you describe more than one type of work (for example, carpentry and painting, or personnel and budget), write the approximate percentage of time you spent doing each.*

For Agency Use (skill codes, etc.)

Page 2   IF YOU NEED MORE EXPERIENCE BLOCKS, USE SF 171-A *(SEE BACK OF INSTRUCTION PAGE).*

← ATTACH ANY ADDITIONAL FORMS AND SHEETS HERE

EDUCATION

25 Did you graduate from high school? *If you have a GED high school equivalency or will graduate within the next nine months, answer "YES".*

26 Write the name and location *(city and state)* of the last high school you attended or where you obtained your GED high school equivalency.

| YES | ▶ | If "YES", give month and year graduated or received GED equivalency:............. _____ |
| NO | ▶ | If "NO", give the highest grade you completed: . _____ |

27 Have you ever attended college or graduate school? YES ▶ If "YES", continue with 28. NO ▶ If "NO", go to 31.

28 NAME AND LOCATION *(city, state and ZIP Code)* OF COLLEGE OR UNIVERSITY.. *If you expect to graduate within nine months, give the month and year you expect to receive your degree:*

	Name	City	State	ZIP Code	MONTH AND YEAR ATTENDED From	To	NUMBER OF CREDIT HOURS COMPLETED Semester	Quarter	TYPE OF DEGREE *(e.g. B.A., M.A.)*	MONTH AND YEAR OF DEGREE
1)										
2)										
3)										

29 CHIEF UNDERGRADUATE SUBJECTS *Show major on the first line*

	NUMBER OF CREDIT HOURS COMPLETED Semester	Quarter
1)		
2)		
3)		

30 CHIEF GRADUATE SUBJECTS *Show major on the first line*

	NUMBER OF CREDIT HOURS COMPLETED Semester	Quarter
1)		
2)		
3)		

31 If you have completed any other courses or training related to the kind of jobs you are applying for *(trade, vocational, Armed Forces, business)* give information below.

NAME AND LOCATION *(city, state and ZIP Code)* OF SCHOOL		MONTH AND YEAR ATTENDED From	To	CLASS-ROOM HOURS	SUBJECT(S)	TRAINING COMPLETED YES	NO
School Name 1)							
City	State ZIP Code						
School Name 2)							
City	State ZIP Code						

SPECIAL SKILLS, ACCOMPLISHMENTS AND AWARDS

32 Give the title and year of any honors, awards or fellowships you have received. List your special qualifications, skills or accomplishments that may help you get a job. Some examples are: skills with computers or other machines; most important publications (do not submit copies); public speaking and writing experience; membership in professional or scientific societies; patents or inventions; etc.

33 How many words per minute can you:
TYPE?   TAKE DICTATION?
Agencies may test your skills before hiring you.

34 List job-related licenses or certificates that you have, such as: registered nurse; lawyer; radio operator; driver's; pilot's; etc.

LICENSE OR CERTIFICATE	DATE OF LATEST LICENSE OR CERTIFICATE	STATE OR OTHER LICENSING AGENCY
1)		
2)		

35 Do you speak or read a language other than English *(include sign language)?   Applicants for jobs that require a language other than English may be given an interview conducted solely in that language.*   YES   NO   If "YES", list each language and place an "X" in each column that applies to you.   If "NO", go to 36.

LANGUAGE(S)	CAN PREPARE AND GIVE LECTURES Fluently	With Difficulty	CAN SPEAK AND UNDERSTAND Fluently	Passably	CAN TRANSLATE ARTICLES Into English	From English	CAN READ ARTICLES FOR OWN USE Easily	With Difficulty
1)								
2)								

REFERENCES

36 List three people who are not related to you and are not supervisors you listed under 24 who know your qualifications and fitness for the kind of job for which you are applying. At least one should know you well on a personal basis.

FULL NAME OF REFERENCE	TELEPHONE NUMBER(S) *(Include Area Code)*	PRESENT BUSINESS OR HOME ADDRESS *(Number, street and city)*	STATE	ZIP CODE
1)				
2)				
3)				

Page 3

BACKGROUND INFORMATION -- *You must answer each question in this section before we can process your application.*

		YES	NO
37	Are you a citizen of the United States? *(In most cases you must be a U.S. citizen to be hired. You will be required to submit proof of identity and citizenship at the time you are hired.)* If "NO", give the country or countries you are a citizen of: _____		

NOTE: It is important that you give complete and truthful answers to questions 38 through 44. If you answer "YES" to any of them, provide your explanation(s) in Item 45. Include convictions resulting from a plea of nolo contendere *(no contest)*. Omit: 1) traffic fines of $100.00 or less; 2) any violation of law committed before your 16th birthday; 3) any violation of law committed before your 18th birthday, if finally decided in juvenile court or under a Youth Offender law; 4) any conviction set aside under the Federal Youth Corrections Act or similar State law; 5) any conviction whose record was expunged under Federal or State law. We will consider the date, facts, and circumstances of each event you list. In most cases you can still be considered for Federal jobs. However, **if you fail to tell the truth or fail to list all relevant** events or circumstances, this may be grounds for not hiring you, for firing you after you begin work, or for criminal prosecution (18 USC 1001).

		YES	NO
38	During the last 10 years, were you fired from any job for any reason, did you quit after being told that you would be fired, or did you leave by mutual agreement because of specific problems?.		
39	Have you **ever** been convicted of, or forfeited collateral for **any felony violation**? *(Generally, a felony is defined as any violation of law punishable by imprisonment of longer than one year, except for violations called misdemeanors under State law which are punishable by imprisonment of two years or less.)*		
40	Have you **ever** been convicted of, or forfeited collateral for any **firearms or explosives violation**?		
41	Are you **now** under charges for any violation of law?.		
42	During the **last 10 years** have you forfeited collateral, been convicted, been imprisoned, been on probation, or been on parole? Do not include violations reported in 39, 40, or 41, above.		
43	Have you **ever** been convicted by a military **court-martial**? If no military service, answer "NO".		
44	Are you **delinquent** on any Federal debt? *(Include delinquencies arising from Federal taxes, loans, overpayment of benefits, and other debts to the U.S. Government plus defaults on Federally guaranteed or insured loans such as student and home mortgage loans.)*		

45 If "YES" in: 38 - Explain for each job the problem(s) and your reason(s) for leaving. Give the employer's name and address.

39 through 43 - Explain each violation. Give place of occurrence and name/address of police or court involved.

44 - Explain the type, length and amount of the delinquency or default, and steps you are taking to correct errors or repay the debt. Give any identification number associated with the debt and the address of the Federal agency involved.

NOTE: If you need more space, use a sheet of paper, and include the item number.

Item No.	Date (Mo./Yr.)	Explanation	Mailing Address
			Name of Employer, Police, Court, or Federal Agency
			City State ZIP Code
			Name of Employer, Police, Court, or Federal Agency
			City State ZIP Code

		YES	NO
46	Do you receive, or have you ever applied for retirement pay, pension, or other pay based on military, Federal civilian, or District of Columbia Government service?.		
47	Do any of your relatives work for the United States Government or the United States Armed Forces? Include: *father; mother; husband; wife; son; daughter; brother; sister; uncle; aunt; first cousin; nephew; niece; father-in-law; mother-in-law; son-in-law; daughter-in-law; brother-in-law; sister-in-law; stepfather; stepmother; stepson; stepdaughter; stepbrother; stepsister; half brother; and half sister.* If "YES", provide details below. If you need more space, use a sheet of paper.		

Name	Relationship	Department, Agency or Branch of Armed Forces

SIGNATURE, CERTIFICATION, AND RELEASE OF INFORMATION

YOU MUST SIGN THIS APPLICATION.   Read the following carefully before you sign.

* A false statement on any part of your application may be grounds for not hiring you, or for firing you after you begin work. Also, you may be punished by fine or imprisonment (U.S. Code, title 18, section 1001).
* If you are a male born after December 31, 1959 you must be registered with the Selective Service System or have a valid exemption in order to be eligible for Federal employment. You will be required to certify as to your status at the time of appointment.
* **I understand** that any information I give may be investigated as allowed by law or Presidential order.
* **I consent** to the release of information about my ability and fitness for Federal employment by *employers, schools, law enforcement agencies and other individuals and organizations, to investigators, personnel staffing specialists, and other authorized employees of the Federal Government.*
* **I certify** that, to the best of my knowledge and belief, all of my statements are true, correct, complete, and made in good faith.

48 SIGNATURE *(Sign each application in dark ink)*	49 DATE SIGNED *(Month, day, year)*

Page 4

☆ U.S. GOVERNMENT PRINTING OFFICE: 1992 312-071/50114

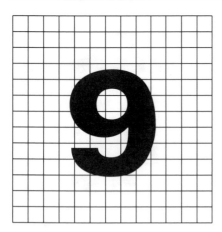

THE RESUME

The resume's primary goal is to sell you as a viable candidate for a specific position. The most important part of writing a resume is knowing what the job description is of the position you are applying for, because you need to tailor your qualifications and experience to suit it. Resumes are most often used in applying for state, county, and municipal positions, even though many posts require completion of their own application form.

The purpose of a resume is twofold. First, you want to demonstrate that your goal, experience, and education make you a very good candidate for a particular position. Second, you want to qualify for an interview, where you will have a one-on-one meeting and the opportunity to sell yourself.

The resume should pique a potential employer's interest, rather than present a comprehensive summary of your capabilities. Since you will undoubtedly apply for different types of jobs, you will require different resumes. Your experience and education remain the same. What changes is how you present or describe your experience and education (perhaps it is more accurate to say how you emphasize or highlight various parts of your past and recent work responsibilities).

Your worksheet is invaluable in preparing a strong resume as it contains all the information. You simply need to decide which items will best present your qualifications for a particular position and how you will describe them to suit the employment you are seeking. Since each job differs, the three critical questions you need to answer before beginning a resume are:

What duties and responsibilities are required for the position you are seeking? This is critical, since you will want to describe your background in a manner that best suits what the position requires. Also, you will want to answer in the same language used in the job description. By repeating key words in recounting your abilities, you send a strong message that you understand what they are looking for and that you are qualified and interested in being hired for the position.

Sometimes, the announcement is vague. To obtain the information you need, simply call the agency, department, or bureau and ask for a full description of the duties involved for that particular job.

What are the required levels of experience and education? You may find that you need to have more schooling or additional work experience to be hired for the government position you desire. For some situations, if you are enrolled in appropriate courses, your application is considered seriously because you show a commitment and willingness to acquire the necessary credentials for a particular post. However, government officials, especially at the federal and state level, rarely make exceptions for what they consider requirements for specified positions.

On the other hand, if you feel you can do the job, even though your background does not match the requirements, you should prepare a resume that reflects your desire and the confidence you have in your ability. You truly have nothing to lose and everything to gain—more information about the position you want, practice applying for a job, even an interview.

If your academic and work credentials match or are close to the requirements stated in the announcement, then you can highlight or present the information on your resume in a way that will attract attention.

What is the pay scale or range? Knowing the pay scale or range of the position you are applying for is not only helpful but necessary. If it is not listed in the job announcement or description, phone the agency, department, or bureau and request the salary range.

Salary requirements do not belong on a resume. However, they form a critical part of your background knowledge in seeking a particular position. Sometimes, you may decide not to apply for a position or even pursue a particular career path because the beginning pay scale does not enable you to meet your responsibilities.

You have to be able to judge if the trade-offs, e.g., an investment in a long-term government career for less money in the first year or two, are worth the effort. Sometimes earning less money will mean more change in your current life-style than you originally anticipated. When a potential employer realizes this, he or she will be concerned that you are ready to make that commitment. You have to be convinced first before you can convince anyone else, especially a future employer, that you will undertake the challenge because you want a long-term career.

Once you have satisfactorily answered the above three questions, you are ready to write your resume. A sample of how to arrange the information on a one-page resume is shown on the facing page.

Recent graduates or those with less than 5 years' experience need to condense their resume to a single page. Applicants with more than 5 years may also find it appropriate to have a one-page resume, particularly if their job responsibilities have not changed dramatically during their working years.

The two-page resume is recommended only for individuals with considerable experience or education that is relevant to the job they are seeking. Since the resume should motivate employers to want to interview you, to learn more about you, you want the resume to capture their interest, not to divulge everything.

Today, more and more applicants use a computer, word processor, or professional resume service to prepare their resumes. This is by no means essential. What is important is to have a clean, neat, organized resume that effectively presents your capabilities and looks professional.

The standard order of a resume is to put your name, address, and phone number at the top (see sample resume), then organize relevant information under headings in the following order: position sought/goal, experience, education, and special abilities (if applicable).

Optional considerations are volunteer or extracurricular experience (if applicable), and references or the statement "Upon request." The rules of thumb to follow are to remember that a one-page resume is generally more appropriate, information on a resume should interest the potential employer, not divulge everything, and the information given should directly tie into the job description.

Government hiring personnel at the state, county, and municipal level differ from their counterparts in the private sector in that they do not regard resumes as sacred cows. Resumes are important because generally they are the first significant means of evaluating you as a candidate for a particular job. Having stated this, it is important to realize that resumes are critical tools. A resume offers the best means of interesting a potential employer in wanting to meet with you. Since you want to have every opportunity to convince an employer that you are the right choice for a position, each encounter, written, verbal, or in person, becomes a golden opportunity to use to your advantage.

The reason for putting the goal first is to capture the attention of the person reading your resume. The goal will tell the reader whether you are a potential candidate before considering your qualifications. The next most critical component of your resume is your experience.

Experience is the practical application to date of your abilities and skills. This is the part of your resume that will change the most frequently. To adapt your experience to the various types of positions you are seeking, you need to repeat the words used in the job description to describe the responsibilities you held and the tasks you successfully completed. Each major job change is identified separately, even if it is with the same employer.

SUSAN R. COCHRANE
1650 N. Street Name
Anytown, IL 60637
312-245-2446
(Add another number, if needed)

POSITION SOUGHT: xxxxxxxxxxxxxxxxxxxxxxxxxxx
xxxxxxxxxxxxxxxxxxxxxxxxxxx
xxxxxxxxxxxxxxxxxxxxxxxxxxx

EXPERIENCE:

19xx–Current   (Most recent) job title, employer's name, city.
List key duties and accomplishments. Use language that relates to words in the ad.

19xx–19xx   List as separate positions all major job changes with the same employer, if applicable, or with the different employers you have worked for in sequential order.

EDUCATION:

19xx–19xx   School, city, degree (M.B.A. or B.A.), year of degree (1994), major (finance).

19xx–19xx   Repeat format for each school attended.

TRAINING:

19xx–19xx   Sponsor or school, city, title of course or study, year of certificate or other recognition.

19xx–19xx   Repeat format for all pertinent training.

CIVIC & OTHER AWARDS:

19xx   Award, origin, brief description. Repeat format for recognitions you have received that relate to this particular position.

LANGUAGES: Spanish (fluent), French (reading fluency).

REFERENCES: Furnished upon request.

Traditionally, the dates you held each position are put in the left margin adjacent to the first line of the description of your job. There is a trend today to submit resumes without dates because of the age discrimination issue. However, legislation prohibits discrimination because of age. Since you are applying for a governmental position, they will have access to your age and other records. There is no point in fudging.

Education is generally a simple listing of the years a school was attended, the name of the school, the location, the degree or certificate received, the year it was awarded, and the subject in which it was received. Unless a certain course or specified series of courses relates directly to the position you are seeking, no more information is given on a resume.

If you have certain specialized training or capabilities that relate directly to the position you are applying for, then they should be included immediately after education. List the year or years of study in the left column; on the right side, describe your specialty or training, and where and when you took or acquired it. Be brief. You will have better opportunities (the cover letter, the interview) to explain these capabilities. Your goal is to show you have the desire, the ability, and the experience for a particular position.

Some tips to use in writing your resume are:

- Use plain white or slightly off-white paper, preferably 24-pound bond.
- Use a standard typeface for your resume whether you type it or print it.
- State your goal to reflect the position you are seeking.
- Word your experience to demonstrate you have the qualifications necessary; be succinct but interesting.
- Omit controversial or negative facts, but be prepared to discuss them in a positive way at the interview.
- Proofread your resume carefully.
- Ask someone to proofread your resume.
- Have a third person proofread the resume.
- Read your resume one more time for content and errors.
- Use the best-quality photocopier to make several photocopies of your resume. File one with a copy of the cover letter, keep one to modify for the next position you apply for, and send one with your cover letter for the position you want.

PROFESSIONAL SERVICES

Many people choose to use professional resume or typing services in their job search. If you elect to hire a service for your resume, cover letters, and other correspondence, be sure it uses a laser printer (dot matrix printer quality is unacceptable) and that you are aware of the full cost in advance. Some questions to ask are:

1. What flexibility do you have to produce several variations of a resume?
2. What is the cost of having several different resumes?
3. What is the cost for proofing resumes and correspondence?
4. What is the standard turnaround for producing resumes, envelopes, and letters—one and two pages? What is the rush charge?
5. What is the charge if the stationery is supplied? If not supplied?
6. Is there a quantity discount? Is it cumulative?

The decision to hire a professional service to produce your resume or other written materials is a personal one and can be expensive. Apart from cost, the most important aspect of writing your resume is having the flexibility to tailor your qualifications to suit the position you desire, to describe your background so it reflects the qualities in the job description.

During your job search, you may find what you would like to do or the type of work you prefer changing. That alone is sufficient reason to plan for flexibility in redoing your resume. Your resume is a tool, one that needs to be adapted to meet your needs whenever you feel the situation calls for it.

Professional services often make suggestions about the wording, the organization, or other factors of your resume. Sometimes the suggestions are helpful, sometimes not. To help you evaluate the worth of their advice, remember that you are the one to decide what you want as a career and what your qualifications are. It is also your responsibility to write the resume describing your abilities so they will coincide with those listed in the job description. Arbitrary changes rarely serve anyone.

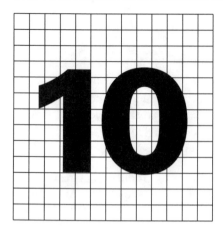

APPLICATION FORMS

Government agencies typically make more use of application forms than they do resumes. At first glance, the forms will seem rigid and appear to offer little flexibility to demonstrate why you are an excellent candidate. Governmental agencies, especially at the federal level, tend to operate in a set manner. As a result, they want to see the same information in the same place.

Their saving grace is that they want to hire someone. When they start to read an application form, they are thinking, "Maybe this is the person we can hire." You should use the experience blocks, the education blocks, and the other blocks on the application form to show that you are the person for the job.

You can get an application form to complete when you stop by an agency to inquire about positions, when you go on an interview, or on similar occasions. Frequently, when you phone to inquire about a position, you will be sent an application form to complete. Whenever you receive an application form, be sure you have a copy of the job description. If you do not, simply request one. The job description will enable you to tailor your responses to match those in the announcement.

The worksheet you so painstakingly prepared is extremely useful in filling out an application form. Carry at least one copy with you when you are looking for work or go for an interview. As obvious as it may seem, do not put all the copies of your worksheet in the same place.

Looking for employment is stressful. In a very real sense, you have to anticipate the unexpected and prepare for it. Having two or more copies of your worksheet with you in two separate places, perhaps in your wallet and in your pocket, will protect you against losing or misplacing the only copy when you most need to have the information on it.

In completing an application form, it is to your advantage to know the wording of the job description you want. Job descriptions for government positions are prepared with considerable thought and reflect the qualities desired for a particular post. As with a resume, it is smart to word your responses describing your abilities and experience in the same language used in the official announcement.

Some general advice for completing application forms:

1. Request two copies of the form. Immediately make several photocopies you can use for rough drafts. Do not touch the originals and use a very good quality photocopier.

2. Read the whole form in its entirety before you even begin to fill in basic information. Always put the information on a draft first.

3. Prepare a master copy if the same application form is used by several agencies. Be sure to leave certain items blank, e.g., the job description you are applying for, your signature, and date, as well as any other items that need to be current or tailored to a particular position. Make several copies of the master with the appropriate items left blank to be completed when you are ready to apply for a position.

4. Fill in the general information first, then photocopy it. On the copy, tailor your responses to fit the job you are seeking. When you have finished the form, photocopy the whole form, sign it, and date it.

5. Type your responses. If there does not appear to be sufficient room, type your information on a separate sheet of plain, white paper, then paste or glue it onto the application form. Photocopy it when you have completed the form, then sign, date, and submit it.

6. Answer everything. If a question does not apply to you, be sure to put *n/a,* not applicable. This will show the people reviewing your form that you read and answered each item.

7. Complete the form at home whenever possible. When you mail it in, send a cover letter and a copy of your resume written with this position in mind. If you have to fill it out at the agency, be sure to carry a copy of your worksheet with you so that you will have all the information needed to complete the application. Always ask if you can have or make a copy of the completed application form before handing it over to the agency.

8. Make use of the fact that applications for government positions almost always allow for extra information to be included on separate sheets of paper that can be attached to the official application. Follow the instructions exactly regarding adding information on separate attachments. More than likely, the instructions will be included at the beginning or end of the application. Often they will require you to type or print in dark (black or blue only) ink your name, Social Security number, name or classification of the position, and the item num-

ber to which you are adding supplemental information. As each form is different, please read carefully all the instructions on each application before completing. Then photocopy the additional sheets for your records before attaching them to the application and mailing them.

If you are required to fill out an application in the office of the agency, bureau, or department, remember to ask for a photocopy of the application before (in case you make mistakes) and after you have completed it (for your files). Having an extra copy will make you less nervous as you can use one for a draft. Drafts allow you to practice. In doing so, you are able to see what works on a specific application. The end result is a better application.

Referring to your worksheet will help with pertinent information and make it easier to adapt your qualifications to match the ones asked for in the job description. When you have completed the draft, check it carefully for content and other errors. Then fill out the application for good. Proof it carefully for spelling errors and omissions before signing and dating it. Ask for a photocopy of the completed form before turning it in. This is a standard request and will be treated as such.

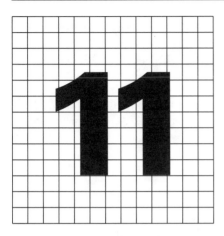

LETTERS

Every time you send in a resume or a completed application form, you will need an intriguing cover letter. The letter is an excellent opportunity to get the attention of your potential employer and to demonstrate why you are the right choice for a particular position. Instead of dreading writing a letter, be glad you have another chance to show why you are the person to hire.

A couple of pointers to remember in writing an effective cover letter are:

Address the letter to the person with whom you want to speak. This is the person that will hire you. For that reason, it will most likely be your future supervisor, not the head of personnel or the head of a department. Verify the spelling of this person's name and title by calling the agency or bureau. If you have any doubts about the information, call again and ask the personnel department to verify the spelling and title.

Write a sales letter. This is a great opportunity to sell yourself. Use it to your advantage. Sales letters are short, informative, and grab the attention of the reader. They are divided into four parts—the opening, the body, the request, and the closing. You can either center your name, address, and phone number at the top of the page or use the more traditional placement in the upper right corner; center the date in the middle of the letter; and place the address four spaces down from the date (see the sample cover letter on the facing page). As you become more confident, you will develop your own format for cover letters.

THE OPENING

You are the product, so sell yourself by capturing the reader's attention right away. The best way to do this is explain in the first sentence why you are writing the letter. You then want to refer to one of the employer's projects or an award it has recently won; end with a personal message. In Appendix A we list numerous periodicals and associations that publish periodicals. Check them for any information that will help you write a personalized opening.

If you are responding to an ad and you know someone influential who suggested you apply, mention her or his name. But only do this if you have first obtained permission to do so. Be sure and thank the person in a brief, handwritten thank-you note—immediately. If your handwriting is not easily read, you can type your message.

THE BODY

The second and third paragraphs are considered the body of the letter, where you toot your own horn. As shorter is better, consider a brief three- to four-sentence paragraph about your special qualifications; focus on the attributes and experiences that best match those used in the job announcement. You should interest the reader enough to want to know more about you, to want to meet you. This is not the time for full disclosure.

THE REQUEST

In the paragraph immediately following the body of the letter, ask for an interview. State a day and date that you will phone to arrange an appointment for an interview. Because you have declared your intentions, you are giving the reader several options.

The reader can plan to see you and make the necessary arrangements, such as giving the secretary times for a meeting if he or she is unavailable when you phone or asking that you phone back at a specific time, or direct the secretary to discourage you.

Just as it is critical to phone when you say you will, it is equally important to be courteous, regardless of the reception you receive. Always thank the person for his or her time and consideration. People have a way of remembering; besides, situations always change. Should an opening occur after you phone, you would like to be remembered and asked to come in for an interview. People tend to remember the pleasant, polite caller even though they might forget their own attitude was less than cordial.

When you call, introduce yourself and explain that you are following up on your letter requesting an appointment for an interview. Identify the position for which you are applying by title and classification. While this may be the most important call you make that day or even that week, remember that your call is but one of many that will be received that day. Speaking directly avoids wasting the time of the person answering the phone and helps you establish a professional, businesslike image.

Approach each contact with a potential employer as a golden opportunity to present yourself as a reliable and competent employee. Avoid stating that

Mr. Barry Dillen
2332 S. Edgar
Anytown, MA
Phone Number

Date

Ms. Louise Johnson
Manager of Special Events
Street Address
City, State, Zip

Dear Ms. Johnson:

Your announcement of an opening for an assistant in the Special Events Department–Neighborhoods for a six-month temporary assignment beginning April 10, 19xx, is of great interest to me. Your section has consistently done an outstanding job for the past five years with the Summer Festival Program. I would like to work with your team.

My goal is to have a career in municipal government bridging the gap between the different ethnic communities that enrich our city. On March 15, 19xx, I will have completed my B.A. in the work/study program of Community Affairs at Columbia College with a minor in Spanish. As the final phase of my program, I am working as a facilitator in Family Relations at the Adams Neighborhood Center.

Two years ago, I was awarded the Maxwell Cup for Outstanding Achievement because of the work I did as an intern managing the visual arts program at the Garcia Foundation. Although I grew up here in the city, I was an exchange student in Mexico twice during my high school years.

My fluency in Spanish has enabled me to be a volunteer at the Northside Children's Hospital on Saturday mornings for the past 15 months. I translate and serve as a patient/family advocate for Spanish-speaking patients and their families.

For your review, I am enclosing my resume. I will phone your office on Friday, March 3, 19xx, to arrange for an appointment for an interview for the position of assistant.

Sincerely,

Mr. Barry Dillen

you would like an interview on a specific day or during a certain week. This makes your request sound more like a demand, and often is misinterpreted as being presumptuous or too pushy. Practically speaking, you have no way of knowing if that person is available to meet then, as people often take vacations or are out of the office on business.

THE CLOSURE

A conservative complimentary close—"Sincerely" or "Cordially"—is always preferable. It is better to sign your name in black ink, although blue is acceptable. Avoid other colors. Under your signature, type your name; this ensures it will be read correctly.

Send a clean, business-looking letter. The appearance of your letter describes you. As you want to be hired, your cover letter should look clean, neat—absolutely free from typos or misspelled words—and professional. For appearance, choose a 24-pound plain white or slightly off-white bond paper (available in office supply stores) for your letter. You can use the same stationery for your resume.

In addition to proofing your own letter, be sure to have at least one other person carefully check your letter for errors and typos. Check your own name and address carefully and verify that the day and date you are to phone coincide. Glaring errors frequently occur where they are least expected.

Develop a system for your follow-up. Photocopy your letter before sending it. Before putting it in your *Active* file, mark your calendar with the name and phone number of the person you are to call on the appropriate day. In parentheses, insert the date you wrote the letter so you know where it is in your file.

Before phoning, pull the letter from your file to review what you wrote. Even though you have a format for your cover correspondence, you will want to refresh your memory as to what you wrote in the opening and body of the letter.

THANK-YOU LETTERS

Thank-you correspondence is as essential to your career as brushing your teeth is to your dental well-being. For some reason, writing thank-you notes seems to be a task that most people tend to delay or avoid, especially when it concerns small favors.

A favor, regardless of size, is essentially an action that benefits you. That benefit can be as varied as using someone's name to open a door, having the advantage of using a high-profile person as your reference, or hearing of a position that is available. Whatever it is, your first reaction must be to thank the person for his or her effort.

In pursuing a career in government, you have decided to become part of a special segment of our society. Networking and building your reputation start with your first job. A practical gift you can give yourself is the lifelong habit of thanking those who help you, directly and indirectly. This will enrich your own life and enhance your professional life. Most people enjoy helping others, especially if they are not inconvenienced and their efforts are appreciated.

Job-related favors require that thank-yous be written. Their importance can not be overstated. Appearance and content are the two essential components. Clean, neat handwritten notes are acceptable, unless your handwriting is illegible. Then you will have to type them. Although a thank-you note is informal, there are certain guidelines for content that will help you in writing them.

1. In the first sentence, state why you are writing (to thank the individual for suggesting you contact a particular person or for her or his willingness to recommend you for a particular position, et cetera). Your first sentence often is your first paragraph.

2. In the second sentence, describe your interest in having a career in government (See the example at the end of this chapter). Follow this with a statement that you will notify her or him of the appropriate developments.

3. The next paragraph should focus on the personal connection that exists between you. This can include seeing the person or one of her or his family at a recent function, congratulating her or him on news you have heard, or any similar type of message that reinforces your relationship. Then go to the next guideline.

4. This is your closing where you wish the person well. This is particularly easy to do if there is a holiday in the near future, or a new season is beginning. If you do not have the benefit of any of these opportunities, simply send your very best wishes. Sign off with a closing that is formal—"Sincerely" or "Cordially"—if your relationship is not a personal one. If you do have a personal relationship, use whatever closing is appropriate—"Best regards," "Fondly," et cetera.

When you start to wind your workday down—and looking for a job is work—use the last hour or so to write all your thank-you correspondence for that day's activity. Making it a part of your daily routine will help you avoid the pitfalls of postponing.

315 N. Glenview
Anytown, State, Zip

Date

Mr. Jason Edwards
Director of Customer Services
First National Bank
445 N. Madison
Anytown, State, Zip

Dear Mr. Edwards:

Thank you for notifying me that there is a mid-level administrative position available in the county's program for the homeless. I appreciate your offer to recommend me to Mr. Homer Jefferson, the supervisor in charge of the program.

My long-term goal is to have a career in government, specializing in community affairs. Having successfully worked for the city's shelter programs until the recent budget cuts, I am most interested in this opportunity as it relates closely to the work I did over the past four years.

What a wonderful article that was on the First's scholarship program in last night's paper! You and your staff are running an excellent program that is truly making a difference.

Have a terrific Fourth of July.

Cordially,

Ms. Rachel Horner

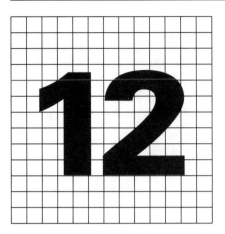

THE INTERVIEW

As soon as you have an appointment for an interview, congratulate yourself. You have achieved an important interim goal. Now you need to prepare for another success—the interview. Having a positive interview significantly increases your chance of receiving a job offer. It is worth your time and effort to prepare carefully for every interview, even if you think you do not want a particular job. You will learn valuable information that will help you turn the job you accept into a successful career.

Three objectives are normally realized in an interview. First, you will learn more about the position. You then will be in a position to decide whether this is a job you want and whether it is one you can do well. You will also begin to see how it will help build your career.

Second, you will know if you would like to work for this particular agency; each agency and bureau has its own energy, its own personality. By asking the right questions during the interview, you will be able to evaluate how you will fit in this environment. You may find that the position is desirable, but that your immediate supervisor would be too domineering or that the atmosphere is too stifling. Because these conditions would seriously handicap your performance, you may decide to pursue another offer or look for a similar position, but in a different section of the agency.

Third, the interviewers will be deciding if you are the person for the job. They will be investing in the individual they hire. Training a new employee affects coworkers, supervisors, and other staff members. Supervisors are responsible for the person who is hired.

If they make a mistake in judgment, it reflects badly on their own record. No one wants to make a mistake. Naturally, they want the person hired to succeed. Careful scrutiny is both a protection and a necessity to avoid wasting valuable time, energy, and other resources. The interview is a major step or hurdle in the decision to hire an individual.

You want a position where you can do well; the employer wants an employee who will do well and remain with the organization. Hiring and accepting a job is a risk for everyone because of the investment involved for both parties. For the employer, it represents a potential loss in productivity, training time and money, and the cost of finding a replacement. For you, it represents the potential loss of time, self-esteem, and money, plus the effort, anxiety, and cost of finding a new position.

You can reduce your risk by preparing for the interview. Begin by approaching the interview in your mind. See it as an opportunity to learn about the people you could be working with on a daily basis. Then imagine yourself greeting the individual. Picture what you are wearing, what you are saying, how you are reacting. Play out different scenarios—see the interview in a small office, a small conference room, a cluttered office, a large office. Always try to envision the details of the situation, including the background noise of the office, the temperature, the color of the walls.

See yourself as being professional, courteous, interested, and responsive under all these circumstances. Imagine hearing yourself asking and responding to questions in a forthright manner. The more you do this, the greater is your opportunity to shine in an interview, regardless of what happens.

Essentially what you are doing is creating a sense memory of doing well, of successful behavior. The more you imagine it, the more you are training yourself to respond positively.

The next step is to work on the content of the interview. Ideally, you want to understand their expectations as well as what the job actually is all about and the types of responsibilities you will have. You also want to explore the possibilities for long-term promotion, further training, and advancement within the current job classification.

Some questions that you need to explore are: Do they expect you to be fully functional within 4 to 6 weeks or 6 months? Is there a formal training program already set up? Will your duties increase over time or will they remain the same? Your focus is to discover as much as possible about what they expect from the person holding this post. You also want to know if they encourage or discourage promotion. As you interview, you will form your own list of questions that you will want answers to before accepting a position.

Since interviewers look for highly motivated people who understand what the job entails and demonstrate they can do it, the following are tips for a successful interview:

Show you are a highly motivated person. A clean, neat appearance is the first thing you will be judged by, so make sure your hair is freshly washed and that you are well groomed. Blue jeans, runs in stockings, chipped nail polish, heavy makeup, wrinkled shirts and so on all send a negative message.

Greet the interviewer by his or her proper name. Do not presume to use his or her first name; wait for the interviewer to suggest it.

Listen attentively.

Avoid smoking and chewing gum.

Thank the interviewer at the end and state your interest in being hired for this position—"I would like to come to work for you," or "I am very interested in being hired for this position." Be sure to end the interview on a positive note.

Write a brief thank-you when you get home, saying you enjoyed your meeting and are interested in being hired.

Also include some point raised in the interview and elaborate on it, relating one or more of your capabilities to it. (See the example at the end of the chapter.)

Demonstrate your interest in and your understanding of what the job entails.   Ask questions that show you read the announcement and want to know more. Some questions to ask are:

What is the most important function of this position?

In addition to (repeat certain qualifications mentioned in the ad), what additional skills are needed or would you like a person to have?

Who would be my supervisor?

When can I meet the supervisor?

What training programs are offered?

How important is this job to the agency?

Why is the position vacant?

What is that person doing now?

What are the opportunities for advancement?

Sell yourself by tying in your responses to your qualifications. For example, if asked what your weaknesses are, your reply could be that you work too hard, you need to see the big picture, you worry too much about details. If asked about your disabilities, a police conviction, a failure in school, or being fired, stress how much you have learned from your mistakes, how you have overcome your shortcomings, and how you are and will continue to be a better employee because of what you have learned.

Do not discuss salary. Wait until you have a job offer to discuss salary and benefits. Show your interest in performing the job well, not in what you can receive in benefits and salary. Besides, municipal, county, state, and federal positions generally have defined ranges for benefits and salary with minimal leeway. Normally, they will be advertised in the job announcement. You should know this information well before the interview.

Practice interviewing.   One of the better ways to succeed at an interview is to practice. You can role-play with a friend or relative as the interviewer. You should also practice being the interviewer to gain a better understanding of what he or she would like and how it feels. Use the questions we have suggested in the previous pages and add to them.

Another good way to practice is to go on interviews, even if you feel you do not want the position. Go on every interview you can since it will build your confidence by giving you practical experience.

AFTER THE INTERVIEW

As soon as you get home, make notes about the interview—what went well, your impressions about the job, the person who interviewed you, the names of the other people you met, and what you thought about them. Include what did not go so well, and carefully note what you can do to have a better interview. Then be sure to practice these points before going on your next interview.

Immediately write your thank-you note to the person who interviewed you, even if you have decided that you do not want the job. The network in government is very active. Although you might decide that you do not want this particular job, you never know when you will meet up with that person again or whom she or he might know. Your goal is to have the interviewer think highly of you, your professional behavior, and your capabilities. Promptness is pleasantly received and creates a favorable impression. It is an excellent means of building or keeping a favorable impression associated with your name.

Before going to bed, read your notes for tomorrow's appointments, review your schedule of activities, and imagine yourself doing well at the next interview. Your agenda should include job search tasks such as reading the local papers for news items (references to agencies where you have applied, the people who work there, anyone recommending you, et cetera), checking for available positions, calling to verify names and titles, preparing cover letters and resumes, completing applications, and practicing interviewing.

428 N. Sechwag
Anytown, State, Zip

Date

Ms. Carmen Jacobs
State Supervisor—Secondary Education
The Johnson State Building
Street Address
Anytown, State, Zip

Dear Ms. Jacobs:

Thank you for meeting with me today and explaining your long-term goals for language awareness in the northern part of our state. I am most interested in being considered for the position of administrative coordinator of the language program for the seven counties that comprise the northern portion of Missouri.

Your emphasis on developing a program that includes the parents of our Spanish-speaking students is very exciting. My volunteer work in teaching English to adults at the Lincoln Community Center has made me keenly aware of the sensitivities involved in undertaking this type of project.

In today's mail, I received my quarterly copy of *Outreach*. There is an excellent article on a dynamic new program being run in the Miami area by Maria Cortez. Because it approximates many of the ideas we discussed, I am enclosing a copy for your review.

I would welcome having the opportunity to work with you and your staff. If you would like me to submit additional information on my work at the Lincoln Community Center, I will be happy to do so.

Sincerely,

Ms. Stephanie Horan

Section III
Jobs, Jobs, Jobs

Some say a career is made up of a series of jobs. In working for the government, this rings particularly true as many agencies and most supervisors prefer to hire from within rather than hire an unknown person from outside. The path a number of people take is to accept a position, even if it is for less pay or rated lower than they anticipated. Then they concentrate on being promoted within the system.

The purpose of this section is to give you an overview of the thousands upon thousands of positions available in government. More than 18 million civilians are employed by the federal, state, county, and municipal governments. At the federal level, there are the agencies (employing millions of workers), Congress, and the courts. The vast majority of jobs, almost 15 million, are with the state, county, and municipal branches of government.

The seven chapters in this section are divided into two principal subsections (first federal, then the state, county, and municipal portion). Within the federal subsection, the first chapter considers white-collar jobs in the administrative, professional, and scientific sectors and the second chapter covers clerical, technical, and blue-collar positions. Chapter 3 recaps 39 different federal agencies. Chapter 4, the last portion of the federal material, looks at Congress and the courts.

The following three chapters comprise the state, county, and municipal section. Chapter 5 provides an overview of the opportunities available at the state, county, and municipal level. Chapter 6 covers the administrative, professional, and scientific positions while Chapter 7 delves into the clerical, technical, and blue-collar jobs. The job descriptions and information in the seven chapters are for nonelected and non-appointed positions.

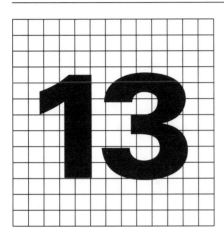

PROFESSIONAL, ADMINISTRATIVE, AND SCIENTIFIC CAREERS IN THE FEDERAL GOVERNMENT

College graduates generally enter the positions described in this chapter, although people without a college degree but with the right kind of experience also qualify and are hired for them. The sheer size of the federal government distinguishes it from individual state, county, and municipal governments. To maintain some type of uniformity in hiring and promoting individuals, the federal government and its agencies use the GS classification system and GS ratings. Generally, state, county, and local governments follow less standardized practices for hiring and promoting.

Since no one book can actually represent all the jobs that 3 million people do, each category of position defined in this chapter offers employment opportunities for at least 5,000 people. Other occupations with fewer than 5,000 employees are listed at the end of this chapter to give you a better insight to what is available.

THE PERSONNEL CLASSIFICATION SYSTEM

The government's Personnel Classification System includes an occupational group structure that places like jobs together. There are 22 occupational groups, ranging from GS-100 to GS-2100.

Each occupational group has a three-part identifier: the pay system, occupational group number, and title. For example, when you read GS-400, Biological Sciences, GS means the job is in the General Schedule (white-collar) pay system; 400 is the group number; and Biological Sciences is the group title.

A list of the 22 federal occupation groups follows.

Occupational Group Number	*Occupational Group Title*
GS-000	Miscellaneous
GS-100	Social Science, Psychology, and Welfare
GS-200	Personnel Management and Industrial Relations
GS-300	Administrative, Clerical, and Office Services
GS-400	Biological Sciences
GS-500	Accounting and Budget
GS-600	Medical, Hospital, Dental, and Public Health
GS-700	Veterinary Medical Science
GS-800	Engineering and Architecture
GS-900	Legal and Kindred
GS-1000	Information and Arts
GS-1100	Business and Industry
GS-1200	Copyright, Patent, and Trademark
GS-1300	Physical Sciences
GS-1400	Library and Archives
GS-1500	Mathematics and Statistics
GS-1600	Equipment, Facilities, and Service
GS-1700	Education
GS-1800	Investigation
GS-1900	Quality Assurance, Inspection, and Grading
GS-2000	Supply
GS-2100	Transportation

Federal government employees generally fall into a certain pay grade. All the jobs in this chapter are in what is called the *General Schedule* (GS). Grades in the General Schedule go from GS-1 to GS-18. Almost all the occupations described here start at GS-5, which denotes a salary similar to those offered to new college graduates by private companies. The lower grades are assigned to clerical and technical employees, whose jobs are described in the next chapter.

Accountants and auditors (GS-510) keep track of how much money an agency spends and receives. They also evaluate the performance of contractors and offices within the agency to make sure that the taxpayers get what they pay for. They are found in almost every agency. Since some agencies are responsible for auditing the work of many other agencies, they employ large numbers of accountants and auditors. These auditing agencies include the Air Force Audit Agency, the Army Audit Agency, the Defense Contract Audit Agency, the Navy Audit Agency, and the General Accounting Office.

The departments of Agriculture, the Treasury, Health and Human Services, and Energy also employ large numbers of the government's accountants and auditors, about one-fourth of whom work in Washington. To qualify for these positions, applicants should have majored in accounting or taken at least 24 semester hours of college-level courses in accounting or auditing. Many government accountants are certified public accountants.

Administrative assistants and officers (GS-341) have many different duties, depending on their particular job. They manage an office so that others can do the work required of the agency by Congress and the president. For example, the function of NASA is the exploration of outer space and many of its employees work directly on that task. In order for them to do their work, administrative assistants in the agency organize the inner space of the office building, manage the hiring and paying of employees, administer contracts, arrange for office supplies and computer equipment, provide for office security, and take care of any number of other necessary but mundane tasks.

Because the duties of administrative officers are so varied, these employees usually specialize in a particular aspect of a job. Entry positions (GS-5) are open to college graduates regardless of major.

Administrative officers are employed throughout the government. Only the Defense Department and Postal Service employ more than 1,000, but each of the large agencies employs a substantial number.

Aerospace engineers: See Engineers in this chapter.

Air traffic control specialists (GS-2152) make sure that planes do not fly into each other. They are the "tower" that the pilot talks to when taking off or landing; they function as a control center telling pilots where to fly when going from one point to another. As they track several planes at once, they must be able to keep calm and make decisions quickly in an emergency. When you consider the number of planes that hover around a major airport, you will realize how stressful an occupation air traffic control is. The work is so demanding that applicants must meet stricter physical requirements than usual for federal jobs.

Applicants for terminal and center specialties must not have reached their 31st birthday. All applicants must have 20/20 vision, at least with the use of glasses, and have excellent peripheral vision. In addition, applicants must have excellent hearing and the ability to speak clearly and concisely. They must have a medical history free of heart disease, diabetes mellitus, and mental disorders. All must pass written and oral examinations.

A college degree is required of most applicants, but experience can be substituted for education if it is related to air traffic control. Acceptable experience includes things such as providing pilots with information about weather and airport conditions or doing research on new air traffic control systems. Despite the strict requirements for this occupation, competition for these jobs is intense.

Air traffic control specialists work at airports and control centers throughout the United States. Since planes are in the air around the clock, shift work is required. The Federal Aviation Administration, which is part of the Department of Transportation, employs most of the controllers, but the Army, Navy, and Air Force also employ at least 200 civilians each in this job. To make sure that all airports and control centers are adequately staffed, air traffic controllers may have to move from one city to another.

Attorneys: See Lawyers in this chapter.

Budget analysts or officers (GS-560) see that an agency spends no more than Congress said it could. Putting together a budget for an agency is a complicated business, since every agency has many different programs, and the people in charge of each program estimate how much money their program needs. Budget analysts review these estimates and plan one budget for the whole agency. They also review requests for funds throughout the year, ensuring that the requests do not exceed the amount of money available. Finally, they regularly evaluate the cost of a program in relation to its success.

A college degree qualifies people for GS-5. Budget clerks and accounting technicians may be promoted into these positions. Budget analysts work for almost every agency; the larger agencies naturally employ more of them. More than one-third of the government's estimated 9,800 budget analysts and officers work in Washington.

Chemists (GS-1320) study the nature of the elements and their components—the way they are put together, their properties, and the way they interact with each other. The Office of Personnel Management used to say, "Highly advanced government programs of research and investigation are of such diversity of approach and interest as to include practically any special preferences a prospective employee may have." In other words, no matter what problems chemists wish to solve, the federal government probably has jobs for them.

Chemists qualify for entry positions (GS-5) on the basis of their education. A college degree is required for most positions, including 30 semester hours in chemistry and 6 in physics. Chemists, the largest group of scientists in the government, work for a variety of agencies.

Civil engineers: See Engineers in this chapter.

Civil rights analysts (GS-160) conduct research on voting rights, housing, and other civil rights issues as well as recommend policies for the government to implement. A bachelor's degree in any field qualifies an applicant for the entry level (GS-5). These workers are widely dispersed among the various governmental agencies.

Computer specialists (GS-334) include computer programmers, computer systems analysts, and computer equipment analysts. These three occupations are closely related, and the performance of any one of them requires substantial knowledge of the others.

Programmers write detailed instructions for the computer so it can accomplish a given task one step at a time. Every instruction must be presented to the computer in an either/or format; it cannot choose among three or more possibilities.

Systems analysts are usually responsible for determining which agency tasks can be accomplished by the computer. They do not actually write programs, but they must know whether or not a particular job can be programmed.

Equipment analysts study the kinds of work an agency does and determine what kind of computer equipment the agency should purchase.

College graduates are usually hired for entry-level positions in these occupations. Courses in data processing are helpful, but not required. Many positions require people with special knowledge of the subject that the computers will deal with, such as physics or mathematics.

The federal government pioneered the development of computers and is still the largest single user of computer systems. The departments of the Treasury, Defense, and Health and Human Services employ large numbers of computer specialists; however, computer specialists can be found in nearly every agency.

Contact representative (GS-962) is one of those job titles that keeps the job's duties a secret. These workers might better be called "explainers," because they explain government programs to people. For example, contact representatives who work for the Treasury Department tell people how to figure their taxes; contact representatives who work for the Department of Health and Human Services explain Social Security benefits to people.

College graduates are usually recruited for these positions (even though the Office of Personnel Management classifies them as technical), but you can qualify for the lower grades (GS-4) with only 2 years of education after high school. These jobs are scattered widely throughout the United States; there are only about 200 contact representatives in Washington.

Contract and procurement specialists (GS-1102) buy goods and services that other government workers need to do their jobs. This is one occupation that people thinking of a government career rarely consider, yet some 21,000 people are employed as contract and procurement specialists. When the government needs to purchase something—and it purchases billions of dollars' worth of goods and services each year—someone has to make sure that the taxpayers get the best buy for their money. This responsibility rests with contract and procurement specialists. Some contracts, e.g., one with a printer for a single publication, are fairly simple; others, e.g., building a new jet fighter plane, require complex negotiations and careful administration.

College graduates are preferred no matter what their majors. Contract and procurement specialists work in every agency, but the armed forces, Defense Logistics Agency, and General Services Administration are among the larger employers.

Criminal investigators (GS-1810 and GS-1811) are responsible for providing legal evidence to prosecute individuals who break the law. When a law has been breached, the investigators gather proof, talk to witnesses, trail suspects, and make arrests. The work is physically difficult, involves personal risks, demands considerable travel, and requires irregular, unscheduled hours. It is a demanding occupation that offers a variety of challenges as well as good opportunities for advancement.

Applicants must be at least 21 years old. A college degree, in any field, is usually required, but law school graduates are preferred. Almost every large agency employs a few criminal investigators, but about half work for the Department of Justice, and several thousand work for the Department of the Treasury, which includes the Bureau of Alcohol, Tobacco, and Firearms, the U.S. Customs Service, and the Internal Revenue Service.

Economists (GS-110) track the way people spend their money by studying what people buy and how much they pay for products. They also estimate how large a supply there is of things to buy. Economists with the government use this information for two purposes: to regulate prices and to determine policies that will help the country's economy grow. For example, if a company that sells electric power across state lines wants to raise its rates, economists in the Federal Power Commission must determine whether the rate increase is fair. Or, if unemployment or inflation rates are high, economists try to figure out how to bring them down. Of course, such policy decisions are made only at the highest level of government and must be approved by Congress and the president. Economists at lower levels might be principally engaged in finding out what the unemployment rates actually are, among other things.

The lowest grade for economists is GS-5. College graduates with 21 semester hours in economics and 3 in statistics, accounting, or calculus qualify. Economists work for a large number of agencies, but the departments of Labor and Agriculture have the most.

Electrical/electronics engineers: See Engineers in this chapter.

Engineers (GS-800 series) are among the most numerous employees in the federal service. More than 90,000 engineers are employed by almost every agency, with jobs scattered throughout the country. In general, people qualify for GS-5 entry-level positions if (a) they have graduated from a school of engineering; (b) they are registered as professional engineers; (c) they have completed 60 semester hours in an engineering curriculum and have had 1 year of professional experience; or (d) they have passed the *Engineer-in-Training Examination.* (The Engineer-in-Training Examination is administered by the Board of Engineering Examiners in each state. *Do not write the Office of Personnel Management or any other federal agency for information; write to the secretary of your state's board.*)

Since there are so many different types of engineering, it might be helpful to examine the duties of the major engineering fields separately. Among the specialized engineers the federal government employs are *aerospace engineers, civil engineers, electronics* and *electrical engineers*, and *mechanical engineers.*

Aerospace engineers design and develop aircraft and spacecraft for optimal performance. Planes, helicopters, rockets, space shuttles, and satellites are some of the products they produce. Most of these employees, naturally, are with the National Aeronautics and Space Administration, Air Force, and Navy.

Civil engineers plan military bases, roads, and dams. The Army Corps of Engineers employs more than 9,000 engineers—6,000 of them civil engineers—which makes the Corps "the largest concentration of professional construction talent in the world," according to the Office of Personnel Management. Other major employers include the Department of Transportation and its Federal Highway Administration, the Department of Agriculture, the Navy, and the Department of the Interior, which is responsible for many of the dams and canals built in this country.

Electronics and electrical engineers design the equipment that keeps the U.S. government in touch with the world, whether it be an ordinary telephone line or a sophisticated radar device. Although electronics and electrical engineers might work on the design and manufacture of any kind of electrical equipment, most of those employed in the federal service are concerned with communications equipment. The major employers are the armed forces, the National Aeronautics and Space Administration, and the Coast Guard, which is part of the Department of Transportation.

Mechanical engineers work with engines, some that power a ship through ice floes in the North Atlantic and some that merely air-condition an office building in New Mexico. The armed forces are the largest employers, but almost every agency employs at least a few mechanical engineers.

Equipment specialists (GS-1670) are administrators and technicians who approve designs, negotiate contracts, and instruct people in the use of equipment. They must be able to read blueprints and understand technical language as well as have a practical knowledge of equipment and mechanics. They are usually specialists in a particular kind of equipment, such as aircraft, missiles, or ships. Positions start at GS-5, and require a college degree in engineering, physics, or a related subject. The Defense Department employs almost all of the equipment specialists in the government.

FBI special agents are investigators. Because their job requires that they look for evidence when a crime is suspected, they interview witnesses, examine records, and keep watch over suspects. They are on call 24 hours a day, may have to travel anywhere in the United States, and frequently work overtime. These jobs are hard to obtain because the turnover of agents is low and the requirements are high.

Lawyers and accountants are the preferred applicants, although physicists, language specialists, and experienced police officers are sometimes hired. Applicants must be between the ages of 23 and 35 and pass a rigid physical examination. The only employer of agents is the Federal Bureau of Investigation, which has almost 60 field offices located throughout the country. Agents are attached to a particular field office, so the jobs are widely scattered.

Financial institution examiners (GS-570) audit savings and loan associations, credit unions, farm credit associations, cooperative banks, investment firms, national banks, and other financial institutions. To perform an audit, examiners study the assets or holdings of the institution and determine their value. Then the examiners balance the assets against the institution's liabilities.

Applicants with a college degree can qualify for most entry-level positions (GS-5) if they have 24 semester hours in business-related subjects. Between them, the Federal Deposit Insurance Corporation and the Department of the Treasury employ almost all of the government's examiners, but a few work for such small, specialized agencies as the Farm Credit Administration. Very few of these jobs are in Washington; most require extensive travel within a region.

Foresters (GS-460) manage more than 100 million acres of federal property, an area larger than any of the states except Texas and Alaska. The United States' forests serve many ends. They must be available for recreation and also yield wood and other products for fuel, building material, and paper. Foresters are responsible for seeing that the woodlands are as productive as possible while protected from fire, disease, and erosion.

College graduates qualify as foresters (GS-5) if they have majored in subjects such as forestry, silviculture (the development and care of forests), or range management. No exam is necessary. Competition is usually keen for these positions, most of which are with the Department of Agriculture's Forest Service. The Department of the Interior and several other agencies also employ foresters.

Internal revenue officers (GS-1169) see that people pay their taxes. They review the tax returns of private citizens and corporations whose claims are unusual for some reason—for example, because they gave an uncommonly large sum of money to charity. The agents next look over the taxpayer's financial records and, if necessary, try to collect information from other sources. Agents also advise taxpayers and government attorneys about tax matters and prepare rulings concerning taxes.

To qualify, a college graduate must have taken at least 24 semester hours in accounting and auditing. All the government's internal revenue agents work for the Treasury Department. According to the Office of Personnel Management, "A very substantial portion of the top executive positions in the various Internal Revenue Service offices throughout the country are held by persons who began their careers as agents." Only a few hundred agents work in Washington; the rest are assigned to the 60 district offices located around the country.

Inventory managers: See Supply Management Specialists in this chapter.

Lawyers (GS-905) are critical to the effectiveness of the government, which ensures the safety and welfare of Americans by enacting and enforcing laws that require or forbid certain acts. Lawyers become involved both when the laws are written and when they are broken.

Lawyers are among the workers who are not hired through the Office of Personnel Management. When an agency needs lawyers, it looks for them itself.

Applicants must have an LL.B. or J.D. degree and pass their state's bar exam before they are hired. Degree holders who have not passed the bar exam may be hired as law clerks; law clerks must then pass the bar within 14 months of being hired or they will be fired.

Every government agency hires lawyers, but the departments of Justice and the Treasury together employ about one-third of the government's general attorneys. The regulatory agencies, such as the Securities and Exchange Commission and the Equal Employment Opportunities Commission, also employ many lawyers. Although government lawyers work throughout the country, almost half of them are stationed in or near Washington.

Loan specialists (GS-1165) examine and analyze financial factors and credit risks, counsel loan applicants, and investigate problems with repayment.

The qualification standards do not require any particular college courses for the GS-5 level. However, the phrase "ability to gather and analyze facts and figures" is generally interpreted to mean that an applicant should have taken some finance or accounting courses. The government's loan specialists are concentrated in three agencies: Agriculture, Housing and Urban Development, and the Small Business Administration. Few of the positions are in Washington.

Management analysts (GS-343) study the way an office is organized. They interview the employees, learn what work has to be done, and discover what procedures are followed. They then make a report recommending improvements in the organization of the office. College graduates are usually hired for beginning jobs in this field. Analyst positions are found in all the larger agencies.

Mechanical engineers: See Engineers in this chapter.

Medical officers: See Physicians in this chapter.

Nurses (GS-610) care for the sick and injured. Except for doctors, they are the most highly trained health professionals and have the widest range of jobs. About 35,000 nurses work for the federal government, making them the largest group of professional employees in the federal service after engineers.

The work nurses do depends largely on whether they are employed by a large hospital or small clinic. A large hospital—such as the 150 or so run by the Department of Veterans Affairs, and the many others run by the armed forces and the Public Health Service—offers a great variety of jobs for clinical nurses. At such a hospital, one nurse may work in an intensive care unit, while another works in orthopedics or surgery. Health clinics in government office buildings employ occupational nurses who treat people who become sick or are injured on the job. Occupational nurses also practice preventive medicine, which means they test people for illness before any symptoms exist, suggest diets, and recommend activities for continued health.

To qualify for a government job, an applicant must be a *registered nurse.* Since health and illness are not limited to any geographic area, there are government jobs for nurses all over the country. To learn about local opportunities, first find out which federal hospitals are near you. Their names will be listed in the telephone book under *U.S. Government.* Then write or call the personnel office of the hospital.

Personnel management specialists (GS-201) hire, promote, and train the government's labor force. Despite their title, these employees are less specialized than other kinds of personnel administrators; their jobs combine the duties of two or more of the following personnel workers: personnel staffing specialists, position classification specialists, employee development specialists, labor-management relations specialists, and employee relations specialists. An individual personnel management specialist might interview people looking for a job, review a supervisor's recommendation that someone be promoted, determine the pay scale for a particular job, plan training programs, or try to settle disputes between supervisors and those who work under them.

College graduates qualify for entry-level positions. Only the Army employs more than 1,000 personnel management specialists, but almost every agency employs some.

Physicians, called medical officers (GS-602) by government agencies, treat patients, conduct research, and advise government officials on health-related subjects. To qualify, applicants must usually be graduates of medical schools who have finished their internships and are licensed to practice, although some residencies and internships are available.

The vast majority of the physicians employed by the federal government work for the Department of Veterans Affairs in the Department of Medicine and Surgery, although the Department of Health and Human Services also employs several thousand, mostly in the Public Health Service and the National Institutes of Health.

Physicists (GS-1310) study the laws of nature that control matter, motion, and energy. Some of the areas of specialization are atomic energy, atmospheric phenomena, and electricity.

All applicants must have at least 24 semester hours of college-level courses in subjects such as electricity and magnetism, heat, light, mechanics, sound, and other aspects of physics. Many positions are open only to applicants who have graduate degrees.

About a score of agencies employ the government's physicists, including such unexpected ones as the Department of Commerce, to which the National Bureau of Standards and the National Weather Service belong. The Navy and the Army employ the most physicists.

Production controllers (GS-1152) are concerned with the manufacture and repair of equipment. When the equipment can be made or repaired by use of mechanical production methods, production controllers are in charge of planning the process and estimating its cost. College graduates qualify for a GS-5 rating in this occupation. Most of the production controllers work for the Navy, Air Force, and Army.

Program analysts (GS-345) determine how well the government works by evaluating particular programs and recommending improvements. "Program," a rather vague word, can refer to a project as vast and complex as building the space shuttle or as relatively simple as collecting information about the amount of wheat being grown this year. Program analysts must determine the purpose of the program, its cost, and its success in fulfilling its purpose.

Program analysts need experience in management analysis, statistics, and financial management. They are fairly high-level employees. Positions start at GS-9, which usually means that a college graduate must have at least 2 years of experience. The government has more than 13,500 program analysts spread throughout dozens of agencies.

Programmers: See Computer Specialists in this chapter.

Quality assurance specialists (GS-1910) make sure that everything bought by the government is as good as it should be. To do this, they are stationed in the manufacturer's plant, so that problems can be spotted before the finished product is delivered.

To qualify, an applicant must be a college graduate who majored in a field such as business, engineering, or production management. The Army, Navy, Air Force, and Defense Logistics Agency employ almost all of these workers.

Social insurance representatives and administrators (GS-105) explain the Social Security program to the general public, interview claimants, and review claims. College graduates qualify for the entry level (GS-5), no matter what their major. All work for the Department of Health and Human Services, and all but about 200 work outside Washington.

Social insurance claims examiners (GS-993) assist people filing for Social Security benefits. They interview people making claims, obtain the information needed, and explain the social insurance program to the general public. A college education qualifies people for GS-5.

More than 11,000 of these jobs are located throughout the United States in more than 1,300 local offices. All but a few are with the Social Security Administration of the Department of Health and Human Services.

Supply management specialists (GS-2003) and *inventory management specialists* (GS-2010) are in charge of seeing that government employees have the material they need to do their jobs at the lowest cost to the taxpayers. Specialists must figure out how much is needed, buy it, store it, and distribute it. Any college graduate can qualify. The Defense Department, which includes the Defense Logistics Agency, is the largest employer of these workers.

Systems analysts: See Computer Specialists in this chapter.

Teachers (GS-1710) One of the largest American school systems is not even in the United States. It is in the score of foreign countries where American servicemen and women are stationed with their families. The schools in this system, administered by the Department of Defense Dependents' Schools, offer classes from kindergarten through the senior year of high school. They employ the same types of teachers, counselors, librarians, and administrators found in schools in this country. Another large school system run by the U.S. government is under the direction of the Department of the

Interior's Bureau of Indian Affairs. These schools are on Indian reservations. Many of the teachers in these schools work more than 30 miles from the nearest large town.

Teachers qualify for jobs in the schools run by the government on the basis of their education and experience. In general, they must have a college degree and at least 18 semester hours of education courses, plus additional course work in elementary education or their subject specialty.

Training instructors (GS-1712) make a living teaching other people how to make a living. They are the instructors in occupational, trade, and craft-worker training programs run by the federal government. In general, training instructors must have practical and teaching experience in the trade they are going to teach even for the lowest pay grade (GS-5). The Army and the Air Force employ the largest number of these workers, very few of whom work in the nation's capital.

OTHER OCCUPATIONS

A complete list of the professional, administrative, and scientific jobs in the federal government would be about as long as a list of these jobs in the private sector. Such a list would not serve any purpose here, however, because very few people are employed in many of those occupations and, in most cases, there is intense competition for the few openings that exist. The following list, therefore, is restricted to occupations in which 1,000 or more people are employed.

OCCUPATION	CLASSIFICATION
Agricultural management specialist	GS-475
Appraiser	GS-1171
Architect	GS-808
Aviation safety officer	GS-1825
Biologist	GS-5401
Cartographer	GS-1370
Communications manager and management specialist	GS-391
Consumer safety officer	GS-696
Correctional officer	GS-007
Customs inspector	GS-1890
Dental officer	GS-680
Dietitian	GS-630
Digital computer systems administrator	GS-330
Educational assistant, education officer, educational specialist, and adviser in education	GS-1720
Employee development specialist	GS-235
Employee relations specialist	GS-230
Environmental protection specialist	GS-028

Facility manager	GS-1640
Financial analyst assistant	GS-1160
Financial manager	GS-505
Fingerprint clerk and fingerprint examiner	GS-072
Fishery biologist	GS-482
Food assistance program specialist	GS-120
Foreign affairs analyst	GS-130
Foreign service information officer	GS-1085
General health science workers	GS-601
General inspection, investigation, and compliance workers	GS-1801
Geologist	GS-1350
Housing manager	GS-1173
Hydrologist	GS-1315
Immigration inspector and examiner	GS-1816
Import specialist	GS-1889
Industrial specialist	GS-1150
Intelligence research specialist and operation specialist	GS-132
Labor relations specialist	GS-233
Librarian	GS-1410
Logistics management specialist	GS-346
Manpower development specialist	GS-142
Mathematician	GS-1520
Medical technologist	GS-644
Meteorologist	GS-406
Microbiologist	GS-403
Military personnel specialist	GS-205
Park ranger and park manager	GS-025
Personnel staffing specialist	GS-212
Pharmacist	GS-660
Physical scientist	GS-1301
Plant protection and quarantine officer	GS-436
Position classification specialist	GS-221
Printing management officer	GS-1654
Program manager (title varies with program)	GS-340
Property utilization, marketing, or disposal specialist	GS-1104
Psychologist	GS-180
Public health program specialist	GS-685
Public information officer	GS-1081
Range conservationist and range specialist	GS-454
Realty officer	GS-1170
Recreation/therapeutic recreation specialist	GS-188
Safety management specialist	GS-018
Security administration officer	GS-080
Social science analyst	GS-101
Social worker	GS-185

Soil conservationist	GS-457
Soil scientist	GS-470
Statistician	GS-1530
Supply cataloger	GS-2050
Support services administrator	GS-342
Technical writer/editor	GS-1083
Traffic manager and traffic management officer	GS-2130
Transportation specialist	GS-2101
Veterans claims examiner	GS-99
Veterinary medical officer	GS-701
Visual information officer	GS-1084
Wage and hour compliance specialist	GS-249
Wildlife biologist	GS-486
Writer/editor	GS-1082

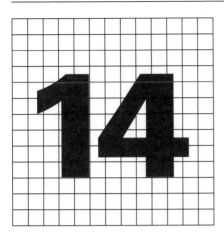

CLERICAL, TECHNICAL, AND BLUE-COLLAR CAREERS IN THE FEDERAL GOVERNMENT

Clerical, technical, and blue-collar workers assist administrators, scientists, and other professionals employed by the federal government. The occupations listed in these areas employ at least 10,000 workers. Each entry gives the job's title, the numerical code listed in government manuals and job announcements, the general duties and qualifications, the number employed, and the major employers.

CLERICAL OCCUPATIONS

Clerical occupations usually involve office work: typing, filing, keeping records, and processing forms. Clerical workers make up the largest group of government employees. More than 400,000 work in the executive agencies alone. Always in short supply, these jobs in the *General Schedule* (GS) start at GS-2, which usually requires a high school diploma. Some, however, begin at GS-1.

Clerical occupations offer people good opportunities for advancement for two reasons. First, the government offers many training programs for clerical workers. Second, hiring new people is a complicated process in the government; firing old ones is even harder. When possible, supervisors prefer promoting a well-qualified person whose habits and abilities are known to hiring from the outside. This way, the supervisor runs less risk of making a mistake and being stuck with a marginal worker who cannot be fired for incompetence. Of course, not every clerk becomes an administrator, and many clerical positions are rather dull. But clerical jobs do offer talented people, including college graduates, a way to get into the system and move up over time.

TECHNICAL OCCUPATIONS

Technical occupations are those frequently called *paraprofessional.* The work involves fewer routine tasks and requires practical knowledge of a specialized subject. Technical workers often start at GS-4 and can either advance in their technical specialty or move into the professional, scientific, or administrative area to which their work is related. Additional formal education may be needed to make such a move.

BLUE-COLLAR WORKERS

Blue-collar workers are defined by the type of work they do, not the difficulty of the work. Many of these workers are very highly skilled and become proficient in their craft only after years of experience.

The variety of blue-collar jobs offered by the government does not equal that of private industry; many blue-collar jobs are in manufacturing, and the government does not manufacture much. Nevertheless, many opportunities still exist for the blue-collar worker, as almost half a million workers can attest. Just three agencies—the Navy, Army, and Air Force—employ about 7 out of 10 of the government's blue-collar workers. The Postal Service is also a major employer of these workers.

The pay scale for these workers is very different from that of other federal employees. Secretaries and scientists who work for the government make the same amount of money whether they live in Washington, D.C., or Washington state. But the wages of government blue-collar workers vary from place to place, so the wage will be about the same as that of other blue-collar workers in the surrounding area. This pay scale is called the *Wage Board Schedule* (WG). Most government workers are under the *General Schedule* (GS). Grades in the Wage Board Schedule go from WG-1 to WG-15. WG-10 is the equivalent of journeyworker status for most blue-collar occupations.

To qualify for a blue-collar position, applicants must be able to do the work required for the particular job; length of experience or training doesn't matter. People not qualified for the journeyworker level can be hired as trades helpers. Trades helpers perform jobs in which they learn how to use tools properly, read blueprints and technical manuals, make adjustments, and rebuild and make parts. Helpers, who are usually under the direction of a journeyworker, have a WG-5 rating. One way to become a journeyworker is through an apprenticeship program. Apprenticeships usually require four years of on-the-job training and classroom work, which shows how demanding many of these occupations are.

SPECIFIC POSITIONS

Accounting technicians (GS-525) maintain records, prepare reports, and balance the books. Essentially, they are bookkeepers who check how much money is owed to the agency, compared with how much the agency owes.

To qualify, applicants should have at least 2 years of education after high school. A test is required for the lowest entry position, GS-4, but not for the next higher grade, which requires a college degree. The experience that accounting technicians receive on the job may make it possible to advance into professional accounting positions.

These jobs are spread all over the United States. Nearly all the agencies employ accounting technicians, but the largest employers are the departments of Defense, the Treasury, and Agriculture.

Aircraft mechanics (WG-8852) keep planes flying by determining what is wrong with the plane, then repairing worn or broken parts. They start at WG-10. Aircraft workers have a lower rating and perform simpler tasks than mechanics. The Air Force employs about 10,000 aircraft mechanics; the Navy and Army employ more than 2,000 each.

Claims clerks (GS-998) examine the person's claim, make sure that the right information is included, verify that the claim is submitted in time, and see that the claim can be authorized for payment. More than 7,000 claims clerks work for the Department of Health and Human Services, which includes the Social Security Administration, and more than 1,000 work for the Department of Veterans Affairs. The rest are scattered among several agencies and the jobs are located throughout the United States. In fact, there are only a few hundred claims clerks in Washington. The lowest grade is GS-2, for which high school graduates qualify upon passing a test.

Clerks (GS-300 series and GS-500 series) number in the hundreds of thousands in the federal government; the Army alone employs nearly 30,000. Clerks check records and documents, put together information based on the records and documents, and provide information to the general public about the office in which they work. In addition to general clerks, the government employs many other clerical workers whose jobs are described elsewhere in this chapter. (See the following job titles: clerk-typists, data transcribers, mail and file clerks, reporting stenographers, shorthand reporters, clerk stenographers, and secretaries.)

Applicants must be interested in clerical work and show that they can be successful at the job. High school graduates qualify for GS-2. A test is given for this and all other grades. Many of the other clerical positions require little or no experience and only a high school diploma. However, some, such as reporting stenographer, require considerable skill.

Clerks who wish to move up to professional or administrative jobs can take advangage of the government's training programs or enroll in college courses and have their tuition paid by the government.

Clerk stenographers: See Reporting Stenographers and Shorthand Reporters in this chapter.

Clerk-typists (GS-322) are employed by the thousands by the Army, Air Force, Navy, Defense Logistics Agency, Department of Veterans Affairs, Tennessee Valley Authority, and the departments of the Treasury, Justice, the

Interior, Agriculture, Labor, Health and Human Services, Housing and Urban Development, and Transportation. Total employment exceeds 60,000.

A high school diploma qualifies applicants for the entry-level position (GS-2). Applicants should be able to type 40 words a minute. Since no typing test is given, new clerk-typists must show their ability to the satisfaction of their supervisor during a probation period. A general test, which deals with verbal and clerical aptitude, is required.

Computer operators (GS-332) load the computer with magnetic tapes or disks for a particular program or operation, start the machine, and watch while it processes the program. The operators look for signs that the computer is not working properly; if it is not, they find the source of the trouble and fix it or call the service technician.

All applicants must pass a written test. A high school diploma or a 200- or 300-hour computer-training course qualifies applicants for the lowest grade (GS-2). Training courses are offered by a large variety of schools. If you consider taking one, remember that *no school is licensed by the Office of Personnel Management,* and *no school can guarantee that you will get any job,* much less a government job, when you finish the course.

Computer operators work in almost every agency, but the majority of positions are with the departments of Defense and the Treasury. Computers must also operate around the clock because people in the government need constant access to the information they analyze. As a result, computer operators must often be available for work at night and on weekends.

Data transcribers (GS-356) talk to computers through punched cards, magnetic tapes, and disks. Data transcribers, working at machines that have keyboards similar to a typewriter's, transfer information and directions onto the tapes or disks that are fed into the machine by computer operators. Transcribers also do general clerical work when necessary.

No experience, education, or training is required for the lowest grade (GS-1). Employees at this grade do simple, repetitive transcribing. For GS-2, the next higher grade, applicants must pass a test and have a high school diploma. The departments of the Treasury, Defense, and Health and Human Services employ the bulk of these workers.

Electricians (WG-2805) install and repair the electric wiring in offices, hospitals, warehouses, and other buildings. They have to be able to fix electrical fixtures, distribution panels, conduit wiring, high-voltage outlets, searchlights, and electrical appliances. They do not work on outside power lines. Electricians are sometimes exposed to cuts, burns, and electric shocks. More than half the 13,000 electricians employed by the federal government work for the Navy, and both the Army and the Air Force employ more than a thousand.

Electronics mechanics (WG-2604) install and repair radar, missile control, and other sophisticated equipment. They use both simple hand tools and complicated testing devices such as oscilloscopes to do their work. People qualify for these positions solely on the ability to do the work. Almost all of them—about 17,000—work for the Defense Department.

Electronics technicians (GS-856) work with medical equipment, radar, radio transmitters, and computers. Some operate this machinery, while others test it, or determine what is wrong with it when it malfunctions. Electronics technicians must know algebra, elementary physics, and basic electronics. To qualify, they must have at least 2 years of schooling after high school in subjects such as electronics, engineering, physics, and mathematics. Repairing television sets is one kind of experience that qualifies people to be electronics technicians. The Department of Transportation alone employs 8,000 of these workers; another 6,000 work for the Navy; and another 7,000 work at other agencies, notably the Army and Air Force.

Engineering aides and technicians (GS-802) test equipment, operate laboratory instruments, and prepare reports. This occupation has a very wide grade spread, going all the way from GS-1 to GS-15. In the lower grades, aides are closely supervised by engineers or scientists and do simple, repetitive work. At the higher levels, they do work similar to that of professional engineers.

The general experience required of applicants gives a clear idea of the nature of the work. Some examples are apprenticeship training that included drafting and mechanical drawing; surveying experience (chain or rod) as a surveyor's helper; work as a drafter; or being a laboratory mechanic or aide. Specialized experience is also required. A high school graduate qualifies for GS-2; additional technical education qualifies applicants for higher grades. Neither experience nor education is required for GS-1, but there are fewer than a hundred such positions.

Engineering aides and technicians are employed all around the country. Almost all the larger agencies employ some; the Navy, Air Force, National Aeronautics and Space Administration, and the departments of Agriculture, Transportation, and the Interior each employ more than 1,000.

Financial administration workers (GS-503) perform or supervise accounting, budgeting, and financial management tasks that cannot be more specifically classified. The lowest grade is GS-1, but most workers are hired at higher levels. The government employs about 11,600 workers in this category, each of the following employing at least a thousand: Department of the Treasury, Army, Navy, and Air Force.

File Clerks: See Mail and File Clerks in this chapter.

Fire fighters and other fire protection workers (GS-081) combat fires on ships and airfields and in buildings and industrial plants. In addition to fire fighters, this group of workers includes fire communications operators (who work telephone, telegraph, and radio equipment), fire protection inspectors (who locate and remove fire hazards), fire protection specialists (who plan fire prevention programs), and fire chiefs (who supervise the fire fighters and other workers).

Applicants must pass a written test plus a test of stamina and agility for the entry-level grade (GS-3). Many physical conditions may disqualify an applicant.

Almost all of these workers are employed by the Army, Air Force, and Navy at bases throughout the country.

Food service workers (WG-7408) help feed the hungry. They prepare food, serve meals, and clean kitchens and dining rooms. The lowest grade is WG-1. The Department of Veterans Affairs employs more than half the government's food service workers at hospitals all over the country; the Defense Department also employs many of these workers.

Forestry technicians and smoke jumpers (GS-462) help manage the country's woodlands. Smoke jumpers are fire fighters who parachute into areas where there are forest fires. They are seasonal employees who must meet strict physical requirements and be trained parachutists. Not surprisingly, the jobs are few and can be dangerous.

Forestry technicians collect data, take measurements, maintain equipment, look for signs of disease, and help with fire-control activities. Applicants can qualify for the lowest grade (GS-4) if they have had 2 years of experience in forestry, farming, soil conservation, or similar work. Two years of education after high school can also qualify applicants for GS-4 positions. The Forest Service of the Department of Agriculture employs 90 percent of all forestry technicians, few of whom work in Washington.

Heavy mobile equipment mechanics (WG-5803) repair bulldozers, combat tanks, and other heavy duty vehicles. While the qualifications are similar to those for an auto mechanic, these workers must understand hydraulic systems. WG-10 is the equivalent of a journeyworker. Almost all 10,000 of these workers are employed by the Army, Navy, and Air Force.

Janitors or porters (WG-3566; *custodial workers*) keep buildings clean. They collect wastepaper, vacuum rugs, wax floors, and mop hallways. The qualifications for the lowest grade (WG-1) are the ability to read signs, follow simple instructions, and use ordinary cleaning tools. The Army, Navy, Veterans Administration, and Department of Health and Human Services each employ more than 1,000 janitors, as does the General Services Administration, the agency that owns or manages many of the government's buildings.

Laborers (WG-3502) load and unload trucks, move material, clean the grounds surrounding buildings, collect garbage, and help skilled craft workers as directed. Workers are called "laborers" because the job is easily learned, not because it requires heavy work.

Laborers can usually learn their particular job in just a few days, so applicants usually do not need any experience to qualify for the lowest grade (WG-1). More than half a dozen agencies employ at least a thousand laborers each, including the Army, the Navy, the Department of the Interior, and the Air Force.

Machinists (WG-3414) make metal parts for machines. They read blueprints, set up their tools, and make the finished product. Their work must be very precise, since the measurement of the product may need to be correct within a thousandth of an inch. Two-thirds of the machinists employed by the government work for the Navy. The Air Force, Army, and Tennessee

Valley Authority also employ a large number of these workers.

Mail and file clerks (GS-305) are often grouped together, although they perform fairly different tasks. Mail clerks collect, route, and distribute letters, memos, publications, telegrams, and packages. File clerks classify material and organize it in an easily accessible manner.

Willingness to perform routine work is required of applicants for the lowest grade (GS-1). Applicants for the next higher grade must have a high school diploma and pass a written test. Although there are more than 23,000 workers employed in these positions throughout the government, the average grade is quite low, and the chances for advancement are not as good as those of secretaries or typists. These jobs are located all over the country.

Maintenance mechanics (WG-4749) care for government vehicles. Major employers include the Army, the Department of Transportation, and the General Services Administration.

Medical technicians (GS-600 series) assist physicians and other health care workers in doing their jobs. Naturally, the agencies with hospital systems, such as the armed forces and the Veterans Administration, are the major employers.

Motor vehicle operators (WG-5703) drive cars, ambulances, trucks, and buses. They must know how to drive, read maps, and load cargo. The lowest grade is WG-5. The Army, Navy, Air Force, and Department of Veterans Affairs each employ more than a thousand of these workers.

Nursing assistants (GS-621) help registered nurses care for patients. Nursing assistants at lower grades (GS-1 and 2) are often called nursing aides or orderlies outside the government. At the next higher grades (GS-3 and above), they may be called licensed practical nurses or licensed vocational nurses. Nursing assistants take temperatures and blood pressure readings, assist in operating rooms by passing instruments and positioning patients, prepare patients for examinations, set up equipment, bathe patients, and empty bedpans. At higher levels, the work is more complex.

No education or experience is needed for the lowest grade (GS-1). There is a test for GS-2 and GS-3, but it can be waived if the applicant has a high school education or is trained as a practical nurse.

Almost 35,000 nursing assistants work for the federal government, 30,000 of them in hospitals run by the Department of Veterans Affairs. Any local federal hospital can provide further information about employment.

Personnel clerks and assistants (GS-203) do the clerical and technical work that must be done so that the government can hire people. They may also be called staffing clerks or specialists, classification clerks or specialists, employee development clerks or specialists, or employee relations clerks or specialists. They check the forms that applicants fill out, maintain lists of applicants who are eligible for a job, prepare reports, and provide basic information about personnel regulations. The assistants specialize more than the clerks, either assisting a personnel specialist or working independently.

Clerks begin at the GS-4 level, which requires a year of general office experience and a year's experience in a job that involved a knowledge of personnel practices. Assistants start at GS-5. Applicants need one year of general and two years of specialized experience to qualify as assistants. A college degree qualifies applicants for GS-5 if they have majored in subjects such as statistics, the social sciences, journalism, public administration, personnel administration, industrial relations, or management analysis. About half these workers are employed by the departments of Defense and Agriculture.

Pipe fitters (GS-4205) install pipes used to carry air, water, oil, gas, and other materials from one location to another. The pipes have to be bent, cut, and threaded so that they fit tightly together. Pipe fitters must be able to read blueprints and plan the layout for a system of pipes. The Navy employs half the pipe fitters in the government.

Reporting stenographers, shorthand reporters, and *clerk stenographers* (GS-312) make records of conferences, hearings, interviews, and speeches. They take notes either in shorthand or with a shorthand writing machine. Reporting stenographers must be able to record 120 words per minute. Shorthand reporters make word-for-word records of conferences and meetings. They must be able to take dictation at 160 words per minute for the lowest grade (GS-6) and 175 words per minute for all higher grades. *There is no experience or particular training required for entry-level positions in either occupation.* The Army and the Air Force each employ more than one thousand of these workers.

Secretaries (GS-318) answer letters, maintain records and files, make travel arrangements for other staff members, track their supervisor's appointments, and usually, though not always, type. The lowest grade for a secretary is GS-3; the highest is GS-11. The grade of a particular secretary's position depends on the grade of the supervisor.

Secretaries must have a high school diploma and one additional year of education or clerical experience. They must also be poised, neat, discreet, and able to work alone and with others. These qualities cannot be tested, so the Office of Personnel Management recommends that would-be secretaries be hired first as clerk-typists. Clerk-typists who have the appropriate personal characteristics can then be placed in secretarial jobs.

The demand for secretaries has been great for many years and is likely to remain so. All the large agencies employ at least one thousand. The total number employed exceeds 80,900.

Secretaries have a chance to advance into professional and administrative positions if they take advantage of government training programs. Advancement is not easy and sometimes requires being in the right position at the right time, but it is possible.

Sheet metal mechanics (WG-3806) or sheet metal workers make the ducts through which air moves from one part of a building to another, repair tin roofs, and make all kinds of flat metal objects. They cut the metal with power saws or hand shears and then rivet or weld it together. Almost all 13,300 of these workers are employed by the Defense Department.

Shorthand reporters: See Reporting Stenographers in this chapter.

Supply clerks and technicians (GS-2005) prepare orders, keep records, update inventories, and perform the many other tasks necessary to make sure that government employees have the materials they need to do their jobs. The work can be fairly routine at lower levels, but it requires the mastery of complicated regulations and procedures at higher levels. Applicants must usually pass a written test to qualify. To qualify for GS-4, applicants must also have one year of general clerical experience and one year of experience as a supply clerk; two years of experience as a supply clerk; or two years of education after high school. The Department of Defense and the Veterans Administration are the largest employers of these 31,500 workers.

Typists: See Clerk-Typists in this chapter.

Warehouse workers (WG-6907) unload trucks, move material around the warehouse, and keep records of what was shipped and received. More than 24,800 people hold these jobs, mostly with the Department of Defense and the Department of Veterans Affairs.

OTHER OCCUPATIONS

In addition to the occupations described above, there are many other clerical, technical, and blue-collar occupations offered by the federal government. The following occupations employ 5,000 to 10,000 workers.

OCCUPATION	CLASSIFICATION
Air-conditioning equipment mechanic	WG-5306
Aircraft engine mechanic	WG-8602
Automotive mechanic	WG-5823
Biological technician	GS-404
Carpenter	WG-4607
Computer clerk and assistant	GS-335
Education and training technician	GS-1702
Electrician, high voltage	WG-2810
Equipment specialist	GS-1670
Food inspector	GS-1863
Guard	GS-085
Industrial equipment mechanic	WG-5352
Legal clerk and technician	GS-986
Medical clerk	GS-679
Military personnel clerk and technician	GS-204
Miscellaneous transportation/mobile equipment	

FEDERAL AGENCIES

The more than 100 federal agencies are as diverse as ACTION and the Department of Veterans Affairs. Changes in the White House, shifts in political parties and in the balance of power in the legislature, and emerging policy trends based on consumer and constituent demands result in agencies, their numerous commissions, and boards passing in and out of existence regularly.

Every county in the United States has at least one federal employee—at the post office. While federal employees live and work in 150 foreign countries, the largest concentration of government jobs is in Washington, D.C. About 15 percent of all federal white-collar workers are in the nation's capital and the percentage of professionals working there is much higher than anywhere else.

The more important the job, the more likely it will be in Washington. The more directly a job influences an individual, the greater the chances are that it will be outside Washington. If you plan a career with the federal government, you will probably spend some time in the capital planning and administering programs and some time in the field (outside Washington, D.C.) putting these programs into action.

This chapter will provide you with basic information on 39 federal agencies—the agency's function, major occupations, principal divisions, sources of employment, and, when appropriate, its address. The following agencies are listed in this section:

ACTION	Central Intelligence Agency
Agriculture	Commerce
Air Force	Defense
Army	Education

Energy
Environmental Protection Agency
Equal Employment Opportunity
  Commission
Federal Communications
  Commission
Federal Deposit Insurance
  Corporation
Federal Emergency Management
  Agency
Federal Trade Commission
General Services Administration
Health and Human Services
Housing and Urban Development
Interior
International Communications
  Agency
Interstate Commerce Commission
Justice

Labor
National Aeronautics and Space
  Administration
National Labor Relations Board
Navy
Nuclear Regulatory Commission
Office of Personnel Management
Peace Corps
Railroad Retirement Board
Securities and Exchange
  Commission
Small Business Administration
Smithsonian Institution
State
Tennessee Valley Authority
Transportation
Treasury
U.S. Postal Service
Veterans Affairs

ACTION

ACTION has four major components: *VISTA (volunteers in Service to America),* the *Foster Grandparents Program, Retired Senior Volunteer Program,* and the *Senior Companion Program,* all of which are staffed primarily by volunteers.

ACTION employs about 400 paid workers in a wide variety of white-collar occupations. Information on employment can be obtained from ACTION, Personnel Management Division, 1100 Vermont Ave. N.W., Washington, D.C. 20525. Information on volunteering can be obtained from the ACTION office in each state.

AGRICULTURE

The *Department of Agriculture (USDA)* employs about 117,000 people. Even though the number of farms is decreasing, the responsibilities of the department have grown.

Within the department, each of the following occupations has at least 1,000 workers: accountant, agricultural commodity grader, agricultural management specialist, biological technician, civil engineer, clerk-typist, food inspection technician, forester, forestry technician, loan specialist, plant protection and quarantine officer, secretary, soil conservation officer, soil scientist, and veterinarian. The department's central employment office is in Room 1080, South Building, Washington, D.C. 20250.

The department has seven main divisions, each of which has major subdivisions of its own: *Small Community and Rural Development, Marketing and Inspection Services, Food and Consumer Services, International Affairs and Commodity Programs, Science and Education, Natural Resources and Environment,* and *Economics.*

Small Community and Rural Development

Principal components within *Small Community and Rural Development* are the *Farmers Home Administration,* the *Rural Electrification Administration,* and the *Federal Crop Insurance Corporation.*

The *Farmers Home Administration* lends money to people who wish to own family farms or need to make improvements on farms they already own. It employs agricultural management specialists who determine whether the purpose of a particular loan request warrants granting the loan. Although headquartered in Washington, D.C., the agency carries on most of its work at the local level. It has 2,200 county offices, usually located in the county seat, spread through all 50 states, Puerto Rico, and the Virgin Islands. Information on employment is available from the Director, Personnel Division, Farmers Home Administration, USDA, Washington, D.C. 20250.

The Federal Crop Insurance Corporation does what its name says: It sells farmers insurance against the loss of crops caused by bad weather, disease, or insect plagues. It employs people like crop insurance specialists, who sell the insurance and inspect damaged crops to determine the amount of the loss, and the underwriters, who sell the insurance premiums. Jobs are available in all 50 states. Employment information is available from the Personnel Office, Federal Crop Insurance Corporation, USDA, Washington, D.C. 20250.

Marketing and Inspection Services

Marketing and Inspection Services comprise the Agricultural Cooperative Service, the Agricultural Marketing Service, the Animal and Plant Inspection Service, the Federal Grain Inspection Service, the Food Safety and Inspection Service, the Office of Transportation, and the Packers and Stockyards Administration.

The *Animal and Plant Inspection Service* employs about 14,000 people throughout the world. This agency is responsible for controlling pests and diseases that threaten the country's plants and farm animals. Its employees must be able to identify diseased animals and plants, control the outbreak, and impose a quarantine if necessary.

To perform their jobs efficiently, officials are stationed throughout the country carrying on inspection and eradication programs. Quarantine inspection officers work at all major ocean, Great Lakes, air, and border ports of entry in the continental United States, Hawaii, Alaska, Puerto Rico, the Virgin Islands, the Bahamas, and Bermuda. In addition, inspectors in the Netherlands, Belgium, Germany, Italy, France, and Japan supervise the certification of flower bulbs being shipped to this country. There are also officials in Mexico who supervise the fumigation of fruit before it is sent north.

Employees of the Veterinary Service Program—the Animal part of the Animal and Plant Inspection Service—not only look for signs of disease in animals on farms and ranches, but also inspect animals being imported, and administer federal laws for the humane handling of animals that cross state borders, including the elephants in the circus and the puppies at the pet store. The Animal and Plant Inspection Service hires specialists in many scientific fields, such as veterinary medicine, botany, and plant pathology. Information about employment can be obtained from the Personnel Division, Field Servicing Office, Animal and Plant Inspection Service, USDA, 100 N. Sixth St., Butler Square West, Minneapolis, MN 55403.

The *Food Safety and Inspection Service* touches the life of every American. It is responsible for the *"Inspected USDA"* stamps you see on meat and poultry. Its employees set standards of quality for more than 300 agricultural products. They enforce the standards by inspecting animals when they are slaughtered and food when it is processed.

Other agencies within Marketing Services are responsible for ensuring that farmers are charged reasonable freight rates, protecting the rights of people who develop new varieties of plants, ensuring that different kinds of grain meet official standards, and inspecting stockyards. An indication of the challenge facing the Department of Agriculture can be seen from its responsibility in administering the *Packers and Stockyards Act of 1921.* This job alone entails the supervision of 2,000 public stockyards, 3,000 private livestock buying yards, 5,500 meat packers, 15,000 livestock commission firms and dealers, and 400 poultry dealers and processors.

Information about each of the agencies within Marketing Services can be obtained from the Personnel Division, USDA, P.O. Box 96456, Washington, D.C. 20250.

Food and Consumer Services

Just three agencies make up *Food and Consumer Services:* the *Food and Nutrition Service,* the *Human Nutrition Information Service,* and the *Office of the Consumer Advisor.* The *Food and Nutrition Service* runs the *Food Stamp, School Lunch and Breakfast,* and *Supplemental Food* programs. It employs home economists and specialists in management, finance, food distribution, and nutrition. It has regional offices in Atlanta, Chicago, Dallas, Princeton, and San Francisco, as well as branch offices in many cities and towns throughout the country. Information on employment is available from the Employment Branch, Personnel Division, Food and Nutrition Service, USDA, Alexandria, VA 22302.

International Affairs and Commodity Programs

International Affairs and Commodity Programs include the Agricultural Stabilization and Conservation Service, the Commodity Credit Corporation, the Foreign Agricultural Service, and the Office of International Cooperation and Development.

Raising crops and animals is a boom-or-bust operation for many farmers; the programs administered by the *Agricultural Stabilization and Conservation Service* and the *Commodity Credit Corporation* are designed to help farmers weather disasters and prevent economic loss due to overproduction.

The *Foreign Agricultural Service* of the department assigns agricultural attachés and secretaries to 65 posts throughout the world. The department has more than 1,000 employees overseas. The Foreign Agricultural Service primarily needs agricultural economists and secretaries, but it also recruits agricultural marketing specialists. Like the other agencies that employ people abroad, it prefers to transfer workers already employed by the government, rather than to risk sending an untested employee overseas.

Science and Education   *Science and Education* is made up of the Agricultural Research Service, the Cooperative State Research Service, the Extension Service, and the National Agricultural Library.

The *Agricultural Research Service* looks for ways to improve crops, livestock, soil, and overall farm production. It recruits agronomists, botanists, chemists, entomologists, geneticists, pathologists, physiologists, microbiologists, parasitologists, animal scientists, engineers, veterinarians, soil scientists, physicists, horticulturists, and nutritionists. Information about employment is available from regional offices in Peoria, Illinois; New Orleans; and Oakland, California; as well as from the Personnel Division, Agricultural Research Service, USDA, Beltsville, MD 20705.

The policies of the *Extension Service* reach into almost every county in the country. Working through the land grant universities in each state and through the county governments, the Extension Service provides the public with expert advice through educational programs on gardening, farming, home economics, and related subjects. You will find the Extension Service listed in local telephone directories under the name of your county.

Natural Resources and   *Natural Resources and Environment* has only two components: the Forest
Environment   Service and Soil Conservation Service.

The *Forest Service* is responsible for 191 million acres of federally owned woods and grasslands in 44 states, the Virgin Islands, and Puerto Rico. These areas are not simply a chain of parks and preserves. They are a national heritage which the Forest Service manages, so that they serve the purposes of recreation and conservation at the same time that they produce raw material for the lumber industry and provide forage for livestock. The Forest Service employs foresters, landscape architects, range conservationists, civil engineers, and wildlife biologists. Information about employment can be obtained from the Forest Service, USDA, P.O. Box 96090, Washington, D.C., 20090. All Forest Service field offices also accept employment applications.

The *Soil Conservation Service* works with state and local governments to develop ways to prevent the depletion of nutrients from the soil and other effects of poor soil management. Administrators, botanists, economists, engineers, farm managers, foresters, and many other specialists work for the Soil Conservation Service. Information about employment can be obtained from the Chief, Employment Branch, Personnel Division, Soil Conservation Service, USDA, P.O. Box 2890, Washington, D.C. 20013.

AIR FORCE

The work of the *Air Force* needs little explanation: Its task, in collaboration with the other branches of the armed forces, is to defend the national and overseas interests of the United States. To perform this task, it employs several hundred thousand people—226,000 of whom are civilians—in more than a thousand occupations. Since the machinery the Air Force uses is so complicated, it needs a wide range of engineers and scientists. Because of its size, it also employs a wide range of management specialists, accountants, management analysts, and attorneys, as well as procurement specialists, computer experts, nurses, and intelligence workers.

The following white-collar occupations employ more than 1,000 workers each: accountant, aerospace engineer, budget analyst, clerk-typist, computer specialist, electronics engineer, fire protection worker, general engineer, inventory manager, production controller, secretary, and training instructor.

Blue-collar occupations with at least 1,000 workers include the following: air-conditioning equipment mechanic, aircraft electronics system installer and repairer, aircraft engine mechanic, aircraft mechanic, aircraft ordinance systems mechanic, automotive mechanic, carpenter, electrician, electronic integrated system mechanic, electronics mechanic, food service worker, heavy mobile equipment mechanic, instrument mechanic, laborer, machinist, meat cutter, miscellaneous warehousing and stock handling worker, motor vehicle operator, painter, powered support systems mechanic, sheet metal mechanic, store worker, and warehouse worker.

Among the major commands and agencies within the Air Force are the Logistics Command, Audit Agency, Office of Special Investigations, Medical Services, Manpower and Personnel Center, Information and News Center, Inspection and Safety Center, Accounting and Finance Center, Operational Test and Evaluation Center, Engineering and Service Center, Intelligence Service, and Commissary Service.

Information about jobs at nearby bases can be obtained from the *civilian personnel office* of the base. Information about employment in the Washington area is available from the Directorate of Administration, U.S. Air Force, the Pentagon, Washington, D.C. 20330.

ARMY

The *Army* is the biggest department in the federal government, employing 375,000 civilians in more than 1,200 occupations. For 17 groups of occupations, the Army has a career internship program that provides training and opportunities for promotion. These occupational groups are personnel administration, comptrollership, safety management, supply management, procurement, quality and reliability assurance, education and training, material maintenance, engineering and science, intelligence, ammunition surveillance, library science, information and editing, automatic data processing, communications management, manpower management, and transportation. College graduates are usually hired for these internships.

All the following occupations have at least 1,000 civilian workers in the Army: accountant, air-conditioning equipment mechanic, aircraft mechanic, automotive mechanic, budget analyst, carpenter, civil engineer, clerk-typist, computer specialist, contact and procurement specialist, custodial worker, education and vocational training specialist, electrician, electronics engineer, electronics mechanic, engineering equipment operator, engineering technician, explosives operative, fire protection worker, food service worker, forklift operator, general engineer, general physical scientist, heavy mobile equipment mechanic, guard, inventory management specialist, laborer, lock and dam operator, maintenance mechanic, mechanical engineer, material sorting and classifying worker, machinist, miscellaneous transportation and mobile equipment mechanic, motor vehicle operator, nurse, packing worker, painter, quality assurance specialist, secretary, sheet-metal mechanic, store worker, supply management specialist, training instructor, warehouse worker, and welder.

Information about local opportunities can be obtained from the civilian personnel office of the Army installation where you wish to work. In addition, each of the agencies described below can provide employment information.

Army Subdivisions

Given its size, the Army naturally has very large subdivisions. Some of the larger ones are the Audit Agency, the Communications Command, the Corps of Engineers, the Finance and Accounting Center, the Army Forces Command, the Material Command, and the Medical Department.

The *Army Audit Agency* once did nothing more than check pay and property records, but now it performs sophisticated internal audits on every phase of the Army's operations to ensure that the taxpayers' money is well spent. A major employer of accountants and auditors, it has offices throughout the United States and Europe. Considerable travel is often required. Further information about its training program for college graduates in auditing is available from the Personnel and Employment Service—Washington, Recruitment and Placement Branch, the Pentagon, Washington, D.C. 20310.

The *Army Communications Command* builds and operates communications systems all over the world. It employs more than 30,000 people—civilian and military—who are experts with computers, communications satellites, all types of radio transmitters, automatic switching equipment, telephone lines, undersea cables, and electronic coding and decoding equipment. Employment information is available from the headquarters: U.S. Army Communications Command, Attn: CC-PA-CP, Fort Huachuca, AZ 85613.

The *Army Corps of Engineers* does more to develop the country's water resources than any other government agency. It builds dams, reservoirs, levees, harbors, locks, and many other structures. It also manages the construction of family housing, office buildings, barracks, and other buildings for the Army. To do these jobs, the Army Corps employs about 40,000 civilians, nearly 9,000 of whom are engineers. The jobs are very widely scattered, the Corps having learned long ago that nothing makes a congressional representative approve an agency's budget faster than having a project in the home district. Further information is available from the Civilian Personnel Division, Army Corps of Engineers, 20 Massachusetts Ave. N.W., Washington, D.C. 20314.

Among other things, the *U.S. Army Finance and Accounting Center* keeps track of the pay due the Army's millions of soldiers. It hires people in administration, comptrollership, automatic data processing, and other specialties. All the jobs are in *Indianapolis,* where the center is. Information about employment is available from the Civilian Personnel Office, U.S. Army Finance and Accounting Center, Fort Benjamin Harrison, Indianapolis, IN 46249.

The *U.S. Army Forces Command* is the largest component of the Army. Its head, a four-star general, commands all the soldiers in the United States. The kinds of jobs available in so large an organization number more than 1,000 and include just about all the occupations described in this book. Information can be obtained from the civilian personnel office of any local army installation; from the regional headquarters at Fort George G. Meade, Maryland, Fort Sam Houston, Texas, and the Presidio of San Francisco, California; and from the national headquarters: Commander, U.S. Army Forces Command, Attn: AFPR-Cpt, Fort McPherson, GA 30330.

The *Army Material Command* has more than 115,000 civilian employees, which is more than most cabinet-level departments can claim. In addition to large numbers of clerical and administrative workers, it employs engineers, scientists, procurement and supply specialists, and computer experts. They work together to develop, test, buy, produce, store, distribute, maintain, and keep track of the thousands of different kinds of equipment the Army needs, from ration kits to tanks. For further information, contact the commanding general, United States Army Material Command, 200 Stovall St., Alexandria, VA 22333.

The *Army Health Services Command* is part of the Medical Department. As the largest single medical organization in the world, it operates hospitals and health programs for soldiers and their dependents at Army bases throughout this country and overseas. Professionals, technicians, and paraprofessionals in every health occupation are employed. For civilian professionals, information can be obtained from Health Services Command,

Civilian Health Occupations Recruiting Office, Fort Sam Houston, TX 78234. For reserve and active duty positions with the Army Medical Department, contact AMDDDPERSA, Attn: Procurement Division, 1900 Half St. S.W., Washington, D.C. 20324.

CENTRAL INTELLIGENCE AGENCY

One of the country's principal gatherers of information crucial to the nation's security, the *Central Intelligence Agency* is cloaked in secrecy. Neither the amount of its budget nor the number of its employees is a matter of public record. Naturally, however, it does have workers—about 25,000—and it does have a personnel office you can contact: Central Intelligence Agency, Office of Personnel, Washington, D.C. 20505.

The CIA usually hires college graduates in economics, international trade, auditing, political science, international relations, history, physics, chemistry, electronics, medicine, and library science. Employees are not within the regular civil service system administered by the Office of Personnel Management, but their pay and other benefits are claimed to be similar to those received by most government workers. The CIA often does its own recruiting through college placement offices.

COMMERCE

The *Department of Commerce* and its 35,000 employees promote the growth of the nation's businesses and industries. Some agencies within the department promote business directly. Examples of these are the *International Trade Administration* and *Minority Business Development Agency.* Other agencies serve business by registering patents (the *Patent and Trademark Office*) and setting uniform standards (the *National Bureau of Standards and Technology*). Still other agencies gather the information businesses need to plan their activities; these include the *Bureau of Economic Analysis,* the *Bureau of the Census,* and the *National Oceanic and Atmospheric Administration.* Finally, the *National Technical Information Service* runs a publishing operation that issues 70,000 titles a year.

The larger occupations in the department include the following: attorney, cartographer, chemist, computer specialist, economist, electronics engineer, fishery biologist, meteorologist, patent examiner, secretary, statistician, and trade specialist. Information is available from the U.S. Department of Commerce, 14th St. and Constitution Ave., N.W., Washington, D.C. 20230.

The *International Trade Administration* tries to expand overseas markets for U.S. goods by promoting products in the United States and encouraging companies to enter foreign markets. It also serves as an advocate within the government for policies favorable to business. Employment information is available from the Personnel Office, Room 4808, Hoover Building, 14th St. and Constitution Ave. N.W., Washington, D.C. 20230.

The *Economic Development Administration* stimulates business in depressed localities by lending money and providing technical assistance to local businesses. The personnel office is in Room 7316, Hoover Building, 14th St. and Constitution Ave. N.W., Washington, D.C. 20230.

The *Patent and Trademark Office* issues 60,000 patents each year that give inventors—or their employers—the exclusive right to sell the fruits of their ingenuity and creativity. Before a patent can be issued, however, records of existing patents must be checked to make sure that the invention really is new. Information is available from the Office of Personnel, Patent and Trademark Office CPK-1, Suite 700, Washington, D.C. 20231.

The *National Bureau of Standards and Technology* tests consumer products, looks for ways to improve the country's technology, and sets the standards for weights and measures. It also runs some of the largest physics laboratories in the country at Gaithersburg, Maryland, and Boulder, Colorado. More than half of its 3,000 workers are technicians or scientists. For information, contact the Personnel Division, Gaithersburg, MD 20899.

The *Bureau of the Census* keeps count of the country's population and production. It hires statisticians galore to work at its headquarters in Suitland, Maryland. The address of the Personnel Division is Suitland, MD 20233.

The *National Oceanic and Atmospheric Administration* studies the oceans and runs the National Weather Service. It hires cartographers, physicists, geodesists, engineers, meteorologists, and fishery biologists. For employment information, contact the Personnel Officer, National Oceanic and Atmospheric Administration, Room 716, 6010 Executive Blvd., Washington, D.C. 20852.

DEFENSE

One out of every three civilians in the executive agencies works for the *Department of Defense*. In addition to the agencies described here, see the sections of this chapter on the Air Force, Army, and Navy to get a more complete picture of the kinds of workers employed by the department.

The *Defense Logistics Agency* provides supplies for the armed forces. It buys, stores, and distributes food, clothing, gasoline, electronics equipment, and more. Just fewer than 49,000 civilians work for this agency. It hires experts in supply and inventory management, procurement, contract administration, and quality assurance, as well as in clerical and administrative specialties. Warehouse workers, material sorting and classifying workers, and packing workers are also numerous. More than 90 percent of the agency's employees are with field offices located throughout the United States. Its headquarters, across the Potomac River from Washington, can provide information about employment. Contact the Defense Logistics Agency, DLA Administrative Support Center, Cameron Station, Alexandria, VA 22304.

Most United States citizens employed overseas started working for their agency at home. The *Department of Defense Dependents' Schools* is one agency that cannot recruit from its home-based staff, because it has none.

The school system employs several thousand teachers to instruct the children of military and civilian personnel stationed abroad. It recruits teachers and other education specialists who have had at least 2 years of active work experience within the last 5 years and meet other requirements. More information about the positions available in these schools can be obtained from the Chief, Teacher Recruitment, 2461 Eisenhower Ave., Hoffman Building I, Alexandria, VA 22331.

The *Defense Mapping Agency* employs about 7,000 civilians to make maps, nautical charts, and filmstrips for target positioning and missile directional systems. About half its employees are cartographers. Most positions are in Washington or St. Louis, but there are small offices in several states and foreign countries. Employment inquiries should be sent to the Director, Personnel Office, at DMA Aerospace Center, St. Louis Air Force Station, MO 63118; or DMA Hydrographic/Topographic Center, 6500 Brookes Lane N.W., Washington, D.C. 20315. Executive/managerial applications should be addressed to Chief, Civilian Personnel Division, Headquarters, DMA, 8613 Lee Highway, Fairfax, VA 22031.

The *Defense Contract Audit Agency* employs about 3,000 accountants and auditors whose job is to evaluate the costs claimed by contractors and review the efficiency of the contractors' operations. Agency headquarters are located near Washington, but more than 90 percent of its 3,500 employees are stationed in its 350 field offices in the United States and abroad, or in one of the regional offices in Marietta, Georgia, Waltham, Massachusetts, Philadelphia, Chicago, Los Angeles, and San Francisco. Information is available from the Personnel Director, Defense Contract Audit Agency, Cameron Station, Alexandria, VA 22304.

The *Defense Intelligence Agency* collects and distributes intelligence information. Not quite half its 2,300 employees are intelligence specialists; most of the rest are general administrative and clerical workers. For employment information, contact the Defense Intelligence Agency, Washington, D.C. 20340.

The *Defense Investigative Service* conducts security investigations of Defense Department personnel. It has 2,000 employees, about half of whom are investigators. For more information, contact the Assistant Director for Personnel and Security, Defense Investigative Service, 1900 Half St. S.W., Washington, D.C. 20324.

The *Defense Communications Agency,* with 1,500 workers, operates a worldwide system of communications for intelligence gathering, weather reporting, administration, and other purposes. One of its fields organizations is the *White House Communications Agency,* which makes sure that the president is always in touch with the major centers of the government. It employs electronics engineers, computer specialists, operations specialists, and administrative, clerical, and technical workers. Information about employment can be obtained from the Civilian Personnel Division (Code 306), Headquarters, Defense Communications Agency, Washington, D.C. 20305. The street address is Eighth St. and South Courthouse Road, Arlington, VA 22204.

EDUCATION

The *Department of Education* became a separate cabinet-level department in 1979 and employs 5,000 or so workers. The department conducts a wide range of programs designed to improve elementary, secondary, and higher education—especially for the disadvantaged. Besides working with institutions and agencies of state and local governments, it runs programs that aid students directly, such as *Basic Education Opportunity Grants* and the *Guaranteed Student Loan Program.* Educational specialist and civil rights analyst are the largest occupations in the department. *There is a single source of employment information,* the Office of Personnel, 400 Maryland Ave. S.W., Washington, D.C. 20202.

ENERGY

The *Department of Energy* is responsible for research into new sources of energy, the regulation of energy production, and the nuclear weapons program. The department was created by bringing together existing agencies, such as the Energy Research and Development Administration, the Federal Power Commission, and the Bonneville Power Administration, which is basically a hydroelectric company. It employs 16,300 people in a wide range of clerical, administrative, and blue-collar positions, notably secretary, accountant, general engineer, electrical engineer, and attorney. For more information, contact the Personnel Office, Department of Energy, 1000 Independence Ave. S.W., Washington, D.C. 20585.

ENVIRONMENTAL PROTECTION AGENCY

The *Environmental Protection Agency* is both regulatory and research-oriented. As a regulatory agency, it sets and enforces standards such as those in the *Toxic Substances Control Act.* As a research organization, it strives to discover ways of improving our natural surroundings. Both its functions aim at the reduction of air, water, and soil pollution. Among its 15,000 employees are environmental specialists, environmental engineers, general physical scientists, chemists, biologists, medical doctors, lawyers, and secretaries. Employment information is available from the Personnel Management Division, Gallery 1, West Tower, 401 M St. S.W., Washington, D.C. 20460.

EQUAL EMPLOYMENT OPPORTUNITY COMMISSION

The laws of the United States *forbid job discrimination based on race, color, creed, or national ancestry.* The *Equal Employment Opportunity Commission* and its 3,200 employees enforce these laws. Its employees (1,400 of whom are civil rights analysts, and almost 500 of whom are lawyers) investigate complaints and negotiate settlements. It has offices in 40 cities, including Washington, where the headquarters is located. In addition to the usual staff of clerical and administrative employees, the commission hires lawyers and equal opportunity specialists. More information can be obtained from the Equal Employment Opportunity Commission, Personnel Office, 1801 L St. N.W., Washington, D.C. 20507.

FEDERAL COMMUNICATIONS COMMISSION

The airways through which radio and TV broadcasts travel are public property, and it is the responsibility of the *Federal Communications Commission* to see that our property is not misused. It has jurisdiction over AM and FM radio stations, television networks, cable television companies, and even ham radio operators. The FCC employs lawyers, electronics engineers, economists, accountants, administrators, computer specialists, and clerical personnel, about 2,000 people altogether. Most of the entry-level positions are located in the Washington headquarters, but much of the investigative and enforcement work is done at 40 different field offices and monitoring stations throughout the country. Requests for employment information can be sent to the Chief, Staffing and Employment Services Branch, Personnel Management Division, Federal Communications Commission, 1919 M St. N.W., Washington, D.C. 20554.

FEDERAL DEPOSIT INSURANCE CORPORATION

The *Federal Deposit Insurance Corporation* guarantees depositors of member banks—and 97 percent of all banks are members—that they will get their money back if the bank fails. To make sure the money is safe, the corporation regularly examines all member banks. Because of the banking problems that surfaced after federal deregulation in the 1980s, the FDIC has grown more rapidly than any other federal agency. From 1980–1989, the FDIC grew by almost 150 percent, jumping from about 3,500 workers in 1980 to almost 9,000 in 1989. It employs several thousand bank examiners. Examiners start as trainees; they are usually college graduates who majored in accounting, business administration, finance, or economics. Examiners travel extensively. Information on these and 1,400 other jobs is available from the Director, Office of Personnel Management, Federal Deposit Insurance Corporation, 550 17th St. N.W., Washington, D.C. 20429.

FEDERAL EMERGENCY MANAGEMENT AGENCY

The *Federal Emergency Management Agency* coordinates the preparation for and response to emergencies such as floods and nuclear war. It has only about 2,700 employees in various administrative, clerical, and engineering positions, most of which are in Washington. Information on employment can be obtained from the Office of Personnel, Resource Management and Administration Directorate, 500 C St. S.W., Washington, D.C. 20472.

FEDERAL TRADE COMMISSION

The *Federal Trade Commission* is the government's consumer protection service. Its 1,000 workers administer such laws as the truth in lending legislation and enforce antitrust laws. Among its employees are the usual administrative and clerical workers, 100 economists, and 500 lawyers. For information about employment, write the Director of Personnel, Federal Trade Commission, Room 151, Sixth St. and Pennsylvania Ave. N.W., Washington, D.C. 20580.

GENERAL SERVICES ADMINISTRATION

The *General Services Administration* is a conglomerate with 21,000 employees. Among the larger occupations are accountant, archivist, clerk-typist, contract and procurement specialist, general engineer, inventory management specialist, mechanical engineer, miscellaneous administration, police officer, property disposal specialist, quality assurance specialist, realty appraiser, secretary, and transportation specialist.

The work of each major division is largely unrelated to the work of the others. For example, different agencies within the administration run Federal Information Centers, build government office buildings, and maintain the memorial libraries for former presidents. Its five divisions are the Public Buildings Service, Office of Federal Supply and Services, National Archives and Records Service, Office of Information Resource Management, and Federal Property Resources Service. The address of the central office is Personnel Office, General Services Administration, Room 1100, 18th and F Streets N.W., Washington, D.C. 20405. However, applications are not kept on file; they are accepted only for announced vacancies. Furthermore, hiring is highly decentralized, much of it occurring in the regions.

The *Public Buildings Service* owns or leases more than 7,000 buildings. Its responsibility begins when the decision to erect a new building is made and ends only when the building is no longer needed by the government. Among the employees of the service are engineers, architects, and property management and disposal specialists, as well as a large number of guards and building maintenance workers. Information about local employment is available at local government office buildings.

Federal Supply and Services (often referred to as the Federal Supply Service) spends an estimated $3 billion a year to provide government workers with the materials they need to do their jobs. It is a major employer of procurement specialists and other workers in supply-related occupations. For information about employment, contact Federal Supply and Services, Office of Personnel, Washington, D.C. 20406.

The *Information Resources Management Service* runs the Federal Data Processing Center, Automatic Data Processing Procurement Programs, the government's telephone system, and the Federal Information Centers. Engineers, computer programmers, and telecommunications experts are among the people it hires. Information about employment can be obtained from the regional offices of the General Services Administration.

The *Federal Property Resources Service* manages the National Defense Stockpile of Strategic and Critical Materials and sells off real estate it no longer needs. For employment information, contact the regional offices of the General Services Administration.

HEALTH AND HUMAN SERVICES

The *Department of Health and Human Services,* with 126,400 workers, is one of the largest government agencies outside the Defense Department and the Postal Service. It employs more than 1,000 workers in each of the following occupations: accountant, chemist, computer specialist, consumer safety officer, contact representative, medical officer, nurse, program analyst, public health program specialist, secretary, social insurance claims examiner, social insurance representative and administrator, and social science analyst. As its name indicates, however, its functions fall into two distinct categories: *Health* (the *Public Health Service*) and *Human Services* (the *Social Security Administration*). It also operates an *Office of Human Development Services,* a *Health Care Financing Administration,* an *Office of Child Support Enforcement,* and other agencies.

The *Public Health Service* goes back to 1798, when hospitals were set up for the United States' merchant sailors. Running hospitals is still one of its functions, but it has many others as well. Among the major agencies with the Public Health Service are the *Health Resources and Services Administration,* the *Centers for Disease Control,* the *National Institutes of Health,* the *Food and Drug Administration*, and the *Alcohol, Drug Abuse, and Mental Health Administration.*

The *Health Resources and Services Administration* provides direct medical care in communities and on Indian reservations not served by private or local government hospitals. It employs physicians, nurses, and many other health care professionals who are members of the Commissioned Corps of the Public Health Service. For information on medical, scientific, and technical positions, contact the Commissioned Personnel Operations Division, Room 4-35, Parklawn Building, 5600 Fishers Lane, Rockville, MD 20857.

The *Centers for Disease Control* plan nationwide programs designed to eliminate or control communicable diseases. The staff includes many doctors, scientists, and technicians. More information about employment in most occupations is available from the headquarters in Atlanta. Contact Recruitment and Placement, Room 1055, Centers for Disease Control, 1600 Clifton Road N.E., Atlanta, GA 30333. As with the Public Health Service, many medical, scientific, and technical workers are members of the Commissioned Corps of the Public Health Service. The address for information about the corps is given in the previous paragraph.

The *National Institutes of Health* are a collection of a dozen institutes, such as the National Cancer Institute and the National Heart, Lung, and Blood Institute. The Institutes are responsible for health education and medical research. They run their own laboratories and also administer grants to universities and medical schools. The highly trained staff of the Institutes includes physicians, scientists, and medical engineers. Further information can be obtained from the Division of Personnel Management, NIH, Bethesda, MD 20892. Like the Public Health Service, the National Institutes of Health have a Commissioned Officer Program. Information on this program is available from the Division of Personnel in Bethesda; ask for a copy of "Associate Training Programs in the Medical and Biological Sciences."

The *Food and Drug Administration* is a regulatory agency that sets quality standards for medicines, cosmetics, food, and medical devices. It employs consumer safety officers, pharmacologists, microbiologists, physiologists, chemists, statisticians, animal caretakers, and many other workers. Employment information for local areas is available at the 30 *Food and Drug Administration Consumer Affairs* offices around the country; for information about work at the headquarters, contact the Personnel Office (HFA-400), Food and Drug Administration, 5600 Fishers Lane, Attn: Personnel, Room 4B18, Rockville, MD 20857.

The *Social Security Administration* runs the largest pension fund in the world. To function efficiently, it has a 70,000-person army of claims authorizers, benefit examiners, economists, social insurance representatives, statisticians, and computer specialists. The agency has more than 1,300 offices throughout the country, any of which can provide employment information. Or you can contact the national headquarters: Office of Human Resources, Social Security Administration, 6401 Security Blvd., Baltimore, MD 21235.

HOUSING AND URBAN DEVELOPMENT

The *Department of Housing and Urban Development* administers programs that encourage the improvement of housing and the planned growth of towns and cities. It has field offices in many cities, and the majority of its 15,000 workers are located in the field offices. Construction analyst, loan specialist, and appraiser are among the larger occupations in the department. Information on employment is available from the personnel divisions of the regional offices and from the Headquarters Office of Personnel, U.S. Department of Housing and Urban Development, 451 Seventh St. S.W., Washington, D.C. 20410.

INTERIOR

The *Department of the Interior,* the nation's principal conservation agency, is responsible for most of the public lands owned by the federal government. It controls more than 500 million acres, an area twice the size of Texas. It conducts land surveys, manages the national parks, protects wildlife, and is the government's official agency for Indian affairs. The department's 75,000 employees work in occupations such as the following: cartographer, civil engineer, clerk-typist, computer specialist, education and training specialist, education and training technician, fishery biologist, forester, general biologist, geologist, hydrologist, maintenance mechanic, park manager and park ranger, police officer, range conservationist, realty appraiser, secretary, and wildlife biologist.

The department has many major components, such as the Bureau of Indian Affairs, the Fish and Wildlife Service, the Geological Survey, and the National Park Service.

The *Bureau of Indian Affairs* has the responsibility of encouraging Indians and native Alaskans to develop their full potential. To this end, it operates schools, provides technical assistance, and subsidizes projects like the construction of roads. Indian applicants receive preference in appointments. Information on employment can be obtained from the area personnel offices of the bureau.

The *Fish and Wildlife Service* operates fish hatcheries and wildlife refuges and regulates the hunting of migratory birds. Employment information is available from regional offices in Atlanta; Albuquerque, New Mexico; Anchorage, Alaska; Denver; Portland, Oregon; Newton Corner, Massachusetts; and Minnesota's Twin Cities. The address of the Office of Personnel at the Washington headquarters is Room 3454, 18th and C Streets N.W., Washington, D.C. 20240.

The *Geological Survey* systematically maps the United States and identifies areas likely to be rich in minerals, oil, and gas. Employment information can be obtained from the Recruitment and Placement Office, 215 National Center, 12201 Sunrise Valley Drive, Reston, VA 22092.

The *National Park Service* manages national parks, monuments, historic sites, and recreational areas—about 330 different places that range in size from a small stone house to Yellowstone National Park. Its employees develop and maintain these areas and conduct educational programs. Information on employment is available from the Personnel Office, National Park Service, U.S. Department of the Interior, 18th and C Streets N.W., Washington, D.C. 20013. Applications for seasonal (summer) employment should be sent to the regional offices in Boston, Philadelphia, Atlanta, Omaha, Denver, San Francisco, Seattle, and Washington. These offices, including the Washington office, will have information about jobs in their respective regions only.

INTERNATIONAL COMMUNICATIONS AGENCY

The *International Communications Agency,* formerly called the United States Information Agency, runs informational and cultural programs designed to promote greater understanding of the United States. It has its own Foreign Service made up of more than 1,000 foreign service information officers. The agency, which employs a total of 3,800, also hires secretaries, foreign affairs analysts, writers, electronics technicians, audiovisual production specialists, and other workers. For information on all these positions, contact the Recruitment and Examining Division, International Communications Agency, 301 Fourth St. S.W., Washington, D.C. 20547.

INTERSTATE COMMERCE COMMISSION

The first article of the Constitution gives the federal government the duty of regulating commerce between the states. The *Interstate Commerce Commission* is one of the agencies that carries out that duty. Trains, trucks, buses, barges, and pipelines that cross state lines are regulated by the commission, one of the oldest of the regulatory agencies. Its major task is making sure that the rates companies charge are fair to both the receiver of the goods and the shipping company. At its headquarters in Washington, and at 56 field offices around the country, it employs one thousand workers, including lawyers, transportation specialists, accountants, and auditors. For more information, contact the Director of Personnel, Room 1136, Interstate Commerce Commission, 12th St. and Constitution Ave. N.W., Washington, D.C. 20423.

JUSTICE

The largest law firm in the country, the *Department of Justice* provides legal advice to the president and to government agencies, represents the United States in court cases, and investigates possible violations of federal law. Among its 80,000 employees are lawyers, criminal investigators, accountants, immigration inspectors, chemists, computer specialists, border patrol agents, correctional officers, and teachers. Its major divisions are the Federal Bureau of Investigation, the Immigration and Naturalization Service, and the Bureau of Prisons, though there are many others.

The *Federal Bureau of Investigation* looks for evidence that a crime has been committed. Besides its special agents, the bureau employs fingerprint specialists and many other workers in administrative and clerical positions. For information, contact any field office, resident agency, or the Applicant Recruiting Office, FBI, Tenth St. and Pennsylvania Ave. S.W., Washington, D.C. 20520.

The *Immigration and Naturalization Service* administers the country's immigration laws. Its border patrol is responsible for the 6,000 miles of border between this country and Canada and Mexico. Employment information is available from any regional or district office or from the Central Office, Immigration and Naturalization Service, 1425 Eye St. N.W., Washington, D.C. 20546.

The *Bureau of Prisons* runs 45 federal penitentiaries and other correctional institutions. Medical personnel, such as physician assistants, are among the people employed in the prisons, in addition to the correctional officers. You can obtain information about jobs from any regional or field office or from the Central Office, Bureau of Prisons, 320 First St. N.W., Washington, D.C. 20534.

Among the other divisions of the Department of Justice are the Antitrust Division, Civil Division, Civil Rights Division, Drug Enforcement Administration, Tax Division, and U.S. Marshals Service, each of which has its own personnel office.

Lawyers should make inquiries to the Director, Office of Attorney Personnel Management, Room 4311, U.S. Department of Justice, Tenth St. and Constitution Ave. N.W., Washington, D.C. 20530.

LABOR

One of the smaller cabinet-level agencies, the *Department of Labor* and its 18,000 workers promote the welfare of wage earners and analyze information about the economy and the labor force. Among its major divisions are the *Employment and Training Administration, Employment Standards Administration, Occupational Safety and Health Administration,* and *Bureau of Labor Statistics.* Its largest occupations are computer specialist, economist, general attorney, industrial hygienist, manpower development specialist, mine safety specialist, safety management specialist, wage and hour compliance specialist, and worker compensation claims examiner. Employment information is available from eight different personnel offices for the various divisions within the department, from the regional offices, and from the Reception and Correspondence Unit, Room C5516, U.S. Department of Labor, 200 Constitution Ave. N.W., Washington, D.C. 20210.

NATIONAL AERONAUTICS AND SPACE ADMINISTRATION

NASA, the National Aeronautics and Space Administration, ran one of the nation's most spectacularly successful programs, culminating in the Apollo moon landing. While its recent projects have not been quite as heart-stopping, NASA continues its aeronautics and space research, employing more than 21,000 people—10,000 of whom are engineers, 1,500 of whom are secretaries, 1,400 of whom are scientists, 700 of whom are mathematicians, and the rest of whom are clerical and administrative workers. Inquiries concerning employment can be sent to the Director of Headquarters Personnel, NASA Headquarters, Washington, D.C. 20546. That office will also provide a list of the field offices, which have local information.

NATIONAL LABOR RELATIONS BOARD

The rights of workers to organize in unions are established by various laws. These laws are administered by the *National Labor Relations Board* and its 2,600 workers. Among its employees are lawyers, labor management relations examiners, field examiners, and clerical and administrative personnel. It has more than 50 field offices around the country. Applications for field examiner and attorney positions can be sent to the Personnel Operations Section, National Labor Relations Board, 1717 Pennsylvania Ave. N.W., Washington, D.C. 20570.

NAVY

The *Department of the Navy* employs almost 135,000 blue-collar and more than 164,000 white-collar civilians. They do everything from serving food in mess halls to conducting advanced research into the nature of the ocean. Most of the occupations that are described in the two previous chapters can be found in the Navy. At least 1,000 people work for the Navy in the following white-collar occupations: accountant, aerospace engineer, civil engineer, clerk-typist, contract administrator, education and vocational training specialist, electrical engineer, electronics engineer, electronics technician, engineering technician, fire protection worker, general engineer, inventory management specialist, mathematician, mechanical engineer, naval architect, nuclear engineer, secretary, and supply program administrator.

At least 1,000 blue-collar workers are in each of the following occupations: air-conditioning equipment mechanic, aircraft electronic systems installer and repairer, aircraft engine mechanic, aircraft mechanic, automotive mechanic, boiler plant operating worker, boilermaker, carpenter, custodial worker, electrician, electronics mechanic, equipment cleaner, heavy mobile equipment mechanic, industrial equipment mechanic, instrument mechanic, insulating worker, laborer, machinist, maintenance mechanic, marine machinery mechanic, motor vehicle operator, ordinance equipment mechanic, painter, pipefitter, rigger, sheet metal mechanic, shipfitter, shipwright, tools and parts attending worker, warehouse worker, and welder.

Positions are very widely spread throughout the coastal states. For further information about jobs in the Washington area, write the Director, Naval Civilian Personnel Command, Capital Region, 801 N. Randolph St., Arlington, VA 22203. Each of the Navy's numerous local installations can provide information about jobs at that facility.

When filling overseas jobs, the Navy rarely recruits outside its own body of employees. When it does, it is usually looking for engineers, scientists, skilled trade workers, accountants, and auditors. Information about Navy jobs overseas is available from the civilian personnel officer at the nearest Navy installation.

NUCLEAR REGULATORY COMMISSION

The safe use of nuclear energy is the responsibility of the 3,300 employees of the *Nuclear Regulatory Commission.* This agency licenses companies that want to build or operate nuclear reactors or use nuclear material in other ways. Among the major occupations in the agency are security administration officer, secretary, nuclear engineer, general engineer, lawyer, and health physicist. *The agency is not in the regular civil service system and the Office of Personnel Management cannot give any advice about employment.* Instead, contact the Director, Division of Organization and Personnel, Nuclear Regulatory Commission, Washington, D.C. 20555.

OFFICE OF PERSONNEL MANAGEMENT

The *Office of Personnel Management* is the government's principal personnel office. Although your first contact with it is likely to concern employment, most of its 6,000 workers deal with other matters, such as position descriptions, pensions, and health benefit plans. It employs personnel specialists, computer specialists, civil service retirement claims examiners, general claims examiners, and general investigators. For information about employment, contact the nearest Federal Job Information Center.

PEACE CORPS

More than 6,000 Peace Corps volunteers are currently serving in 70 countries around the world, trying to promote peace and friendship by helping communities develop agricultural, business, health, and education projects. Since the Peace Corps was founded in 1961, more than 125,000 volunteers have gone through the program. More than 300 skills are needed, especially those related to agriculture, industrial arts, engineering, and science. The host country determines which skills are needed where. Volunteers receive room, board, medical care, and transportation to the host country. At the end of their service, they receive a stipend for each month they worked. Only one applicant out of six is chosen for training, which lasts about 3 months. Volunteers normally serve for 2 years, but may serve longer.

The volunteers are supported by a small staff of regular employees. Information on these jobs is available from the Peace Corps, Office of Personnel, 1990 K St. N.W., Washington, D.C. 20526.

RAILROAD RETIREMENT BOARD

In 1935, a law was passed that set up something like a social security program just for railroad workers. That system is still in existence. It is administered by the *Railroad Retirement Board,* which has 1,600 employees in 100 offices across the country. The board hires computer specialists, contact representatives, and social insurance claims examiners, as well as the usual administrative and clerical workers. The headquarters is in Chicago. More information is available from the Director of Personnel, Railroad Retirement Board, 844 Rush St., Chicago, IL 60611.

SECURITIES AND EXCHANGE COMMISSION

The *Securities and Exchange Commission* sets the rules for stockbrokers, mutual fund dealers, and other securities traders. Its staff of 1,900 includes experts in corporate law, financial analysis, accounting, and securities investigation. It was created to prevent the wild speculation that contributed to the 1929 stock market collapse. Additional employment information is available from the Director of Personnel, Securities and Exchange Commission, 450 Fifth St. N.W., Washington, D.C. 20549.

SMALL BUSINESS ADMINISTRATION

Fostering the creation and growth of the small business is the job of the *Small Business Administration.* In more than 100 offices around the country, it employs about 4,500 specialists who can assist the small entrepreneur with finances, planning, legal matters, data processing, and administrative management. Major occupations in the administration include loan specialist, law, and general business and industry specialist. Information about employment can be obtained from the Director of Personnel, Room 300, Small Business Administration, 1441 L St. N.W., Washington, D.C. 20416.

SMITHSONIAN INSTITUTION

The *Smithsonian Institution,* the nation's attic, is a quasi-official agency that runs many different museums and a zoo. Employment totals about 5,000 in such occupations as guard, security officer, curator, and museum technician. Information for most of the Institution's components is provided by the Office of Personnel Administration, Smithsonian Institution, 900 Jefferson Drive S.W., Washington, D.C. 20560.

STATE

The Department of State is responsible for conducting relations with foreign nations and international organizations. It has about 25,000 employees— about 35 percent in Washington and most of the rest in foreign countries. Career foreign service officers fill virtually all the professional positions in the 300-plus embassies and consulates around the world. *The Foreign Service is not under the control of the Office of Personnel Management. It is administered directly by the department.*

Appointments to the Foreign Service are made from among those who pass the *Foreign Service Officer Examination.* Candidates for these examinations must be at least 21 and under 57 years of age, unless they are either college graduates or juniors in college, in which case they can take the exam when they are 20. The test is generally given in December, the deadline for applications being in October. A booklet, "Foreign Service Careers," and information about the exam, which is generally considered difficult, can be obtained from the Foreign Service Officer Recruitment Branch, Box 9317, Department of State, Rosslyn Station, Arlington, VA 22209.

Those who pass the exam and become foreign service officers usually serve in one of four specializations: administration, consular affairs, economic/commercial affairs, or politics. State is interested in people with training in political science, economics, public administration, and business administration. People with experience in business, government, and organizations involved in international activities are also sought.

Secretaries, foreign affairs analysts, general administrative and clerical workers, and passport and visa examiners are among the employees of the department who are not members of the Foreign Service. Requests for information regarding opportunities and qualifications for these positions should be sent to the Recruitment Branch, Employment Division, U.S. Department of State, Washington, D.C. 20520.

TENNESSEE VALLEY AUTHORITY

Controlling floods, developing forests, and producing electric power are among the activities of the Tennessee Valley Authority, a government-owned corporation with about 25,000 workers. Positions with the TVA are not covered by regular civil service procedures, so you must contact it directly. Guard, personnel management worker, miscellaneous administrator, engineering technician, general engineer, civil engineer, mechanical engineer, electrical engineer, facility management specialist, high-voltage electrician, machinist, laborer, structural-ornamental ironworker, boilermaker, pipefitter, and carpenter are the occupations with the largest numbers of employees. Employment information is available at local facilities and construction projects and from the Employment Branch, Tennessee Valley Authority, 400 W. Summit Hill Drive, Knoxville, TN 37902.

TRANSPORTATION

The *Department of Transportation* implements the country's transportation policy through such agencies as the Federal Aviation Administration, Maritime Administration, Federal Railroad Administration, Urban Mass Transit Administration, National Highway Traffic Safety Administration, and Federal Highway Administration. The Coast Guard is also part of the department during peacetime.

The department employs roughly 60,000 people. Air traffic controllers; electronics technicians; engineering technicians; general, civil, electrical, and electronics engineers; aviation safety officers; computer specialists; accountants; secretaries; and clerical workers hold most of the jobs. For employment information, it is best to contact the district or regional offices of the different agencies. Inquiries concerning positions in Washington can be sent to the Central Employment Information Office, Office of Personnel and Training, U.S. Department of Transportation, Washington, D.C. 20590. Applications are accepted only for announced vacancies.

The *Federal Aviation Administration* enforces safety regulations for airplanes and encourages the development of a national system of airports. Air traffic controllers and aeronautical engineers are among the many professional and clerical workers it employs. Further information is available from the Federal Aviation Administration, Employment Branch, APT-150, 800 Independence Ave. S.W., Washington, D.C. 20591.

The *Federal Highway Administration* administers the funding that makes it possible for states to build interstate highways. The FHA also regulates the activities of trucking companies that operate across state lines. It hires employees in a broad range of occupations, including civil engineering. For further information, write the Federal Highway Administration, Office of Personnel Training, HPT-22, 400 Seventh St. S.W., Washington, D.C. 20590.

The *Coast Guard is the only branch of the armed forces not in the Defense Department.* Like the other armed services, it employs many civilians in a variety of occupations. The Coast Guard is primarily responsible for enforcing federal laws in U.S. waters. Information about employment can be obtained from the Commandant (G-PC/ 62), U.S. Coast Guard, 2100 Second St. S.W., Washington, D.C. 20593. Specify whether civilian or military employment interests you.

TREASURY

The *Department of the Treasury* is one of the original departments created by George Washington. With more than 155,000 employees, it is one of the biggest. The following occupations each employ at least 1,000 people: computer specialist, criminal investigator, customs officer, financial institution examiner, internal revenue service agent, internal revenue service officer, lawyer, program analyst, tax accountant, and tax technician.

The department has 11 major divisions: The Bureau of the Mint; Bureau of the Public Debt; Bureau of Alcohol, Tobacco, and Firearms; Bureau of Engraving and Printing; Bureau of Government Financial Operations; Federal Law Enforcement Training Center; Internal Revenue Service; Office of the Assistant Secretary for International Affairs; Office of the Comptroller of the Currency; U.S. Customs Service; U.S. Secret Service; and U.S. Savings Bonds Division. The largest of these divisions are the Internal Revenue Service; U.S. Customs Service; Bureau of Alcohol, Tobacco, and Firearms; and Bureau of Engraving and Printing.

The *Internal Revenue Service* collects more than 90 percent of the money owed the government by its citizens. It has about 4,500 employees in Washington and another 65,000 in the rest of the country. A substantial number of positions are filled by persons who majored in accounting, business administration, finance, economics, and law, but many other fields of study can also be applied to the work of the service. There is an IRS office in or near your hometown to which you can write for additional employment information.

The *U.S. Customs Service* collects revenue from imports and enforces customs and related laws. It has 14,500 employees, about 1,400 of whom are located in Washington. The rest work at seaports, airports, border crossings, and other locations throughout the country. A small number are employed in foreign cities such as Montreal, Mexico City, London, Frankfurt, and Hong Kong. Among the workers it hires are customs patrol officers. Additional information about employment—including summer employment—is available from the Director, Personnel Management Division, Room 6124, U.S. Customs Service, 1301 Constitution Ave., Washington, D.C. 20229.

The *Bureau of Alcohol, Tobacco, and Firearms* has two major functions: preventing the illegal production or sale of alcoholic beverages, tobacco products, and firearms; and regulating the legal producers of these products. Only about 500 of its 3,700 employees work in Washington; the rest are employed throughout the United States. For more information about employment, contact the Employment Branch, Bureau of Alcohol, Tobacco, and Firearms, 1200 Pennsylvania Ave. N.W., Washington, D.C. 20226.

The *Bureau of Engraving and Printing* has 3,000 employees, all of whom work in its Washington plant. They design, engrave, and print every U.S. dollar bill, postage stamp, and food coupon. The bureau employs printing and management specialists; chemists in ink, paper, and general research; mechanical, electrical, and industrial engineers; worker-trainees; apprentices in the mechanical trades; apprentices in the printing crafts; and many other workers. Employment information can be obtained from the Head, Personnel Staffing Branch, Office of Industrial Relations, Bureau of Engraving and Printing, 14th and C Streets, Washington, D.C. 20228.

THE U.S. POSTAL SERVICE

With 835,000 workers, the *U.S. Postal Service is the largest single employer of government workers other than the Defense Department.* Postal workers are the most widespread group of federal employees. There are 30,000 post offices and other postal facilities around the country, ranging in size from the corner of a rural grocery store to the blocks-long building in New York City, where more than 40,000 workers keep the mail moving day and night. There are also 485 mail distribution centers. The range of jobs in the Postal Service is as great as the variety of buildings it owns or uses, but 90 percent of the white-collar workers are in just five occupations: postal clerk, mail carrier, mail handler, supervisor of the mails, and postmaster. Motor vehicle driver and maintenance workers are the largest blue-collar occupations.

Postal Clerks

Postal clerks, who number about 380,000, include distribution clerks, distribution machine clerks, and window clerks.

Distribution clerks sort the mail—some by airmail or surface routes, others by ZIP code, city, or region, and others by delivery route. Some distribution clerks also keep records, cancel the stamps on mail that requires special handling, and work at the public windows in the post office.

Distribution machine clerks run the sorting equipment that helps reduce the need for distribution clerks. They first load the machines, making sure that all the envelopes face the same way. Then, as the machines present each letter to the operators, they read the ZIP Code and press a combination of keys to send the letter into its proper bin. The operator does this 50 times a minute, which requires sharp vision.

Window clerks are much more visible than the other clerks, who work behind the scenes. The window clerks sell stamps and money orders, give out mail, collect postage, listen to and act on complaints, answer questions, and explain the distinctions among first, second, third, and fourth class mail.

Mail Carriers

The nation's 285,000 *mail carriers* are the last link of the chain that connects the letter writer to the letter reader. Carriers take the mail for their route and sort it in the sequence of delivery. They deliver the mail—by foot in cities, by car in rural areas—collect charges for postage and C.O.D. transactions, and pick up mail from people along their routes. Back at the post office, they readdress mail that has to be forwarded, make records of changes in addresses, and take care of other matters. One advantage of a mail carrier's job is being able to set one's own pace, so long as the last delivery is made on schedule. One disadvantage is summed up in the Postal Service motto: "Neither snow nor rain nor heat nor gloom of night stays these couriers from the swift completion of their appointed rounds."

Mail handlers are not nearly so numerous as carriers and clerks, though they still constitute a sizable work force. Mail handlers load and unload trucks, trains, and planes, move bulk mail, operate canceling machines and forklifts, and repackage torn parcels.

Supervisors of the mails are administrators. They oversee the task of distributing and delivering the mail. They evaluate the work loads of carriers, make assignments, recommend changes in routes, see that the proper records are kept, and make sure that service at the public windows is as good as possible.

Postmasters

Postmasters manage post offices. Their duties depend on the size of the post office of which they are in charge. Many postmasters work in very small post offices which are open for only a few hours a day. Such a post office might have window and general delivery operations and a rural delivery route—all supervised by the postmaster. In addition, the postmaster would be responsible for seeing that incoming mail was properly classified and that the proper records were kept. The postmaster's job in a city post office is much more complex. The postmaster needs many subordinates and would have to devote more time to personnel actions, planning, and management than the rural postmaster.

The Postal Service is the only agency of the federal government in which labor unions play an important part. Its hiring practices are also somewhat unusual. For the clerical and carrier positions, each post office and distribution center keeps its own list of eligible job seekers, although employment standards are set nationally.

Clerks and carriers must be at least 16 if they are high school graduates, and at least 18 if they are not. In actuality, relatively few people are hired before they are about 25, because of the length of the waiting periods before and after filing applications. Many postal workers transfer from other occupations. Applicants must pass a four-part written test and show that they can handle 70-pound mail sacks. They often start working part time before advancing to a full-time position. Supervisors of the mails and postmasters are almost always chosen from the ranks of the clerks and carriers, since experience in the distribution and delivery of mail is a major qualification. *Postmasters are not political appointees.*

For more information about employment with the Postal Service, contact the personnel office of your local post office or the nearest mail distribution center. *They are the only places where you can find out when the employment tests are given and how to register for them.* Applications are accepted *only* when the post office decides that a test must be given; therefore, you might need to keep checking back before you actually file an application. The tests are given once every year or two. It may take as long as two years after passing the test to be hired.

General information is available from Headquarter Personnel Division, U.S. Postal Service, 475 L'Enfant Plaza S.W., Washington, D.C. 20260.

VETERANS AFFAIRS

The *Department of Veterans Affairs* provides health care, financial aid, and other forms of assistance to the United States' veterans and their beneficiaries. It runs the largest health care system in the nation, with 172 hospitals, 218 outpatient clinics, 88 nursing homes, and 16 other facilities. The professionals employed in these institutions include physicians, dentists, pharmacists, nurses, physician assistants, psychologists, occupational therapists, physical therapists, social workers, medical technologists, dietitians, audiologists, and medical record librarians. Other major occupations are police officer, secretary, clerk-typist, biological technician, accounting technician, nursing assistant, diagnostic technician, radiological technician, medical machine technician, pharmacy technician, medical clerk, dental assistant, and supply clerk.

Besides providing medical care, the Department of Veterans Affairs administers such far-ranging benefit programs as compensation and pension funds for disabilities and death, home mortgage guarantees, job training, and educational assistance under the GI Bill.

Among the 200,000 white-collar employees of the Department of Veterans Affairs, besides those already mentioned, are veterans claims examiners, contact representatives, and the whole spectrum of clerical and administrative workers. In addition, there are about 45,000 blue-collar workers, mostly in food service and building maintenance occupations. Jobs for physicians, dentists, nurses, physician assistants, optometrists, and podiatrists are not under the jurisdiction of the Office of Personnel Management, but most of the other jobs are. For additional information, contact the personnel officer at any Department of Veterans Affairs facility.

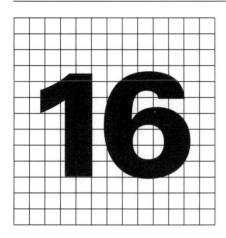

CONGRESS AND THE COURTS

Although the vast majority of jobs in the federal government are with the various federal agencies, Congress and the courts employ thousands of workers in a wide variety of jobs. This chapter describes the career opportunities available in the legislative and judiciary branches of government.

CONGRESS

Congressional employees, more than 38,000 strong, include the staff members who work for individual senators, representatives, or committees and those employed by three agencies—the General Accounting Office, the Government Printing Office, and the Library of Congress.

Working for an elected members of Congress is referred to as being "on the Hill." Positions unique to Capitol Hill and widely sought are administrative assistant, legislative aide, and caseworker. Frequently, members of Congress hire key staff members from their home districts for these positions. They also tend to employ capable constituents for one or more of the clerical posts and for congressional aides.

Since many of these individuals do not know the inner workers of Congress, most elected officials prefer to balance their staff by hiring career individuals. These are the professional cadre, with a reputation for competence, contacts, and a sound knowledge of how business is done on the Hill. Jobs on the Hill do not come under any federal classifications. As a result, the benefits and pay are not uniform. There are no standard hiring procedures and promotions are between the elected member or committee and the individual worker. In fact, workers can be and are fired without notice as they lack the protection employees of federal and congressional agencies automatically receive. Also, when a member loses an election, his or her staff, including the professional cadre, almost always lose their jobs.

The Assistant

The administrative assistant is the chief staff person and the member's right arm. Generally, this person has spent years working closely with the senator or representative. Administrative assistants wield considerable power and work long hours, and their jobs depend upon their boss's being reelected.

The legislative assistant performs more technical tasks—perfecting the language of bills to be introduced, answering constituents' questions about the laws already passed, and researching background on current and proposed bills. Most legislative assistants work directly for members of Congress. But a certain number are also employed by congressional committees. When they work for a committee, they have more research-related assignments, including preparing questions for hearings.

The Caseworker

Caseworkers influence the member's chances for reelection as they are principally responsible for dealing with all the problems that constituents have with the government. For example, they make the phone calls and write the letters that prompt an agency to act or to correct an error. They focus on the practical problems constituents have with the federal government, for example, straightening out a problem with Social Security pensions. In addition, they also send out information on government programs or direct constituents where to obtain the information they are seeking.

Clerical Workers

Clerical workers keep the Hill functioning. Since every office needs receptionists, typists, secretaries, and aides, these jobs are in high demand. Many men and women accept these positions and use them as stepping stones to a career on the Hill or the other opportunities that present themselves, like working for the private firms that deal with Congress.

THE LEGISLATIVE AGENCIES

The three largest legislative agencies are the General Accounting Office, the Government Printing Office, and the Library of Congress.

General Accounting Office

The *General Accounting Office* is Congress's watchdog over the executive agencies. It reviews the particular programs of the agencies and also conducts governmentwide reviews to ensure that programs are not duplicated in different agencies. To perform these reviews, its 5,000-plus employees—3,000 of whom are classified as GAO evaluators (GS-399)—evaluate the cost, efficiency, and success of the programs. Naturally, the General Accounting Office employs many accountants and auditors. It also hires people with backgrounds in business, finance, economics, engineering, statistics, and computer science.

In addition to performing audits, the office is responsible for settling claims against the government and collecting debts. A large staff of lawyers and claims examiners is employed for these purposes. More than half the agency's employees work in Washington. There are also more than 20 offices elsewhere in the United States. Further information is available from the Office of Personnel Management, Room 4452, General Accounting Office, 441 G St. N.W., Washington, D.C. 20548.

Government Printing Office

The *Government Printing Office* is by turns a printer, a publisher, and a contract administrator. It actually prints about 10 percent of all government publications—most importantly, the *Federal Register* and the *Congressional Record*—and operates the largest printing plant in the world. What it cannot print itself, it has printed by commercial firms. It sells its publications through the mails and a chain of 26 bookstores.

The Printing Office employs about 5,000 people, most of whom are blue-collar workers in the printing trades. The bulk of the employees work in Washington, but some are assigned to the regional bookstores and to 14 procurement offices throughout the United States. Information on employment can be obtained from the Chief, Employment Branch, Government Printing Office, North Capitol and H Streets N.W, Washington, D.C. 20401.

Library of Congress

The Library's first responsibility is to conduct research and provide material to members of Congress, but it also administers the copyright law, maintains the *National Union Catalog,* distributes cataloging material for new publications, runs 159 regional and subregional libraries to serve the blind and physically handicapped, provides reference services to the general public, and houses more than 15 million books as well as 45 million other items, including movies and maps. The Library employs about 4,600 people; a large number of them have master's degrees in library science, but other specialists are also hired. Almost all the jobs are in Washington. Information about employment can be obtained from the Recruitment and Personnel Office, Library of Congress, 101 Independence Ave. S.E, Washington, D.C. 20540.

Other Congressional Agencies

Several smaller agencies are also part of the congressional branch. Their names, functions, and addresses follow.

Architect of the Capitol maintains the buildings and grounds for Congress, the Library of Congress, and the Supreme Court; blue-collar employment exceeds 1,500; U.S. Capitol Building, Washington, D.C. 20515.

United States Botanic Garden collects and cultivates plants; 245 First St. S.W., Washington, D.C. 20024.

Office of Technology Assessment identifies the consequences of the use of technology; 600 Pennsylvania Ave. S.E., Washington, D.C. 20510.

Congressional Budget Office analyzes the cost of programs and estimates revenues; Second and D Streets S.W., Washington, D.C. 20515.

THE COURTS

The *judicial branch* of the federal government consists of the *Supreme Court* and a system of special and lower courts. Total employment of the courts is about 20,000. The jobs are very widely scattered around the country; however, each court does its own hiring. The range of occupations is fairly small. Judges, law clerks, bailiffs, guards, and secretaries are among the people employed by the courts.

Federal cases start in the *district courts;* there is at least one in each state. There are more than 400 district judgeships in the United States. Next, a case goes to the *Courts of Appeals,* of which there are 97 divided among 11 circuits. Third and last comes the *Supreme Court.* There are also several special courts, such as the *Court of Claims,* the *Tax Court,* and the *Customs Court.*

Information about employment with a particular court can *only be provided by that court.* The addresses of the courts in any given city are listed in the *United States Government* section of local telephone books. Further information about the lower courts can be obtained from the Director, Administrative Office of the United States Courts, United States Supreme Court Building, Washington, D.C. 20544.

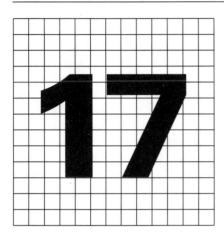

STATE AND LOCAL GOVERNMENTS

State and local governments are major providers of services. They provide education, mass transportation, fire protection, health services, and welfare services. These governments employ more than 14.4 million people in their own operations, more than any other industry in the country. State and local governments account for 1 job in 8.

The size of the state and local government labor force varies from place to place, ranging from almost one and a half million workers in California to fewer than 29,000 in Vermont. Population is the major reason for the differences. Other factors are due to different needs and the willingness and ability of the citizens to pay for government service. For example, rural areas require different services than large cities do. If the private sector traditionally provides hospitals or utilities, the state or local government does not.

One way to look at government employment besides the total number of people working is the number of state and local workers per 10,000 citizens. The average is 490, but even here there is much variation, ranging from 725 in Alaska to 398 in Pennsylvania. Other states with high employment-to-population ratios are Wyoming, Nebraska, New Mexico, and New York; other states with low ratios include New Hampshire, Ohio, Illinois, and Indiana.

The employment-population ratio also varies from function to function within a state. For example, the ratio for Georgia hospitals is very high, but it's a little below average in parks and recreation. Nevada has a low ratio in education and a very high one in correction.

GOVERNMENT IS BIG BUSINESS

Government is a very large industry, with many different employers: 50 states plus 5 territories, Puerto Rico, and the District of Columbia; approximately 3,000 counties; 19,200 municipalities; 16,700 towns; 29,600 special districts; and, finally, 14,700 school districts.

That makes 83,000 different governments or governmental bodies, each of which does its own hiring and may have more than one hiring system. Each state, for example, has an agency similar to the former Civil Service Commission of the federal government that establishes eligibility standards, administers examinations, and maintains registers of eligible applicants. But as many as half the state's employees may be hired according to other procedures. For example, the court system and the legislature are not usually under the civil service system.

TYPES OF GOVERNMENT

State and local governments come in more shapes and sizes than blue jeans. The U.S. Census Bureau conducts an annual survey of government employment. For the survey, it divides governments among the following groups.

- *County.* Organized county governments, called *boroughs* in Alaska and *parishes* in Louisiana.
- *Municipality.* A political subdivision of a county that provides general government services to a concentrated population in a defined geographic area. Municipalities are also called cities, villages, boroughs (except in Alaska), and towns (except in New England, Minnesota, New York, and Wisconsin). Some municipalities have taken over the entire area of a county or, in the case of New York City, several counties. Among these cities are Anaconda; Anchorage; Baltimore; Baton Rouge; Boston; Butte; Carson City; Columbus, Goergia; Denver; Honolulu; Indianapolis; Jacksonville; Juneau; Lexington, Kentucky; Nashville; New Orleans; Philadelphia; St. Louis; Sitka; and San Francisco. Washington, D.C. combines the functions of a city, county, and state government.
- *Township.* A subdivision of a county that provides general government services in a defined geographical area without regard to the concentration of the population. Twenty states use this classification. The governments are called *towns* in New England, New York, and Wisconsin; *plantations* in Maine; and *locations* in New Hampshire.
- *School district.* The census notes that "There is a marked organizational diversity in the types of governmental units that provide for the operation of public schools." School districts that are completely independent of all other local governments are found in 45 states. Dependent school systems are found in Alaska, Hawaii, Maryland, North Carolina, Virginia, and Washington, D.C.; the school system is dependent on a local government or the state government. Eleven states have both independent and dependent school systems.
- *Special district.* A government that provides only one or a few related services, which makes them like school districts. The district may be called

an authority, board, or commission. Among the services provided by special districts are soil conservation, water, bridges, housing, community development, fire protection, and hospitals. These districts, like school districts, vary enormously in size.

Employment Opportunities

Besides hiring workers for new jobs, state and local governments will be hiring huge numbers of workers to replace those currently employed who go to work for private firms, retire, or leave the labor force for some other reason. A turnover rate of about 10 percent is fairly common; given the size of the government labor force, that means that more than 1 million jobs would open up in government service each year. By comparison, all the workers of the nation's two largest corporations in terms of employment now number about 1 million.

Education accounts for far more jobs than any other government function. Local governments—usually special school districts—are the major employers of people who work in education, including teachers, administrators, teacher aides, librarians, and school counselors.

State and local governments employ more people *in their own operations* than any other industry in the country. Thousands of people in the following occupations work for them.

Accountant	Land use manager
Administrative assistant	Lawyer
Accounting clerk	Librarian
Automotive mechanic	Licensed practical nurse
Bookkeeper	Maintenance worker
Building engineer, inspector	Nursing aide and orderly
Civil engineer	Nutritionist
Clerical supervisor	Physician
Clinical lab technician	Police officer
Computer programmer, analyst	Psychiatric aide
Coach	Recreation worker
College and university instructor	Registered nurse
Electrician	Sanitation worker
Emergency medical technician	School principal
Extension service specialist	Sheriff
File clerk	Social worker
Fire fighter	Systems analyst
Food service worker	Teacher
Forester	Therapist
Gardener and groundskeeper	Urban and regional planner
Guard	Water and wastewater conservation
Health inspector	and treatment worker
Heavy equipment operator	Word processor
Highway maintenance worker	

Employees of state governments are not quite as concentrated *by field* as local government workers are, although 30 percent are engaged in higher education. Functions employing at least 5 percent of all state workers are hospitals, highways, correction, and public welfare. This means that state governments employ many college professors, librarians, nurses, psychiatric aides, other medical specialists, engineers, highway construction workers, correction officers or prison guards, social workers, and welfare aides.

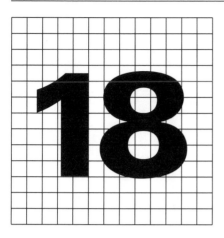

PROFESSIONAL, ADMINISTRATIVE, AND SCIENTIFIC CAREERS IN STATE AND LOCAL GOVERNMENTS

Among the professional, administrative, and scientific occupations available in state and local governments are accountant, lawyer, city manager, purchasing agent, athletic coach, college professor, social worker, and personnel officer. These jobs usually require at least a college diploma in a field related to the occupation, although technical and clerical employees are sometimes promoted into a few of them. The following pages present an alphabetical listing and description for the majority of these positions.

ACCOUNTANTS

Accountants prepare budgets, keep track of incoming money (both taxes and transfers from higher governments) and payments, estimate income and expenditures for the next year or more, and analyze the cost of doing something different ways.

Besides enjoying working with numbers, an accountant must have an interest in detail. In addition, accountants need communication skills to report the results of their analysis in writing and orally.

The majority of accountants have bachelor's degrees in accounting. Many accountants, however, began working as bookkeepers or accounting clerks and were promoted into accounting positions.

The average starting salary for 1991 was $26,600, according to the Bureau of Labor Statistics. The average salary for federal government accountants in 1990 was $40,000. They receive the usual fringe benefits.

In 1990, 90,000 people worked as accountants for state and local governments. Budget agencies, controllers offices, tax assessors' offices, treasury departments, and other agencies that are responsible for financial matters or auditing services have a higher-than-average proportion of accountants. The employment of accountants throughout the economy is projected to increase faster than the average during the next decade.

Several associations provide information about accounting, including the following:

American Institute of Certified Public Accountants
1211 Avenue of the Americas
New York, NY 10036

American Society of Women Accountants
35 E. Wacker Drive, Suite 2250
Chicago, IL 60601

ATTORNEYS

Attorneys are employed in substantial numbers in state and local governments. They are an integral part of the criminal justice system and may work for a state attorney general or in county courts as prosecutors or public defenders.

Lawyers who work for state and local governments draft ordinances and legislation, represent the government in hearings and trials, and teach in public law schools. Most spend much of their time researching legal matters.

In addition, the almost 20,000 municipalities in the United States employ large numbers of lawyers who help develop local statutes, interpret federal and state regulations, establish enforcement procedures, and argue cases on behalf of the city. Smaller communities may retain lawyers who also have a practice that allows them time to work on contract. Special districts, school districts, and townships will also either have their own lawyers or contract on an hourly basis.

Average salaries for lawyers are in the upper third for all wage earners; the average for all attorneys was $110,000 in 1990. The average starting salary for government attorneys was between $25,000 and $31,000 in 1990, according to the Department of Labor.

This is a moderate-size occupation, employing a total of about 120,000 people in 1990. Most lawyers work for firms in the legal services industry. Many other people with law degrees make use of their training in business or government, but do not practice.

To practice, lawyers must be members of the state bar, which requires passing the bar exam; in most states, only law school graduates may take the exam. The American Bar Association publishes *A Review of Legal Education in the United States,* which provides information on all of the law schools approved by the American Bar Association. You can get 1 copy free by writing to Information Services, American Bar Association, 750 N. Lake Shore Drive, Chicago, IL 60611.

CITY MANAGERS

Managers are usually appointed by a council or mayor; their contracts are subject to renewal on a regular basis. Cities and towns have many different departments, each of which takes care of particular functions, such as police protection or street repair. City managers are professional managers who see that all the departments run smoothly.

Depending on the laws of the state and the will of the council, city managers may appoint the department heads, prepare the city budget, submit for approval, and suggest changes in city ordinances or policies.

City managers normally are required to have a master's degree in public administration, which includes courses in municipal law, finance, and political aspects of urban problems. An internship of six to twelve months may be required. They frequently start their careers as assistants before becoming managers.

In 1990, the salary range was from $33,000 to $125,000, according to the International City Manager Association. City and county managers receive standard fringe benefits—such as vacation and sick leave—and many receive additional benefits, such as an automobile, moving expenses, and liability insurance.

This is a small occupation, although about 11,000 worked as appointed managers in cities and counties in 1990, and perhaps 3 times as many worked as management assistants. The major employers are cities ranging from 10,000 to 500,000 in population. Information about this occupation is available from the following organizations:

International City Management Association
777 N. Capitol St. N.E., Suite 500
Washington, D.C. 20002-4201

National Civic League
1445 Market St.
Denver, CO 80202

CIVIL ENGINEERS

Civil engineers are concerned with the design of roads, bridges, and other structures. They determine whether the site is suitable for the structure, what materials are needed, and how much the construction will cost, and supervise construction. As a result, they spend a lot of time writing or delivering reports and consulting with other people working on the project. Specialists within this occupation include structural engineers, highway engineers, construction engineers, hydraulic engineers, traffic engineers, and soil mechanics engineers.

The standard educational requirement for civil engineers is a bachelor's degree in civil engineering. The course of study includes subjects such as physics, calculus, surveying, structural mechanics, and the mechanics of fluids.

Engineers are among the highest-paid workers. Other engineering specialties pay even better than civil engineering on average. In 1990, the average starting salary for civil engineers reported by the College Placement Council was $28,136. Engineers have the usual fringe benefits.

About 48,000 civil engineers work for state and local governments. The major employers are highway and public works departments. Civil engineering is projected to grow 47% by 1995, which is faster than average. Career information is available from the following associations:

American Society of Civil Engineers
345 E. 47th St.
New York, NY 10017

Education Foundation
American Public Works Association
1313 E. 60th St.
Chicago, IL 60637

Society of Women Engineers
345 E. 47th, Room 305
New York, NY 10017

CLINICAL LABORATORY TECHNICIANS

Clinical laboratory technicians are often known by their specialties; for example, they may be called medical laboratory technologists or technicians, bloodbank specialists, or biochemistry technicians. In general, these workers perform chemical and other kinds of tests on body fluids and tissues, such as the measurement of the amount of cholesterol in a blood sample. Some of these jobs require an associate's degree; others—those for technologists—require a bachelor of science degree. The average salary for clinical laboratory technicians was $22,660 in 1990, according to the Bureau of Labor Statistics. Medical laboratory technicians in government had an average annual salary of $21,664 in 1991. This is a moderate-size occupation; total employment in these fields was 258,000 in 1990. The occupations are growing faster than average, and turnover makes many thousands of jobs available each year. To learn more about this occupation, contact the American Society for Medical Technology, 2021 L St. N.W., Suite 400, Washington, D.C. 20036.

COACHES

Athletic coaches teach individuals and groups how to play different sports and improve their performance. They also may select team members, purchase equipment, and organize events. High school coaches usually have teaching duties as well. They must therefore be certified teachers, most often in physical education. Secondary athletic coaches average $30,300 annually; their salaries are comparable with those of other teachers.

This is a small occupation, employing only 16,000 people in state and local government. Little change in employment is likely between now and 1995. Competition is usually keen. To learn more about this occupation, contact unions or associations such as the National Association for Sport and Physical Education, 1900 Association Drive, Reston, VA 22091.

COLLEGE PROFESSORS

College professors teach, conduct research, and perform administrative duties. The proportion of time spent on any one activity varies. College teachers are responsible for specialized subjects, the degree of specialization increasing with the size of the school and its involvement with graduate education. A master's degree is sufficient for some positions; the Ph.D. is usually preferred and often required, however.

The average salary for college professors in 1990–1991 was $56,200 for 9 months, according to the American Association of University Professors. Salaries are lower than the average for the occupation in fine and liberal arts; they are higher in engineering, mathematics and some other scientific fields.

Total employment is projected to decline between now and 1995. The outlook is complicated by the high degree of specialization required; faculty members trained in one discipline are not qualified to teach in another. As a result, colleges may be unable to find enough teachers for certain subjects, such as engineering, while job hunters cannot find any openings in another field.

COUNSELORS

Counselors in schools help students deal with personal or family problems, choose courses, and decide what they will do after graduation. They work closely with teachers, school nurses, and school psychologists. School counselors usually have one to five years of education after college. Teaching experience is usually, but not always, required.

The average annual salary in 1990–1991 was about $38,000, according to the Educational Research Service. Because much of the employment is concentrated in the secondary schools, little growth is likely to occur between now and 1995. Positions will become available because of turnover.

Counselors work in many settings other than schools, such as job service offices and social services agencies. Information on these positions is also available from the American Association for Counseling and Development, 5999 Stevenson Ave., Alexandria, VA 22304.

EXTENSION AGENTS

Extension agents, who are also known as agricultural or home economics extension agents, are teachers without classrooms. They work with individuals and groups to spread information about agriculture and home economics. Specialties include horticulture, grain crops, animal husbandry, disease and insect control, nutrition, human relations, child development, and consumer education. Extension agents also direct 4-H activities and write articles on their specialties. The job requires at least a bachelor's degree in agriculture or home economics. The extension service is a joint endeavor of the federal, state, and county governments, but the employer is the state government, usually the land grant university (of which the service is an extension).

To learn more about this occupation, contact your local agent, the state university that operates the service, or the Extension Office, Science and Education Administration, U.S. Department of Agriculture, Washington, D.C. 20250.

FORESTERS

Foresters ensure that trees are healthy and protected from disease, fire, and infestations of insects. They conduct research, supervise parks, manage watersheds, replant burned-over or harvested forests, and establish guidelines for lumbering operations.

Foresters usually work 8 hours a day, 5 days a week. Much of their work takes place in offices, but they may be required to work outside in all kinds of weather, especially if a forest fire is raging or a hiking party gets lost.

Foresters generally have an aptitude for science and enough physical agility to make their way in the woods. A bachelor's degree in forestry is required for most entry-level positions, and a graduate degree is often preferred.

This is a fairly small occupation, totaling 29,000 in 1990, of whom 44 percent work for the federal government and 33 percent for state and local governments. Lumber companies are the principal employers of foresters outside the government.

Only slow growth is projected for this occupation and turnover is low. These factors, combined with the small number employed to begin with, indicate that relatively few jobs will be available through 1995.

The following organizations can provide further information about forestry:

Society of American Foresters
5400 Grosvenor Lane
Bethesda, MD 20814

American Forestry Association
1516 P St. N.W.
Washington, D.C. 20005

HEALTH INSPECTORS

Inspectors must be able to accept responsibility for their decisions, which can have serious consequences. On the one hand, the duties of their work can close down a business; on the other hand, failure to enforce health codes can result in illness or death. Inspectors must be experts in the field they are going to work in, and they must get along well with a wide range of people under somewhat difficult circumstances.

Consumer safety inspectors check up on food, drugs, and other products, or weights and measures. For example, they might look for mislabeled packages or signs of decomposition or contamination in a product. *Food inspectors* work with veterinarians at meat packing plants, ensuring that the animals and the plant meet state standards. *Environmental health inspectors* or *sanitarians* also check some processing plants, such as dairies, but they also ensure that restaurants, hospitals, and other places that serve food are kept clean and free of vermin. They must also do field work and write reports.

Inspectors usually work a standard 40-hour week. Much of their time is spent at inspection sites, working either alone or as part of a team.

The education required depends on the specialty. Sanitarians must usually have a bachelor's degree in environmental health or a physical or biological science. Most states require that environmental health inspectors or sanitarians be licensed.

About 49,920 health and regulatory inspectors worked for state governments in 1990; 31,200 worked for local governments. City and county health departments are major employers at the local level.

Relatively slow growth is projected for these occupations through 1995; furthermore, turnover is quite low. As a result, the number of jobs available will not be very great.

The following associations can provide further information about this occupation:

> Food Sanitation Institute of the Environmental Management Association
> 255 Detroit St., Suite 200
> Denver, CO 80206

> International Association of Milk, Food and Environmental Sanitarians, Inc.
> 502 E. Lincoln Way
> Ames, IA 50010-6666

HOSPITAL ADMINISTRATORS

Hospital administrators, also known as *health services administrators,* are responsible for seeing that the medical staff has the equipment, working conditions, and personnel needed to treat the patients. Budgeting finances, hiring personnel, keeping the physical plant in shape, coordinating departments, and training the staff all come under their direction.

Most hospital administrators have a master's degree in health care administration, although a bachelor's degree in business and management is sufficient for some positions. Administrators usually start as assistants. Besides hospitals and health departments, health services administrators also work for nursing homes, clinics, health maintenance organizations, and group practices.

To learn more contact unions or associations such as:

American College of Healthcare Executives
840 N. Lake Shore Drive
Chicago, IL 60611

Association of University Programs in Health Administration
1911 Fort Myer Drive
Suite 503
Arlington, VA 22209

National Health Council
Health Career Programs
350 Fifth Ave., Suite 1118
New York, NY 10018

LANDSCAPE ARCHITECTS

Landscape architects design gardens and parks. They determine which plants are suitable for an area, taking the soil, sunlight, water supply, and proposed use into account. They also plan the type and position of roads, walks, fences, lamps, furniture, drains, and sprinkler systems.

A bachelor's degree in landscape architecture—which may take five years to complete—is usually required.

This is a small occupation, with 20,000 workers in 1990. The major employers in state and local government are park departments, school systems, hospitals, city planning agencies, and extension services.

To learn more about this occupation, contact the American Society of Landscape Architects, 1733 Connecticut Ave. N.W., Washington, D.C. 20009.

LIBRARIANS

The job of a librarian is to make information available. Some librarians perform technical services—ordering books, cataloging material, or having sets of magazines bound for the permanent collection. Most librarians provide user services. They explain how the library is arranged, where different kinds of material are kept, and how to use machines such as microfilm and microfiche readers. The majority of librarians work in schools; teaching students how to use a library is an important part of their duties.

Librarians usually work a 5-day, 40-hour week. Depending on the hours the library is open, evening or weekend work may be required. Many librarians—more than 20%—work part time.

Starting salaries of librarians in public libraries who had a master of library science degree were $23,400 in 1990. School librarians had average starting salaries of $26,200 in 1990, according to a *Library Journal* survey.

More than 70% of all librarians are in the educational services sector, whereas less than 11% work in public libraries.

Employment growth in school libraries should be similar to that for teachers; this would mean that growth is likely in the elementary schools and decline is probable in the universities between now and 1995. The employment of librarians in public libraries is projected to grow more slowly than average between now and 1995, but employment in specialized libraries will continue to grow.

The following associations have information on this career:

American Library Association
50 E. Huron St.
Chicago, IL 60611

National Education Association of the United States
1201 16th St. N.W.
Washington, D.C. 20036

PAROLE OFFICERS

Parole officers work with the correction or parole department. Parolees are criminals who have been released from prison before completing their sentences. Early release provides an incentive for good behavior and enables the department to see if people can adjust to society while it still has some control over them. Parole officers keep track of parolees, make certain that parole rules are obeyed, and assist parolees in their search for job training and employment or in other ways. Parole officers usually have a bachelor's degree in sociology, psychology, criminology, or correction, and experience in the correction department. Their salaries are comparable to those of social workers; the average salary for social workers is in the lower third for all wage earners.

PHYSICIANS

Physicians work to prevent illness, restore health, and repair the results of injuries. Some treat the whole person, but most specialize in particular parts of the body, such as the heart or brain. They are among the most thoroughly educated workers, the course of study taking from 4 to 10 years after college, including both medical school and residency requirements.

They are also among the best paid, with an average income of $155,800 after expenses in 1991. Median salaries for hospital interns were $19,800; median salaries for emergency-room physicians were $89,000.

This is a fairly large occupation; 580,000 doctors were working in 1990. Most are self-employed.

To learn more about this occupation, contact associations such as Council on Medical Education, American Medical Association, 515 N. State St., Chicago, IL 60610.

PROBATION OFFICERS

Probation officers work within the court system, although they are employees of the state correction agency. Before a trial, they investigate the accused person's family background and position in the community in order to recommend whether or not a judge should grant bail. Before a person is sentenced, the officer conducts a similar investigation to see if probation rather than prison should be imposed. After sentencing, officers supervise people on probation to ensure that they obey the rules of their sentences. Probation officers usually have a bachelor's degree in sociology, psychology, criminology, or correction, and experience in the department they work for. As of January 1, 1989, the average entry-level salary for probation officers was $19,000 according to the Criminal Justice Institute.

PUBLIC HEALTH NURSES

Many public health nurses work to prevent illness by providing information, health screening, and medications such as vaccines. Public health nurses also care for the injured and ill, either in a clinic or as visiting nurses. Conditions in clinics and schools are similar in that both are indoors and have ready access to medical supplies. Visiting nurses encounter much more varied conditions and must travel throughout the day despite the weather.

A license is required to be a fully qualified public health nurse. To obtain the license, a bachelor of science degree in nursing is usually required. Degree programs usually take 4 to 5 years; they should not be confused with associate programs, which usually take 2 years. People with associate's degrees may complete the requirements to become registered nurses but not fully qualified public health nurses in most cases.

Nurses held approximately 1,727,000 jobs in 1990. Many worked for local governments in public and community health agencies. Other major employers are local health departments and clinics. Three percent of all registered nurses worked in schools.

Nursing is a rapidly growing occupation. The combination of fast growth and large size means that many thousands of jobs should become available between now and the year 2000.

For more information, contact:

American Public Health Association, Inc.
1015 15th St. N.W.
Washington, D.C. 20005

American School Health Association
7263 State Route 43, Box 708
Kent, OH 44240

REGISTERED NURSES

The needs of the patient and the instructions of the patient's doctor determine most of the duties of the nurse. Nurses give people shots, test blood pressure, and bandage wounds, keeping records of everything they do. Some nurses spend their day caring for bedridden patients who, besides medical care, need help with eating and with personal hygiene. Other nurses are primarily concerned with supervisor orderlies, nurse aides, licensed practical nurses, and technicians.

Hours and working conditions for nurses vary. Nursing care must be provided 24 hours a day, so many nurses work nights and weekends. The proportion of nurses who work part time (28 percent) is much higher than for most occupations that require so much education and training.

The educational requirements for *registered nurses* have been the subject of controversy for the past 10 years. Three different kinds of programs enable prospective nurses to take the required licensing exam. Programs in community colleges that last about 2 to 3 years and lead to an associate's degree now train about 45 percent of the new registered nurses. Programs connected to hospitals that last 2 to 3 years and lead to a nursing diploma now train about 8 percent. Programs run by colleges or universities that last 4 to 5 years and lead to a bachelor of science degree in nursing (B.S.N.) now train the balance, about 47 percent.

While graduates of all three types of programs usually qualify for positions as staff nurses, each program has its advantages. The shortest programs are much less expensive both in terms of cost and—even more important—in terms of lost income while you are being trained. Hospital programs are often said to provide more practice working with patients. And B.S.N. degrees are required for public health nursing, admission to graduate school, and some supervisory positions. Graduates of 2- and 3-year programs may go back to school and earn a B.S.N., but the school may require that they retake several courses, adding to the time and expense of their education.

Nurses can advance in two ways, by taking on more supervisory responsibilities or by earning a graduate degree and certification that enables them to provide a higher level of nursing care, such as a nurse practitioner, nurse anesthetist, or clinical nurse.

Hospitals, public and private, employ more than 65 percent of all nurses.

According to the U.S. Department of Labor, job openings for nurses are expected to grow much faster than average through the year 2000.

Information about a career as a registered nurse is available from these organizations:

American Nurses' Association
2420 Pershing Road
Kansas City, MO 64108

American Hospital Association
Division of Nursing
840 N. Lake Shore Drive
Chicago, IL 60611

Career Information Services National League for Nursing
350 Hudson St.
New York, NY 10014

SOCIAL WORKERS

Meeting some of the needs caused by poverty and disadvantage is the social worker's goal. Social caseworkers meet with individuals, families, or groups, try to identify what problems the people have, and suggest ways to solve them.

Some temporary solutions are fairly simple. For example, if a family has no money because the adults are unable to work, the social worker can arrange for welfare payments to be made. Many problems are much more complex—drug addiction, for example. In these cases, social workers may refer the clients to other specialists and programs.

Social workers are trained to recognize that many people with such severe problems may need more intensive and specialized care. Case-workers are also trained in knowing how and where to refer people for special care, and in coordinating the services of different agencies. Most social workers are caseworkers—that is, they work directly with those in need—but some are administrators, teachers, or researchers.

Social workers may specialize in particular fields. About half of all social workers are in just three categories: mental health, child/youth, and medical/health. Similar work is performed by probation and parole officers, whose occupations are described in the chapter on correction departments.

The usual educational requirement is a bachelor's degree in social work, psychology, or sociology. Some positions require a master of social work degree (M.S.W.). More than half the states require that social workers be licensed.

Social workers may advance to supervisory positions or enter teaching. Further education may be necessary for advancement.

In 1990, the average salary was between $23,000 and $36,000. Social workers receive the usual fringe benefits.

About 175,200 social workers were employed by state and local governments in 1990.

The major employers are departments of human resources, social services, mental health, housing, education, and correction.

This occupation is projected to grow about as fast as average through 1995. Many more positions will become available because of turnover, which is relatively high, especially for an occupation that requires a college degree.

The following associations can provide further information:

National Association of Social Workers
7981 Eastern Ave.
Silver Spring, MD 20910

American Federation of State, County and Municipal
    Employees
1625 L St. N.W.
Washington, D.C. 20001

Council on Social Work Education
1600 Duke St.
Alexandria, VA 22314

SCHOOL PRINCIPALS

The principal runs the school in accordance with the rules and policies established by the school board and the superintendent. Principals assign teachers, set schedules, and coordinate school activities. They supervise the maintenance and cafeteria staffs and, of course, the teachers. Principals need the attributes of a good manager: organization and leadership skills, self-confidence, and decisiveness.

Public school principals must be certified by the state. Almost all have teaching experience and graduate school training, such as a master's degree in school administration, which includes such courses as school management, school law, school finance and budgeting, personnel administration, and community relations.

The following, according to the Educational Research Service, were the average salaries in 1990–1991. Elementary school, $51,500; junior high school, $55,100; senior high school, $59,100. Principals receive standard fringe benefits of state and local government workers, although they do not receive the longer vacations of teachers.

These organizations can supply more information about school principals:

Your state's department of education

American Association of School Administrators
1801 N. Moore St.
Arlington, VA 22209

The National Association of Secondary School Principals
1904 Association Drive
Reston, VA 22091

SPEECH PATHOLOGISTS

Speech pathologists work with people who have trouble speaking because of a problem such as a cleft palate, a lisp, or a stutter. They diagnose the problem and plan a course of action, such as teaching the person new ways to use her or his lips.

A master's degree in speech-language pathology is usually required for these workers, although a bachelor's degree is sufficient in some cases. A teaching certificate or certificate to practice speech-language pathology may also be required.

In 1990, according to the American Speech-Language-Hearing Administration, those with 1 to 3 years' experience had average salaries of $25,000; those with 16 or more years' experience earned $38,000, on average.

Schools are the primary employers; others are clinics and hospitals. The occupation is projected to grow as fast as average between now and 1995.

To learn more you can contact the American Speech-Language-Hearing Administration, 10801 Rockville Pike, Rockville, MD 20852.

TEACHERS

In the classroom, teachers have different duties depending on their specialty. Much of their work takes place outside the classroom, however, preparing lessons, grading papers, increasing their knowledge, and attending meetings.

Broadly speaking, elementary school teachers are responsible for all academic subjects while secondary school teachers usually instruct students in a single subject. Even at the lowest grades, however, some division of labor takes place. For example, physical education is almost always conducted by a teacher trained for that subject. English as a second language, special education, music, and art are other specialties within elementary education. As for high school, a secondary school specialist looks like a generalist to a college professor. Social studies teachers in high school, for example, may be called on to teach history, geography, economics, or sociology, all of which are distinct major fields in college.

Besides education, requirements might include citizenship, good health, and good character. Recently, some states have begun to require that new teachers pass competence tests. About half the states require that teachers earn a master's degree within a certain number of years after being hired.

According to the National Education Association, the average salary for public elementary school teachers in 1990–1991 was $32,400, secondary school teachers received $33,700, on average. They receive the usual fringe benefits and more vacation time than most workers.

Public elementary and secondary schools employed more than 2,800,000 classroom teachers in 1990. Even though the total number of elementary school teachers will rise, declines are still possible in certain northeastern areas and other places where overall population is declining. Growth is likely to be fastest in the Southwest.

Contact your local school district and state department of education and other districts or states where you might wish to work to learn the precise requirements for certification in the subjects you wish to teach.

Many teachers are members of associations and unions such as the following:

American Federation of Teachers
555 New Jersey Ave. N.W.
Washington, D.C. 20001

National Education Association of the United States
1201 16th St. N.W.
Washington, D.C. 20036

A list of accredited schools of education is available from the following association:

National Council for Accreditation of Teacher Education
2029 K St. N.W., Suite 500
Washington, D.C. 20006

THERAPISTS

Therapist is a general title for a worker in the health field who helps people overcome physical or emotional difficulties. Specialties within this group are highly specific; a worker trained in one of them is not qualified to work in another one. Among the titles of job specialties are physical, occupational, speech, recreation, art, dance, music, and horticultural therapist; rehabilitation counselor; audiologist; and orientation therapist for the blind. Some therapists diagnose the person's problem and devise ways to conquer it; others work in cooperation with a doctor who diagnoses and prescribes treatment. They usually need at least a bachelor's degree in their specialized field. Salaries ranged in 1990 from $15,000 to $42,000.

URBAN PLANNERS

Urban and regional planners design new or renovated developments. Also known as community or city planners, they juggle the need for housing, schools, industrial sites, business sections, and parks along with requirements for transportation, sanitation, electricity, and natural gas. They must study current conditions, consider long-term development, estimate costs, build models, present plans before authorizing boards, and supervise construction. A master's degree in planning is the usual educational requirement, although some positions require only a bachelor's degree. This is a relatively small occupation with a total employment of 23,000 in 1990; local, regional, and state government planning commissions employ about 75 percent of these workers. Only slow growth is projected between now and 1995. To learn more about this occupation, you can contact the American Planning Association, 1776 Massachusetts Ave. N.W., Washington, D.C. 20036.

CLERICAL, TECHNICAL, AND BLUE-COLLAR OCCUPATIONS IN STATE AND LOCAL GOVERNMENT

Clerical, technical, and blue-collar occupations, by far, represent the largest category of available jobs in state and local government. Of the three, clerical positions (secretaries, typists, and word processors) alone number almost a million and have a high turnover. This means that openings are numerous. Other large occupations that are normally categorized as clerical are accounting clerk and bookkeeper, clerical supervisor, file clerk, and town-country clerk.

Several technical, service, operative, craft, and repair occupations also have large numbers of workers in many different government agencies. These occupations include building custodians, electricians, engineering and science technicians, general maintenance repairers, and guards. Some of these jobs are very routine; others are extremely varied. Some require no particular education or experience; others take years of training. Salaries naturally reflect these differences. In this chapter, we will describe some of the larger occupations that come under this broad category, briefly indicating what the position entails and requires, and what the pay scale is.

AUTOMOBILE MECHANICS

Automobile mechanics find out what is wrong with a car and fix it; they must be able to use tools and read shop manuals; some specialize in certain types of repairs, such as transmissions or tune-ups, but most do a little bit of everything. Average wages are within the middle 40 percent for all wage earners; the average wage in 1990 was $25,800. Employment in state and local governments was about 50,000 that year. Major employers in state and local government would be departments that own many vehicles, such as police and fire departments. The occupation is projected to grow faster than average through 1995; turnover will make even more jobs available. Further information is available in *Opportunities in Automobile Services* by Robert Weber (Lincolnwood, IL: National Textbook Co., 1989), and from these two associations: Automotive Service Industry Association, 444 N. Michigan Ave., Chicago, IL 60611; and Automotive Service Association, 1901 Airport Freeway, Suite 100, P.O. Box 929, Bedford, TX 76095-0929. *Automotive News* and *Motor Service Magazine* are among the many periodicals that carry articles related to this occupation.

BOOKKEEPERS AND ACCOUNTING CLERKS

Bookkeepers and accounting clerks keep track of the money that an organization takes in and pays out. They keep records in journals and ledgers or on computer disks. High school graduates usually qualify for these jobs, especially if they have learned business arithmetic, bookkeeping, and principles of accounting. The average salary for accounting clerks is in the middle third for all wage earners; the median salary in 1990 was $17,600.

BUS DRIVERS

Bus drivers daily carry millions of people, mostly schoolchildren. Drivers inspect the bus before starting, checking such things as safety equipment, fuel supply, and brakes. They follow a specified schedule, being careful not to be early or late. Local transit bus drivers also collect fares, issue transfers, and provide route information. Bus drivers must also be able to make out route and accident reports.

A very large number of bus drivers—45 percent—work part time. School bus drivers usually work 20 to 30 hours a week. The standard work week for local transit bus drivers is 40 hours; however, split shifts, in which the driver is on duty for both the morning and evening rush hours with several hours off in between, are common. Weekend work is also required of local transit bus drivers.

Applicants should have a driver's license; a chauffeur's license is usually required to drive a bus, but you may be able to obtain the license after being hired. You should learn the policy of the company or transportation authority you wish to work for before applying.

A high school education is preferred, but not always required. Indeed, some school bus drivers are as young as 16, although 18 is the usual minimum age. Local transit bus drivers usually must be at least 21.

A driving test and a medical examination may be required. Some states require a background check of school bus drivers to ensure that applicants do not have a history of emotional instability.

After being hired, drivers are trained for 2 to 8 weeks in practical driver training, traffic laws, and bus company regulations.

Average salaries for school bus drivers are much lower than for local transit drivers. In 1990–1991, the average hourly wage for school bus drivers was $9.52, according to the Educational Research Service. According to the American Public Transit Association, the median starting salary for local transit bus drivers in 1990 was $9.90 an hour and the median top—which would be reached after 2 or 3 years—was $13.80 in cities of 1 million or more people. Drivers receive the usual fringe benefits.

The number of school bus drivers—380,000—is very large. Far fewer people—62,000 drive for local transit companies. A driver can tell you where to ask for information.

Many local transit bus drivers are members of unions such as the following:

Amalgamated Transit Union
5025 Wisconsin Ave. N.W.
Washington, D.C. 20016

Transport Workers Union of America
80 West End Ave.
New York, NY 10023

International Brotherhood of Teamsters, Chauffeurs,
    Warehousemen, and Helpers of America
25 Louisiana Ave. N.W.
Washington, D.C. 20001

General information about school bus driving is available from the following association:

National School Transportation Association
P.O. Box 2639
Springfield, VA 22152

General information on local transit bus driving is available from:

American Public Transit Association
1201 New York Ave. N.W., Suite 400
Washington, D.C. 20005

COMPUTER PROGRAMMERS

Computer programmers write detailed descriptions of the steps a computer must follow to solve a problem. After designing the program, the programmer will run sample data through the system to determine if it works correctly or if needs some adjustments. Programmers then prepare instructions for the *operator* who will run the program. Programmers may work alone on a project, or, in the case of large projects, may be part of a team.

Computer programmers usually work from descriptions of a problem presented to them by a *systems analyst*. In some instances, the jobs may be combined and the job will be titled *programmer-analyst*. Others who work in the field are *data entry clerks, data base managers,* and *computer service technicians.*

There are no standard training requirements for computer-related jobs. Depending on the work to be done and the salary you expect to earn, you can come minimally prepared, or you can come with advanced degrees in computer science, mathematics, or engineering.

Computer programming, system analysis, and other courses can be found in high schools, community colleges, vocational and technical schools, colleges, and universities. There are also home-study courses available. Be prepared to take courses throughout your career. This is an area in which the technology changes very quickly. Courses are offered by employers, software vendors, and computer manufacturers. If you expect to advance in your job, get used to the idea of being a periodic student.

Your Job Service Office will have openings listed, as will your local or state offices. Watch newspapers for announcements of openings. Search as you would for any other possibility. Additional sources of information are listed here.

American Federation of Information Processing Societies
1899 Preston White Drive
Reston, VA 22091

Association for Computing Machinery
11 W. 42nd St., Third Floor
New York, NY 10036

Data Processing Management Association
505 Busse Highway
Park Ridge, IL 60068

CONSTRUCTION INSPECTORS

Construction inspectors make sure that a building will not collapse before its time. They are highly specialized, some dealing with public works and others with buildings. Public works inspectors are further categorized by special areas such as highways, streets, bridges, tunnels, dams, and sewer and water systems. Specialties within building inspection include structural, electrical, and mechanical, which concerns plumbing, gas lines, and heating systems.

Inspectors usually check on a project more than once during construction to ensure that it conforms to building codes. Inspectors keep records of their work and write reports. They usually work a standard 40-hour week, spending about half their time in the office and half at construction sites.

Knowledge of the principles of good construction and attention to detail characterize construction inspectors. They must also know the law and be able to communicate. They usually must have experience as a contractor, supervisor, or craftperson. People who have completed an apprenticeship, studied engineering or architecture for 2 years, or earned an associate's degree in a relevant subject are preferred. This is not a job for beginning workers.

This is a fairly small occupation, with 54,000 state and local government employees. Construction inspectors usually work for the building, public works, engineering, or maintenance department of the local government. Those with the state government are most likely to be with the highway department.

Only slow growth is projected for this occupation and turnover is low.

Local governments and the following associations can provide more information about the job of construction inspector:

> International Conference of Building Officials
> 5360 S. Workman Mill Road
> Whittier, CA 90601

> Building Officials and Code Administrations International, Inc.
> 4051 Flossmoor Road
> Country Club Hills, IL 60477-5795

COOKS

Institutional cooks prepare food in large quantities. As they gain experience, they also order food and other supplies, keep records, and supervise kitchen helpers.

Their day might start very early, so they can prepare breakfast, or run late, so they can clean up after dinner; weekend work is also required for some jobs. Most institutional cooks in government, however, work in elementary and secondary schools, where few breakfasts and no suppers are served; these cooks work only on school days.

Cooks are subject to extreme heat from ovens, steam from boiling pots or dishwashers, and cold from walk-in refrigerators. They are on their feet much of the time.

A high school diploma is sufficient for most entry-level positions, although some employers prefer new workers who have earned an associate's degree with courses in subjects such as food preparation or menu planning. Experience working in an institutional or restaurant kitchen is likely to impress an employer more than education, however. A health certificate may be required to screen people with contagious diseases. New workers are usually trained on the job.

In 1990, median hourly earnings for all cooks except short-order cooks were $6.50. This is a fairly large occupation, employing almost 300,000 people in state and local governments. The major employers by far are schools. Hospitals also employ institutional cooks, as do nursing homes, child-care services, and jails and prisons. Employment growth in state and local governments will depend most upon growth of the elementary school population and the growth of hospital employment.

The following associations may be helpful:

Educational Foundation of the National Restaurant
  Association
250 S. Wacker Drive #1400
Chicago, IL 60606

American School Food Service Association
1600 Duke St., Seventh Floor
Alexandria, VA 22314

CORRECTION OFFICERS

Correction officers guard prisoners in state penitentiaries and local jails. Their jobs entail keeping careful watch over the prisoners at all times, whether from towers and guard rooms or while escorting them from place to place. They also inspect the prison, checking for signs of damage to locks, doors, and windows, and for unsafe or unhealthy conditions. Correction officers also supplement the efforts of psychologists and social workers.

The usual educational requirement is a high school diploma. Applicants must usually be at least 18, and take a series of tests including a written examination and a test of physical agility. A medical examination may also be required. Once hired, new officers receive 1 to 6 months of training.

The average salary for correction officers employed by states in 1990 was $22,900, according to CONTAC Inc. They receive standard fringe benefits. Housing is sometimes provided.

Roughly 315,000 correction officers work for state and local governments. About half work at state penitentiaries and the rest at local jails. Turnover averages 24 percent, which is much higher than for most occupations.

The following organizations can provide further information:

CONTACT Inc.
P.O. Box 81826
Lincoln, NE 68501

The American Correctional Association
8025 Laurel Lakes Court
Laurel, MD 20707

COURT REPORTERS

Court reporters are specialized stenographers who, using stenotype machines or shorthand, make word-for-word records of court proceedings, hearings, and legislative sessions. They may also be called shorthand reporters, hearing reporters, or legal reporters. A recording speed as high as

225 words per minute may be required, although 160 is sufficient for some jobs. Besides recording dictation, court reporters may also type, transcribe their notes, or dictate their notes for a typist; increasingly, however, the notes can be transcribed by computer.

Shorthand reporters can learn their skills in 2-year programs at post-high school technical institutes and junior colleges. Salaries are better than those of other clerical workers. This is a relatively small occupation for the clerical field, but demand is often greater than the supply.

`To learn more about this occupation, contact the National Shorthand Reporters Association, 118 Park St. S.E. Vienna, VA 22180. A publication which may be useful to you is the *National Shorthand Reporter.*

CROSSING GUARDS

Crossing guards ensure the safety of children at busy intersections before and after school. A high school diploma is usually required; good character is important, and extensive background checks are often performed. Hourly wages based on the 1990 census and adjusted for inflation were $9.20 in 1989. For more information, contact a local police department.

DETECTIVES

Detectives gather evidence for criminal cases. They interview witnesses and suspects, keep watch over suspects, and assist in arrests. Most have several years' experience as police officers before becoming detectives. Detectives usually earn more than police officers. To learn more about this occupation, consult the sources of information listed under police officers.

DISPATCHERS

Dispatchers who work for police departments, fire departments, and hospitals receive telephone and radio calls from people seeking assistance and broadcast the necessary information to field units. They also keep records, or logs, of the calls they receive and the action they take.

A high school education is usually required of these workers and, frequently, an FCC radio license. National salary data are not available for this occupation; any police department can provide local information, however.

In 1990, about 69,700 people worked as police, fire, and ambulance dispatchers, making this a relatively small occupation. Local governments employ almost all of these workers.

ELECTRICIANS

Electricians are skilled craft workers with years of training. They install and repair the wiring in government buildings. Apprenticeship programs provide training. Electricians must be licensed. Average salaries for electricians are in the middle third for all wage earners; median weekly earnings in 1990 were $524. This is a moderate-size occupation, with a total employment of 548,000 in 1990; state and local governments employed more than 30,000 electricians that year. Large school systems and hospitals also employ many thousands of electricians. You can contact unions or associations such as the International Brotherhood of Electrical Workers, 1125 15th St. N.W., Washington, D.C. 20005.

EMERGENCY MEDICAL TECHNICIANS

Emergency medical technicians (EMTs) may work as dispatchers, ambulance attendants, or paramedics. The paramedics are the most highly trained. Both ambulance and paramedic EMTs give first aid to victims of auto accidents, heart attacks, shootings, and other emergencies. Paramedics are able to give aid that requires more complex medical procedures, such as administering intravenous drugs under the supervision of a physician. Ambulance work requires at least 100 hours of training in a course approved by the U.S. Department of Transportation; training for paramedics takes 4 to 6 times as long. To learn more about this occupation, contact the National Association of Emergency Medical Technicians, 9140 Ward Parkway, Kansas City, MO 64114.

ENGINEERING AND SCIENCE TECHNICIANS

Engineering and science technicians test equipment and use laboratory or engineering instruments. This title refers to a large group of occupations that call for similar levels of skill and training, although the specific duties vary widely. Among these occupations are drafter, electrical and electronics technician, civil engineering technician, surveyor, biological technician, sanitation technician, and pump technician. Drafting, surveying, technical, and laboratory experience or courses in technical schools or community colleges are helpful in qualifying for these jobs, but some openings are available for high school graduates. Salaries depend in part on the specific occupation. The median salary for drafters was $25,900 in 1990. The average salary for electrical and electronics technicians was $24,000 in 1990. The average annual salary for engineering technicians in 1990 was $29,800. Starting salaries for those with no more than a high school diploma are about the same as in entry-level clerical jobs. A pamphlet, *Drafting as a Career,* is available from the American Design and Drafting Association, 5522 Norbeck Road, Suite 391, Rockville, MD 20853. A series of pamphlets on engineering technician occupations is published by the American Association of Engineering Societies, 19th St. N.W., Suite 608, Washington, D.C. 20036.

FILE CLERKS

File clerk is an entry-level job in many large agencies. The clerk sorts letters, bills, contracts, or other documents according to the alphabet, a numerical code, or some other system and puts them where they belong. The clerk also finds and retrieves an item when it is needed. Some clerks classify the material to begin with. A high school education is usually required. The average annual salary was $14,600 in 1990.

FIRE FIGHTERS

There are 260,000 fire fighters employed by state and local governments. Fire fighters are among the most respected employees of local governments. No one questions their courage or the importance of their work.

A fire fighters main duty is to put out fires. All fire fighters must also be prepared to rescue victims and give first aid.

To become a fire fighter, you must usually pass a long series of tests. You begin by submitting an application. If you meet certain minimum qualifications, you will be scheduled to take the first of the tests. Minimum qualifications might include age (usually at least 21 and often no more than 35, although many departments have no upper limit) and residency. You may have to take as many as five different kinds of tests and different kinds of examinations.

Next comes a test of strength and physical agility. The parts of the test are related to a fire fighter's actual duties. You can learn precisely what tests are given by the departments that you want to work for; practice them.

Interviews are another kind of test. At the interview, experienced fire fighters will ask you a series of questions to learn why you want to enter the occupation and what steps you have taken to prepare for it. The board is less concerned about your specific answers than your attitude and personality; they want to see if you keep calm under pressure, follow instructions, express yourself clearly, and are highly motivated.

Medical examinations for fire fighters are stringent. Learn the exact standards for any department you might want to work for before you even apply. Many companies use the National Fire Protection Association Standard 10001. You can obtain a copy of it from the address below and have your own physician examine you so you'll know if you meet the medical qualifications. Among the disqualifying physical conditions are color blindness, poor vision, heart trouble, and back trouble.

Background investigations are conducted by some fire departments, which check for a criminal record, serious driving violations, and credit problems.

Fire fighters are usually trained by the department after being hired. A few departments have formal apprenticeship programs.

The average starting salary in 1990 was $19,700, according to the International City Manager Association; the average salary for nonsupervisory fire fighters was $25,000. Fire fighters are provided with protective clothing by the department and may receive a uniform or uniform allowance. They generally enjoy the usual fringe benefits. Because of the agility needed to perform their duties, fire fighters often are able to retire early; in some cases, they can retire at half pay after 20 years.

This is a moderate-size occupation, numbering about 280,000 in 1990; an additional 60,000 people work as fire officers and inspectors. The numbers of openings projected is smaller than would be expected for an occupation of this size for two reasons. First, turnover is extremely low, an indication of the high degree of satisfaction fire fighters have with their jobs. Second, only slow growth in employment is projected. Competition for fire fighter positions is usually keen.

The following organizations and your local fire department can provide career information on fire fighters:

International Association of Fire Chiefs
1329 18th St. N.W.
Washington, D.C. 20036

International Association of Fire Fighters
1750 New York Ave. N.W.
Washington, D.C. 20006

FISH AND GAME WARDENS

Fish and game wardens make sure that hunters, trappers, anglers, and commercial fishermen obey game laws. Much of their time is spent on routine patrols, but they also investigate complaints and make reports on wildlife. A high school education is usually required. This is a small occupation, employing only several thousand people. State governments are the major employers, although the federal government and some local governments also employ a few wardens.

GENERAL MAINTENANCE REPAIRERS

General maintenance repairers combine the skills of a carpenter, electrician, mechanic, painter, plumber, and plasterer, performing general maintenance and making minor repairs as needed. They work with a great variety of hand and power tools. A high school diploma may be required, but more important is the ability to do the work. The salary range is wide, going from little above the minimum wage almost to the upper third for all wage earners; in 1990, average salaries ranged from $8.70 to $10.40 an hour, depending on the skill required for particular positions. State and local governments employ about 160,000 of these workers, mostly in schools and hospitals. Average growth is projected between now and 1995. Growth combined with turnover should result in thousands of jobs becoming available each year. To learn more about this occupation, visit the Job Service, listed in the state government section of your phone book.

GUARDS

Guards patrol buildings when they are closed and keep watch over their entrances when they are open. A high school diploma is usually preferred, but not always required. In 1990, the average hourly wage was $6.28. There are about 62,000 guards employed in state and local government. Schools, hospitals, and government office buildings frequently employ guards. In 1990 there were 883,000 people employed as guards and security officers. The field is expected to grow at more than the average rate at least until the year 2000.

HEAVY EQUIPMENT OPERATORS

Heavy equipment operators are also known as construction machinery operators or operating engineers. They drive bulldozers, backhoes, paving machines, and other equipment. They usually have experience as construction laborers or helpers before becoming heavy equipment operators. Median weekly earnings in 1990 were $500. Operators employed by state and local governments are less affected by unemployment than are most construction workers. Employment in state and local governments in 1990 was 157,000. To learn more about this occupation, contact the International Union of Operating Engineers, 1125 17th St. N.W., Washington, D.C. 20036.

HIGHWAY MAINTENANCE OPERATORS

Highway maintenance workers have a great many duties. Signs and lines must be painted, potholes filled, cracks patched, grass mown, and snow plowed. A high school education is usually required. This is a moderate-size occupation, employing 151,000 workers in 1990, all of them with state and local governments, which are the major employers. To learn more about this occupation, visit the Job Service, which has job listings and offers employment counseling. You can also contact the American Federation of State, County and Municipal Employees, 1625 L St. N.W., Washington, D.C. 20001.

HOMEMAKERS/HOME HEALTH AIDES

Home health aides, also sometimes called homemakers, will become a bigger and bigger category of workers in the coming decade. By all indicators, the older population will continue to increase and will need home health and homemaking services in increasing amounts. In addition, as the cost of health care skyrockets, more patients will be treated in the home to try to control those costs. Further, new technology will make home care increasingly possible. For example, portable versions of machines, formerly only available in hospitals, are already in use in the home. For further information about this rapidly growing field, write to The National Association for Home Care, 519 C St. N.E., Washington, D.C. 20002.

LIBRARY TECHNICIANS AND AIDES

Library technicians and aides (who may also be called assistants, helpers, or clerks) perform a variety of duties that help a library run smoothly. They check books and other materials in and out, sort and shelve them, calculate fines, locate items for users, issue library cards, repair or bind materials, and provide information. Technicians have more complicated duties and less supervision than aides. Some college coursework (as long as 2 years in a program for technicians) may be required of technicians; a high school education is usually sufficient for aides. Aides with simple clerical duties receive salaries comparable with other clerical workers. To learn more about this occupation, contact the Council on Library-Media-Technicians-Assistants, Cuyahoga Community College, Attn: Margaret R. Barron, 2900 Community College Ave., Cleveland, OH 44115.

LICENSED PRACTICAL NURSES

Licensed practical nurses (LPNs) provide bedside care; they bathe patients, give massages, and change dressings. They also check the patient's vital signs—temperature, blood pressure, pulse, and respiration. Under supervision, they may administer medications. To become an LPN, you must complete a 1-year training program in a vocational school or community college. Average salaries for LPNs are in the lower third for all wage earners. This is a fairly large occupation, employing 644,000 in 1990; more than half these workers were employed by hospitals. Other major employers are nursing homes and physicians' offices. Between now and 1995, fast growth combined with turnover should make thousands of jobs available each year. To learn more about this occupation, you can contact unions or associations such as National League for Nursing, 350 Hudson St., New York, NY 10014; or the National Federation of Licensed Practical Nurses, Inc., P.O. Box 18088, Raleigh, NC 27619.

LIFEGUARDS

Lifeguards are primarily responsible for preventing drownings or other accidents at pools and beaches. They may also teach people to swim, clean the pool, and check the chlorine level of the water. Red Cross Lifeguard Certification is usually required. Applicants for certification must demonstrate the ability to swim and dive to specific degrees, and to rescue swimmers; cardiopulmonary resuscitation or other types of training may also be required. The training for lifeguards is extensive and has been standardized primarily by the Red Cross. Two certifications are the most common: the Advanced Life Saving Certificate and the Water Safety Instructor Certificate. The average salary for lifeguards is in the lower third for all wage earners. Hiring for these positions, most of which are seasonal, frequently begins in January. To learn more about this occupation, contact the U.S. Lifesaving Association, c/o Chicago Park District, 425 E. 14th Blvd., Chicago, IL 60605.

NURSING AIDES

Nursing aides and orderlies take care of many of the patients' basic needs. They make beds, feed, bathe, dress, and transport patients, and set up equipment. High school graduates are usually preferred for these jobs, but a high school diploma is not always required. This is one of the lowest-paid occupations in the country. Median earnings in 1990 were about $13,100. The occupation is projected to grow faster than average between now and 1995. Turnover is high. This combination means that many thousands of jobs will become available each year.

PARALEGALS

Paralegals are sometimes called legal assistants. In general, paralegals do research and background work for lawyers. As costs increase, more and more legal departments in state and local government have only a few lawyers and dozens of paralegals in their employ.

In government, paralegals will analyze legal materials for use within the office, maintain reference files, conduct research, collect and analyze evidence for hearings, and prepare informational material for their own office use and for the public.

Some lawyers will prefer to train their own assistants, or to promote the most capable legal secretaries in the office. Some will search for employees who have completed formal educational programs for the occupation. There are more than 600 of these institutions connected with colleges, universities, community colleges, and proprietary schools. Paralegals need not be certified, but the National Association of Legal Assistants has established standards for voluntary certification.

To learn more about this occupation you can also contact unions or associations such as the American Bar Association, 750 N. Lake Shore Drive, Chicago, IL 60611.

A rapidly growing area of employment is that of the legal assistant— commonly called *paralegal.* As costs increase, the employment of paralegals will increase. To learn more about this profession write to:

American Association for Paralegal Education
P.O. Box 40244
Overland Park, KS 66204

National Association of Legal Assistants, Inc.
1601 S. Main St., Suite 300
Tulsa, OK 74119

National Paralegal Association
P.O. Box 406
Solebury, PA 18963

PARK RANGERS

Park rangers are responsible for maintaining order in public parks, which involves directing traffic, providing information, and patrolling the park to prevent violations of the law or park rules. Administering first aid and assisting with disabled vehicles are common tasks.

Park rangers are outdoors in all kinds of weather. They usually work a 40-hour week, but their shifts are irregular. Since the parks are busiest on weekends and holidays, rangers are likely to work then.

Park rangers must be able to keep calm in emergencies, make decisions rapidly, and remain courteous after the hundredth repetition of the same question.

A high school education is usually required; college-level courses in recreational leadership, environmental science, psychology, sociology, and biology may be helpful.

Applicants are given a series of tests before becoming ranger trainees, including written exams, physical agility tests, medical examinations, and interviews. Rangers are trained after being hired, sometimes at a police academy.

Rangers will probably receive salaries comparable to those of police officers in the same area.

This is a relatively small occupation, employing about 18,000 people. In various states, agencies that employ rangers might be called any of the following names: Department of Parks; Department of Parks and Recreation; Department of Natural Resources; Department of Conservation; Department of Forests and Waters; and even, in Delaware, the Highway Department.

POLICE CLERKS

Police clerks perform various clerical tasks to keep the police department functioning smoothly. They keep records, order supplies, run computers, and operate switchboards. A high school diploma is usually required. According to the 1990 census, about 88,000 people worked as secretaries, typists, file clerks, and record clerks for local governments in justice, public order, and safety. To learn more about this occupation, you should contact local police departments.

POLICE OFFICERS

Most officers are assigned to patrol or traffic control duties. Boredom is often the norm. Patrolling a neighborhood enables officers to know what activities are normal, so that they can spot the unusual; it also tends to prevent crime. At any time, patrol officers may be called upon to stop a burglary, quiet a disturbance, or save a life. Traffic officers direct traffic, give out tickets, and deal with accidents.

Police departments also have divisions that specialize in investigations of certain types of crimes, such as burglaries or homicides, or in other activities, such as juvenile affairs. Other special units are motorcycle patrols, mobile rescue teams, and helicopter divisions. Officers may also be assigned to crime laboratories, record divisions, or police clerk duties.

No matter what their assignment, police officers spend much of their time completing reports of incidents. These reports can serve to build a case or indicate a problem. They are also needed because another important duty of officers is to testify in court.

Many cities have a maximum age limit for job entry of about 35. Most require that applicants be at least 21 years old; some departments hire police cadets, however, who are younger. A high school diploma is almost always required, and some departments look for applicants with at least some college education, often in fields such as law enforcement or the administration of justice.

Prospective police recruits are evaluated in many different ways. A background investigation, medical examination, and interview are almost universal. Psychological evaluation, polygraph testing, physical performance tests, and written tests are also used by many departments. Interviews are designed to determine whether you are highly motivated and can keep calm under pressure. You should learn exactly what is required and practice for all the different types of tests to learn early if you have any disqualifying conditions.

Training usually begins at a police academy run by the department or the state; academy training lasts 6 months in New York. It combines physical conditioning and self-defense with the study of law and police procedure. First aid and marksmanship are also learned and practiced. Training continues when a recruit is assigned to a station. Evaluation continues during both training and a probationary period.

Police officers advance by being promoted through the ranks. Additional testing usually takes place at every rank. Officers may also become more specialized in their work, concentrating on one type of police activity.

According to the International City Management Association, in 1990 the average entrance salary was $22,400, and the average maximum basic salary was $28,700. Officers receive the usual fringe benefits plus a uniform or uniform allowance and required equipment, including weapons. Because of the agility that officers must have, many departments have pension plans that permit an officer to retire at half pay after 20 or 25 years of service.

More than half a million people work as local police officers and detectives; they are ten times more numerous than state police officers.

These occupations are projected to grow more slowly than average during the next decade, in part because of the use of civilian technicians to perform specialized duties once performed by officers. Turnover is also relatively low for this occupation. However, because of the occupation's size, a great many openings will become available. If the past is any guide, competition for those openings will be keen.

Your local police department and state police department or highway patrol are the best places to obtain precise information on job requirements, salaries, and test schedules.

Many police officers are members of unions or professional associations:

Fraternal Order of Police
2100 Gardiner Lane
Louisville, KY 40205-2900

American Federation of Police
3801 Biscayne Blvd.
Miami, FL 33137

National Brotherhood of Police Officers
285 Dorchester
Boston, MA 02127

PSYCHIATRIC AIDES

Psychiatric aides work with the mentally and emotionally ill, usually in hospitals and other health care facilities. They help patients with personal hygiene, if necessary, and encourage them to join in group or recreational activities. A high school education is preferred, though not always required. Salaries are comparable with those of nurse aides, which are among the lower third for all wage earners. This is a moderate-size occupation, employing about 100,000 people in 1990. The occupation is projected to grow at an average rate through the year 2000. To learn more about this occupation contact National Mental Health Association, 1021 Prince St., Alexandria, VA 22314-2971.

RECREATION WORKERS

Recreation workers organize games and other activities to help people make the most of their free time. The kinds of activities they direct depend in part on the place where they work, which can range in size from a city playground to a vast forest. A bachelor's degree is usually required; for some positions, the degree must be in recreation and leisure studies or a special field such as music or art. This is a moderate-size occupation with a total employment of 194,000 in 1990; government employment was about half. To learn more about this occupation, contact the following: National Recreation and Park Association, Division of Professional Services, 3101 Park Center

Drive, Alexandria, VA 22302; American Association for Leisure and Recreation, 1900 Association Drive, Reston, VA 22091.

SANITATION WORKERS

Sanitation workers pick up refuse from homes and businesses and burn it or use it for landfill. Jobs include refuse collector, truck driver, incinerator operator, and landfill operator. Many sanitation workers start as refuse collectors, either emptying trash cans into a truck or operating special trucks that pick up larger bins and dumpsters.

The standard work week is 40 hours. Sanitation workers are outside in all kinds of weather, both winter ice and summer heat, making their job more difficult.

Sanitation workers should enjoy physical labor and working outside, since lifting heavy cans and walking much of the day is their major job. A high school education is usually required, and applicants may have to be licensed drivers.

Sanitation workers start as laborers and can advance to driver and then to supervisory positions.

State and local governments employ about 90,000 garbage collectors, local governments being the major employers.

Government employment in sanitation declined during the 1980s. Some of the decline is due to greater productivity. Another factor is that more and more governments are hiring contractors to collect refuse and perform other sanitation functions.

The following unions can provide further information:

American Federation of State, County and Municipal
  Employees
1625 L St. N.W.
Washington, D.C. 20001

International Brotherhood of Teamsters, Chauffeurs,
  Warehousemen and Helpers of America
25 Louisiana Ave. N.W.
Washington, D.C. 20001

SECRETARIES, TYPISTS, AND WORD PROCESSORS

In some other world, offices might be able to do without secretaries, typists, and word processors, but not in this one. Typists primarily type material either from manuscripts or recorded dictation. Secretaries have many additional duties, including running and maintaining the photocopy machine, organizing files, providing information to callers and visitors, scheduling appointments, and making travel arrangements. Word processors use the latest office equipment to process information and data and to keep records. They are also responsible for editing and storing and revising these materials. Word processors also may be required to function as typists, answer telephones, and operate other office machines. They also need to have good spelling, grammar, and punctuation skills.

Word processing positions are frequently entry-level jobs in the workplace, but they can lead to higher-paying jobs later on. They may become supervisors of their departments, secretaries, statistical clerks, or stenographers.

Successful secretaries are able to handle many things at once, organize their own work, and get along with others. Increasingly, they must be adaptable because of the rapid introduction of new word processing equipment. Each new machine means a change in how to do things, and new machines seem to come along just when the last one has been mastered.

Secretaries and typists, too, should be good spellers and know the essentials of English punctuation and grammar. They also need some mechanical skills to maintain and perform minor repairs to the equipment they use.

Few employers hire typists who cannot type at least 40 words per minute. Higher speeds are preferred. A high school education is usually required.

Typists and secretaries are also able to advance to supervisory positions; some become administrative assistants or office managers. The chances for advancement depend in part on the way an organization is set up, and you may require additional education. Among the sources of dissatisfaction for these workers are low salaries and lack of prestige within the organization.

The average salary for typists in 1990 was $16,000; secretaries earned $24,100. These figures indicate that average salary for typists is in the lower third for all wage earners, and the average for secretaries is in the middle third for all wage earners; government salaries are comparable. Salaries vary widely, however, depending on the skills and responsibilities of the worker. Secretaries and typists receive the usual fringe benefits.

General information about this occupation is available from Professional Secretaries International, 1502 N.W. Ambassador Drive, P.O. Box 20404, Kansas City, MO 64195-0404.

SHERIFFS

Sheriffs combine the duties of a police chief and warden because the county sheriff's department is responsible for traffic control, criminal investigations, and jailing prisoners in the county's jurisdiction. In some states—California, for example—sheriffs also act as coroners. Sheriffs are elected in every state except Rhode Island, where they are appointed. Salaries of sheriffs vary widely, depending upon the size of the county they work for. This is a relatively small occupation, since by definition there can be only one sheriff in a county, no matter how many deputies there are. Deputy sheriffs are grouped with police officers as a vocational category. To learn more about this occupation, consult your local sheriff's office.

STATE HIGHWAY PATROL OFFICERS

State highway patrol officers are chiefly responsible for traffic control on major highways. Officers also perform regular police functions in unincorporated parts of a state. In general, officers must meet the same standards as police officers in city departments. Salaries are comparable to those of police officers. Most of the sources of information listed at the end of the section on police officers also have information on state highway patrol officers.

STENOGRAPHERS

Extensive use of recorded dictation has resulted in a decline in the employment of stenographers throughout the economy, but the decline has not been as great in state and local government. In fact, while state and local governments employ 20 percent of all secretaries and 31 percent of all typists, the 115,000 stenographers they employ represent 43 percent of the people in the occupation. Many of these stenographers are court reporters who operate stenotype machines, which require special training.

TEACHER AIDES

Teacher aides assist teachers by taking care of clerical and housekeeping tasks and also help with instruction by working with individual students or small groups. A high school education is sufficient for some positions, but employers prefer at least some college if the person will work with students on lessons. The average hourly wage was $7.77 for instructional aides in 1990–1991, according to the Educational Research Service. Noninstructional aides earned about $0.25 less an hour, according to the Bureau of Labor Statistics. This is a fairly large occupation, employing 808,000 people in 1990. About half these workers were part-time employees, and most worked in the primary grades.

TOWN CLERKS

Town or county clerks act as secretaries to the governing board, recording the minutes of meetings, answering letters, and preparing reports. They also issue and keep records of official documents, such as marriage licenses, birth certificates, and land deeds. This is usually an elected office. For more information, speak to the clerk in your area.

WATER AND WASTEWATER TREATMENT PLANT OPERATORS

Part mechanic and part technician, these workers operate pumps, adjust valves, inspect pipes and other equipment, check gauges, and adjust controls. They take water samples and test them chemically or perform biological analyses. They make minor repairs to equipment. In larger plants, operators are more specialized, performing only one function; but in small plants, they do everything.

Water treatment plant operators usually work a 40-hour week; weekend and night hours are required, however, since most plants operate around the clock. Operators move around in their work, climbing ladders and scrambling over pipes.

What you should bring to this occupation. Successful operators enjoy working with machinery. They should be agile enough to make their way around a plant and able to use wrenches and other hand tools. Chemical dust can cause trouble for operators with allergies.

A high school education is usually required. Applicants are tested for general intelligence, skill in elementary mathematics, and mechanical aptitude.

Advancement possibilities depend on the size of the plant. Larger plants usually offer more opportunities; the top jobs at larger plants, however, may require a college degree in engineering or science.

Water treatment plant operator is among the lower 30 percent of all occupations in terms of wages. In 1990, average wages were $24,400. Workers in larger plants, with more complicated jobs or with supervisory responsibilities, earn more. Operators receive the usual fringe benefits.

Water and sewage plant operators working for local governments represent almost 90 percent of all the workers in this occupation. Water, sewage, and pollution control departments are the most likely employers.

Slow growth is projected through 1995. New machinery may decrease the need for workers; however, jobs will become available through turnover.

Local employers are the best source of information about this occupation.

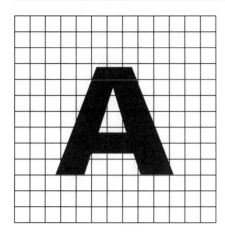

BOOKS AND MAGAZINES

The following books and magazines contain career guidance and occupational information. The bibliographies in these books will lead you to many more publications.

Career Guidance and the Job Hunt

Coming Alive From Nine to Five, Betty Neville Michelozzi, Palo Alto, CA: Mayfield Publishing Co., 1988. Career planning, with exercises for self assessment.

How to Land a Better Job, Catherine S. Lott and Oscar C. Lott, Lincolnwood, IL: VGM Career Horizons, 1989. Covers everything from finding leads to negotiating salaries.

How to Write a Winning Resume, Deborah Perlmutter, Lincolnwood, IL: VGM Career Horizons, 1989. Filled with tips and examples.

What Color is Your Parachute? A Practical Manual for Job-Hunters and Career-Changers, Richard N. Bolles, Berkeley, CA: Ten Speed Press, 1993. (New editions frequent.) Quite possibly the most frequently recommended guide to finding a career (not just a job).

Joyce Lain Kennedy's Career Book, Joyce Lain Kennedy, cuauthored with Dr. Darryl Laramore, Lincolnwood, IL: VGM Career Horizons, 1992.

College Placement Annual, Bethlehem, PA: College Placement Council, annual.

Career World: The Continuing Guide to Careers, Highwood, IL: Curriculum Innovation (9 issues per year). Frequent articles on resumes and job hunting; many articles on occupations.

Occupational Information   *The Complete Guide to Public Employment,* Ronald L. Krannich, Woodbridge, VA: Impact Publications, 1990.

Occupational Outlook Handbook, Washington, D.C.: U.S. Department of
Labor (biennial). Considerable information on 250 or so occupations,
including training requirements, salaries, outlook, and nature of the
work.

Occupational Outlook Quarterly, Washington, D.C.: U.S. Department of
Labor (quarterly). Complementary to the *Handbook,* the *Quarterly* includes material on occupational trends and patterns.

Chronicle of Occupational Briefs, Moravia, NY: Chronicle Guidance
Publications, Inc. A series of more than 400 regularly updated pamphlets, each dealing with a specific occupation such as assessor and
probation officer.

The Standard Periodical Directory, New York, NY: Oxbridge Communications, Incorporated (annual). A guide to more than 60,000 periodicals, thousands of which concern specific occupations.

Information on   *Federal Yellow Book,* Washington: Washington Monitor, Inc., annual.
Federal Positions
Find a Federal Job Fast! Cutting the Red Tape of Getting Hired, Ronald
L. Krannich and Caryl Rae Krannich, Woodbridge, VA: Impact Publi-
cations, 1990.

U.S. General Services Administration, Office of the Federal Register,
U.S. Government Manual, Washington: Government Printing Office,
annual.

"Current Federal Examination Announcements," U.S. Office of Personnel
Management, Washington: Office of Personnel Management, irregular.

How To Get A Federal Job, 5th edition, David E. Waelde, Washington,
D.C.: FEDHELP Publications, 1989.

Washington Information Directory, Washington: Congressional quarterly,
annual.

Information on State and   *The Career Information Center: Public and Community Services,* Vol. 11,
Local Government   Encino, CA: Glencoe Publishing Company, 1984. Descriptions of
occupations often found in governmental agencies.

Careers in State and Local Government, John William Zehring, Garrett
Park, MD: Garrett Park Press, 1980. A general guidebook filled with
sample position announcements, application forms, and sources of additional information.

Pay Rates in the Public Sector, Washington, D.C.: International Personnel
Management Association (annual). Current salary information on 60
occupations.

Public Employment, Washington, D.C.: U.S. Department of Commerce, Bureau of the Census (annual). Current data on employment by function.

Public Sector Jobs, P.O. Box 9, Baldwinsville,NY (biweekly).

The Book of States, Lexington, KY: The Council of State Governments (biennial). Current articles on every function of state government.

The Municipal Year Book, Washington, D.C.: International City Management Association (annual). Current articles and directories of officials for thousands of cities; now includes directories of county officials.

The National Directory of State Agencies, compiled by N.D. Wright, J. G. McCartney, and G.P. Allen, Washington, D.C.: Herner and Company, Information Resources Press (biennial). Names and addresses.

Council of State Governments, Iron Works Pike, P.O. Box 11910, Lexington, KY 40578.

ASSOCIATIONS

Many associations provide a wealth of information to job seekers. Three types of information will probably be most useful: career guidance material in either books or pamphlets; periodicals that contain position announcements, want ads, or articles about new developments in the field; and directories of members, which you can use to find local people to talk to about an occupation.

Besides the associations listed elsewhere in this book, many other associations are listed in the *Encyclopedia of Associations,* an annual 3-volume publication, Gale Research Company, Detroit, MI 48226. Section 3 of the *Encyclopedia* lists associations in government and public administration; the other sections of the *Encyclopedia* list thousands of occupational associations.

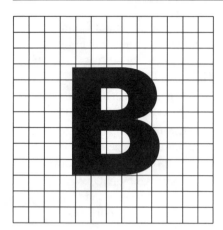

PERSONNEL DEPARTMENTS

States and Territories

Alabama
Department of Personnel
402 Administrative Building
64 N. Union Street
Montgomery, AL 36130

Alaska
Division of Personnel and Labor
    Relations
Department of Administration
State Office Building, Pouch C
Juneau, AK 99811

Arizona
Personnel Division
Department of Administration
1831 W. Jefferson St.
Phoenix, AZ 85007

Arkansas
Office of Personnel Management
Department of Finance and
    Administration
1509 W. Seventh St.
P.O. Box 3278
Little Rock, AR 72203

California
Personnel Board
801 Capitol Mall
Box 94420
Sacramento, CA 94244-2010

Colorado
Department of Personnel
122 Centennial Building
1313 Sherman St.
Denver, CO 80203

Connecticut
Personnel Division
Department of Administrative
    Services
State Office Building
165 Capitol Ave.
Hartford, CT 06106

Delaware
State Personnel Office
Executive Office of the Governor
Townsend Building Federal Street
P.O. Box 1401
Dover, DE 19901

District of Columbia
Personnel Office
South Potomac Building, Room 306
613 G St. N.W.
Washington, D.C. 20001

Florida
Division of Personnel
Department of Administration
330 Carlton Building
Calhoun Street
Tallahassee, FL 32304

Georgia
Merit System of Personnel
    Administration
Floyd Memorial Building West
    Tower, Suite 504
200 Piedmont Ave. S.E.
Atlanta, GA 30334

Hawaii
Department of Personnel Services
Keelikolani Building
830 Punchbowl St.
Honolulu, HI 96813

Idaho
Idaho Personnel Commission
State Office Building
700 W. State St.
Boise, ID 83720

Illinois
Department of Personnel
503 William G. Stratton Office
    Building
401 S. Spring St.
Springfield, IL 62706

Indiana
Personnel Division
Department of Administration
513 State Office Building
100 N. Senate Ave.
Indianpolis, IN 46204

Iowa
Merit Employment Department
Grimes State Office Building
400 E. 14th St.
Des Moines, IA 50319-0150

Kansas
Division of Personnel Services
Department of Administration
Landon State Office Building, Room
    951-5
900 Jackson St.
Topeka, KS 66612

Kentucky
Department of Personnel
373 New Capitol Annex
Frankfort, KY 40601

Louisiana
Department of State Civil Service
Republic Tower
5700 Florida Blvd.
Box 94111-9111
Baton Rouge, LA 70804

Maine
Department of Personnel
214 State Office Building
Augusta, ME 04333

Maryland
Department of Personnel
State Office Building
301 W. Preston St.
Baltimore, MD 21201

Massachusetts
Division of Personnel
    Administration
John W. McCormack State Office
    Building
1 Ashburton Place
Boston, MA 02108

Michigan
Department of Civil Service
Lewis Cass Building
320 S. Walnut St.
P.O. Box 30002
Lansing, MI 48909

Minnesota
Department of Personnel
Space Center Building
520 Lafayette Road
St. Paul, MN 55155

Mississippi
State Personnel Board
301 N. Lamar St., Suite 100
Jackson, MS 39201

Missouri
Division of Personnel
Office of Administration
Harry S. Truman State Office
    Building, Room 430
P.O. Box 388
Jefferson City, MO 65102

Montana
Personnel Division
Department of Administration
130 Sam W. Mitchell Building
205 Roberts St.
Helena, MT 59620

Nebraska
Department of Personnel
State Office Building
301 Centennial Mall S.
P.O. Box 94905
Lincoln, NE 68509-4905

Nevada
Personnel Division
Department of Administration
209 E. Musser St.
Carson City, NV 89710

New Hampshire
Personnel Department
1 State House Annex
Capitol Street
Concord, NH 03301

New Jersey
Department of Civil Service
Arnold Constable Building
215 E. State St.
Trenton, NJ 08625

New Mexico
State Personnel Board
130 S. Capitol St.
Santa Fe, NM 87503

New York
Department of Civil Service
1 W. Averill Harriman Office
    Building
Albany, NY 12239

North Carolina
Office of State Personnel
Department of Administration
Administration Building
116 W. Jones St.
Raleigh, NC 27611

North Dakota
Central Personnel Division
Office of Management and Budget
State Capitol, 14th Floor
Bismarck, ND 58505

Ohio
Division of Personnel
Department of Administration
    Services
State Office Tower
30 E. Broad St.
Columbus, OH 43266

Oklahoma
Office of Personnel Management
G-40 Jim Thorpe Office Building
2101 N. Lincoln Blvd.
Oklahoma City, OK 73105

Oregon
Personnel and Labor Relations
  Division
155 Cottage St. N.E.
Salem, OR 97310

Pennsylvania
Bureau of Personnel
Office of the Governor
517 Finance Building
Harrisburg, PA 17120

Puerto Rico
Central Office for Personnel
  Administration
P.O. Box 8476
Fernandez Juncos Station
Santurce, PR 00910

Rhode Island
Division of Personnel
  Administration
Department of Administration
CIC Complex 289 Promenade St.
Providence, RI 02908

South Carolina
Division of Human Resources
  Management
Budget and Control Board
AT&T Building, Suite 1016
1201 Main St.
P.O. Box 12547 Capitol Station
Columbia, SC 29211

South Dakota
Bureau of Personnel
Department of Executive
  Management

Public Safety Building
118 W. Capitol Ave.
Pierre, SD 57501

Tennessee
Department of Personnel
James K. Polk Office Building,
  Second Floor
Nashville, TN 37219-5185

Texas
Merit System Council
507 Broan Building
P.O. Box 1389
Austin, TX 78767

Utah
State Division of Personnel
  Management
State Office Building
Room 2222
Salt Lake City, UT 84114

Vermont
Department of Personnel
Agency of Administration
State Office Building
120 State St.
Montpelier, VT 05602

Virgin Islands
Division of Personnel
Office of the Governor
St. Thomas, VI 00801

Virginia
Department of Personnel and
  Training
James Monroe Building, 12th Floor
101 N. 14th St.
Richmond, VA 23219

Washington
Department of Personnel
600 S. Franklin St.

P.O. Box 1789
Olympia, WA 98507

West Virginia
Civil Service System
B456 State Office Building 6
1900 Washington St.
East Charleston, WV 25305

Wisconsin
Division of Personnel
Department of Employment
    Relations
P.O. Box 7855
Madison, WI 53707

Wyoming
Personnel Division
Department of Administration and
    Fiscal Control
Emerson Building
2001 Capitol Ave.
Cheyenne, WY 82002

New York

The Ten Largest Cities

City of New York
Department of Personnel
49 Thomas St.
New York, NY 10013

Los Angeles
Personnel Department
City Employment Office
111 E. First St.
Los Angeles, CA 90012

Chicago
Department of Personnel
Room 1100
121 N. Lasalle St.
Chicago, IL 60602

Philadelphia
Employment Application Center
127 City Hall
Philadelphia, PA 19017
(residents only)

Dallas
Civil Service
2014 Main St.
Dallas, TX 75201

San Diego
Personnel
202 C St.
San Diego, CA 92101

Phoenix
Personnel Department
Municipal Building
300 W. Washington
Phoenix, AZ 85003

Baltimore
City of Baltimore
Civil Service Commission
111 N. Calvert St.
Baltimore, MD 21202

Houston
City of Houston
Department of Personnel
P.O. Box 1562
806 Main, Fourth Floor
Houston, TX 77251

Detroit
Personnel
316 City-County Building
2 Woodward St.
Detroit, MI 48226

**The Ten Largest
Counties**

Los Angeles
County of Los Angeles
Personnel Department
222 N. Grand Ave.
Los Angeles, CA 90012

Dade
Metropolitan Dade County
Employment Relations Department
Employment Services division
200 S. Miami Ave., Suite 240
Miami, FL 33130

Harris
Personnel
1 Clark St.
Room 834
Houston, TX 77020

Nassau
Nassau County Civil Service
  Commission
140 Old Country Road
Mineola, NY 11501

Suffolk
Civil Service
65 Jetson Lane
Central Islip, NY 11722

Cuyahoga
Cuyahoga County Board of County
  Commissioners

Personnel Department
1219 Ontario St.
Cleveland, OH 44113

San Diego
Office of Employee Services
County Administration Center
1600 Pacific Highway
Room 207
San Diego, CA 92101

Erie
Personnel Department
95 Franklin St.
Buffalo, NY 14202

Santa Clara
Department of Personnel
70 W. Hedding
San Jose, CA 95110

Orange
Department of Personnel
10 Civil Center Plalza
Santa Ana, CA 92701

Alameda
Civil Service Commission
Personnel Department
1212 Oak St.
Oakland, CA 94612

**The Ten Largest School
Districts**

New York
New York City Board of Education
Division of Personnel
65 Court St.
Brooklyn, NY 11201

Los Angeles
Los Angeles City Board of
  Education
450 N. Grand Ave.
Los Angeles, CA 90012
(also see the telephone directory
  under Los Angeles Board of
  Education)

Chicago
Teacher Personnel
Service Personnel
1819 W. Pershing
Chicago, IL 60609

Detroit
Detroit Public Schools
Teacher Employment Office
5057 Woodward Ave.
Room 440
Detroit, MI 48202

Houston
Houston Independent School
    District
3830 Richmond Ave.
Houston, TX 77027

Broward County
Broward County School District
1320 S.W. Fourth St.
Ft. Lauderdale, FL 33312

Dallas
Dallas Independent School District
3807 Ross Ave.
Dallas, TX 75204

Dade County
Dade County Public Schools
1410 N.E. Second Ave.
Miami, FL 33132

Philadelphia
Board of Education
Department of Personnel
21st and Race Streets
Philadelphia, PA 19103

Fairfax County
Fairfax County Public Schools
The Administration Center
10700 Page Ave.
Fairfax, VA 22030

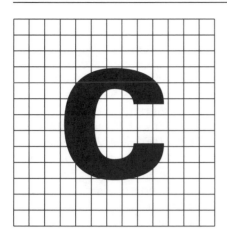

INDEX OF COLLEGE MAJORS AND FEDERAL JOBS

This index can be used like a road map. It will help you locate federal agencies and departments that are seeking individuals with your academic major, related field of study, or experience for their typical entry-level position.

Under each academic major, you will find the names of the agencies and departments interested in individuals with that background. If an agency is a component of a department or larger agency, you will find the parent organization's name in parentheses and boldfaced. Independent agencies stand without parenthetical reference.

This list is reprinted from the Federal Career Directory, published by the Office of Personnel Management, 1990.

ACCOUNTING
Administrative Office of the U.S. Courts
Agency for International Development
Agricultural Stabilization and Conservation Service (**Agriculture**)
Agriculture, Department of
Army Corps of Engineers (**Defense**)
Army Finance and Accounting Center (**Defense**)
Army Material Command (**Defense**)
Army Military District of Washington (**Defense**)

Bureau of Economic Analysis (**Commerce**)
Bureau of Engraving and Printing (**Treasury**)
Bureau of Prisons (**Justice**)
Bureau of the Public Debt (**Treasury**)
Commodity Futures Trading Commission
Defense Contract Audit Agency (**Defense**)
Defense Logistics Agency (**Defense**)
Departmental Offices (**Treasury**)
Drug Enforcement Administration (**Justice**)

Energy, Department of
Equal Employment Opportunity
    Commission
Export-Import Bank of the United
    States
Executive Office of the President
Family Support Administration
    (Health and Human Services)
Farm Credit Administration
    (Agriculture)
Federal Deposit Insurance
    Corporation
Federal Emergency Management
    Agency
Federal Highway Administration
    (Transportation)
Federal Retirement Thrift
    Investment Board
Federal Trade Commission
Financial Management Service
    (Treasury)
General Accounting Office
General Services Administration
Government Printing Office
Health Care Financing
    Administration **(Health and
    Human Services)**
Health Resources and Services
    Administration **(Health and
    Human Services)**
Housing and Urban Development,
    Department of
Interior, Department of the
Internal Revenue Service
    (Treasury)
Labor, Department of
Maritime Administration
    (Transportation)
National Credit Union
    Administration
National Labor Relations Board
National Science Foundation
National Technical Information
    Service **(Commerce)**
Navy **(Defense)**

Office of the Comptroller of the
    Currency **(Treasury)**
Office of Inspector General
    **(Agriculture) (Health and
    Human Services) (Labor)
    (Transportation)**
Office of Justice Programs **(Justice)**
Office of Personnel Management
Office of the Secretary **(Commerce)
    (Health and Human Services)**
Office of Surface Mining
    Reclamation and Enforcement
    (Interior)
Office of Thrift Supervision
    (Treasury)
Public Health Service **(Health and
    Human Services)**
Railroad Retirement Board
Rural Electrification Administration
    (Agriculture)
Securities and Exchange
    Commission
Selective Service System
Small Business Administration
Smithsonian Institution
State, Department of
Transportation, Department of
U.S. Coast Guard **(Transportation)**
U.S. Customs Service **(Treasury)**
U.S. Marshals Service **(Justice)**
U.S. Postal Service
Veterans Affairs, Department of

ACTUARIAL SCIENCE

Employment and Training
    Administration **(Labor)**
Federal Emergency Management
    Agency
Health Care Financing
    Administration **(Health and
    Human Services)**

ADP

Navy **(Defense)**

ADULT EDUCATION AND TRAINING
Federal Emergency Management Agency

ADVERTISING
Labor, Department of

AERONAUTICAL ENGINEERING
National Aeronautics and Space Administration

AEROSPACE ENGINEERING
Army Material Command **(Defense)**
Federal Aviation Administration **(Transportation)**
National Aeronautics and Space Administration
Navy **(Defense)**

AGRIBUSINESS MANAGEMENT
Farm Credit Administration **(Agriculture)**

AGRICULTURAL BUSINESS
Farmers Home Administration **(Agriculture)**
Foreign Agricultural Service **(Agriculture)**

AGRICULTURAL ECONOMICS
Agricultural Stabilization and Conservation Service **(Agriculture)**
Economics Management Staff **(Agriculture)**
Farm Credit Administration **(Agriculture)**
International Trade Commission

AGRICULTURAL ENGINEERING
Agricultural Research Service **(Agriculture)**

AGRICULTURAL FINANCE
Farm Credit Administration **(Agriculture)**

AGRICULTURAL MANAGEMENT
Agricultural Marketing Service **(Agriculture)**
Agricultural Stabilization and Conservation Service **(Agriculture)**

AGRICULTURE (GENERAL)
Agricultural Marketing Service **(Agriculture)**
Agricultural Stabilization and Conservation Service **(Agriculture)**

AGRONOMY
Agricultural Research Service **(Agriculture)**

AIRWAY SCIENCE
Federal Aviation Administration **(Transportation)**

ALL MAJORS
ACTION
Air Force **(Defense)**
Army Information Systems Command **(Defense)**
Army Material Command **(Defense)**
Training and Doctrine Command **(Defense)**
Bureau of Alcohol, Tobacco, and Firearms **(Treasury)**
Bureau of Labor Statistics **(Labor)**
Defense Investigation Service **(Defense)**
Employment and Training Administration **(Labor)**
Employment Standards Administration **(Labor)**

Equal Employment Opportunity
Commission
Federal Aviation Administration
(**Transportation**)
Federal Deposit Insurance
Corporation
Federal Highway Administration
(**Transportation**)
General Services Administration
Immigration and Naturalization
Service (**Justice**)
Labor, Department of
Maritime Administration
(**Transportation**)
Military Traffic Management
Command (**Defense**)
Mine Safety and Health
Administration (**Labor**)
National Science Foundation
Occupational Safety and Health
Administration (**Labor**)
Office of Inspector General (**Labor**)
Office of Personnel Management
Office of the Secretary (**Health and
Human Services**)
Railroad Retirement Board
State, Department of
U.S. Marshals Service (**Justice**)
U.S. Postal Service
Veterans Affairs, Department of

AMERICAN HISTORY
National Archives and Records
Administration

AMERICAN STUDIES
National Archives and Records
Administration

**ANIMAL HEALTH
TECHNOLOGY**
Animal and Plant Health Inspection
Service (**Agriculture**)

ANIMAL HUSBANDRY
Agricultural Marketing Service
(**Agriculture**)

ANIMAL SCIENCE
Agricultural Marketing Service
(**Agriculture**)
Bureau of Land Management
(**Interior**)

ANTHROPOLOGY
Bureau of Land Management
(**Interior**)
U.S. Customs Service (**Treasury**)

ARCHAEOLOGY
Bureau of Land Management
(**Interior**)
Forest Service (**Agriculture**)
National Endowment for the
Humanities
National Park Service (**Interior**)

**ARCHITECTURAL
ENGINEERING**
Navy (**Defense**)
U.S. Postal Service

ARCHITECTURE
Army Corps of Engineers (**Defense**)
Farmers Home Administration
(**Agriculture**)
General Services Administration
Housing and Urban Development,
Department of
National Institute of Standards and
Technology (**Commerce**)
Navy (**Defense**)
Veterans Affairs, Department of

AREA STUDIES
U.S. Information Agency
Voice of America (**U.S.
Information Agency**)

ART (DESIGN)
Government Printing Office

ART HISTORY
National Archives and Records
Administration
Smithsonian Institution

ASIAN LANGUAGES
National Security Agency

ASTRONAUTICAL ENGINEERING
National Aeronautics and Space
Administration

ASTRONAUTICS
National Aeronautics and Space
Administration

ASTRONOMY
Defense Mapping Agency **(Defense)**
Navy **(Defense)**

AUDIOLOGY
Veterans Affairs, Department of

AUDITING
Department Offices **(Treasury)**
Housing and Urban Development,
Department of
National Credit Union
Administration
Office of Inspector General
(Commerce) (Labor)
State, Department of

BANK LAW
Office of the Comptroller of the
Currency **(Treasury)**

BANKING
Farm Credit Administration
(Agriculture)

Office of the Comptroller of the
Currency **(Treasury)**
Small Business Administration
State, Department of

BIOLOGICAL LAB TECHNOLOGY
Animal and Plant Health Inspection
Service **(Agriculture)**

BIOLOGICAL SCIENCES
Environmental Protection Agency
Library of Congress

BIOLOGY
Animal and Plant Health Inspection
Service **(Agriculture)**
Army Corps of Engineers **(Defense)**
Bureau of Indian Affairs **(Interior)**
Bureau of Land Management
(Interior)
Bureau of Reclamation **(Interior)**
Federal Bureau of Investigation
(Justice)
Forest Service **(Agriculture)**
Minerals Management Service
(Interior)
Navy **(Defense)**
Office of Surface Mining
Reclamation and Enforcement
(Interior)
Patent and Trademark Office
(Commerce)
U.S. Fish and Wildlife Service
(Interior)

BOTANY
Bureau of Land Management
(Interior)

BROADCASTING
U.S. Information Agency

BUDGET ANALYSIS
Energy, Department of

**BUDGETING
(GOVERNMENTAL)**
U.S. Marshals Service **(Justice)**

BUSINESS (GENERAL)
ACTION
Board of Governors of the Federal
  Reserve System
Defense Logistics Agency **(Defense)**
Equal Employment Opportunity
  Commission
Executive Office of the President
Export-Import Bank of the United
  States
Federal Highway Administration
  (Transportation)
Federal Maritime Commission
Federal Railroad Administration
  (Transportation)
Financial Management Service
  (Treasury)
Office of the Secretary **(Commerce)**
Patent and Trademark Office
  (Commerce)
U.S. Mint **(Treasury)**
Veterans Affairs, Department of

BUSINESS ADMINISTRATION
Agency for International
  Development
Agriculture, Department of
Agricultural Stabilization and
  Conservation Service
  (Agriculture)
Army Corps of Engineers **(Defense)**
Army Finance and Accounting
  Center **(Defense)**
Army Military District of
  Washington **(Defense)**
Departmental Offices **(Treasury)**
Economic Affairs **(Commerce)**
Economic Development
  Administration **(Commerce)**
Executive Office for U.S. Attorneys
  (Justice)

Farm Credit Administration
  (Agriculture)
Federal Deposit Insurance
  Corporation
Federal Emergency Management
  Agency
Federal Railroad Administration
Federal Retirement Thrift
  Investment Board
Federal Trade Commission
General Accounting Office
General Services Administration
Government Printing Office
Health Care Financing
  Administration **(Health and
  Human Services)**
Housing and Urban Development,
  Department of
Interior, Department of
Internal Revenue Service
  (Treasury)
International Trade Administration
  (Commerce)
International Trade Commission
Justice, Department of
Maritime Administration
  (Transportation)
Minority Business Development
  Agency **(Commerce)**
National Labor Relations Board
National Park Service **(Interior)**
National Science Foundation
Office of the Comptroller of the
  Currency **(Treasury)**
Office of Inspector General
  (Transportation)
Office of Personnel Management
Office of Thrift Supervisors
  (Treasury)
Research and Special Programs
  Administration **(Transportation)**
Rural Electrification Administration
  (Agriculture)
Savings Bonds Division **(Treasury)**
Selective Service System

Small Business Administration
State, Department of
Transportation, Department of
Travel and Tourism Administration
(Commerce)
Urban Mass Transportation
Administration **(Transportation)**
U.S. Coast Guard **(Transportation)**
U.S. Customs Service **(Treasury)**
U.S. Marshals Service **(Justice)**

BUSINESS LAW
U.S. Customs Service **(Treasury)**

BUSINESS MANAGEMENT
Food and Nutrition Services
(Agriculture)
National Credit Union
Administration
Navy **(Defense)**
Office of Inspector General
(Transportation)

CARTOGRAPHY
Bureau of the Census **(Commerce)**
Bureau of Land Management
(Interior)
Defense Mapping Agency **(Defense)**
National Oceanic and Atmospheric
Administration **(Commerce)**
U.S. Customs Service **(Treasury)**

CERAMIC ENGINEERING
National Institute of Standards and
Technology **(Commerce)**
Navy **(Defense)**

CHEMICAL ENGINEERING
Army Material Command **(Defense)**
Agricultural Research Service
(Agriculture)
Drug Enforcement Administration
(Justice)
Environmental Protection Agency

National Aeronautics and Space
Administration
National Institute of Standards and
Technology **(Commerce)**
Navy **(Defense)**
Nuclear Regulatory Commission
Patent and Trademark Office
(Commerce)
Tennessee Valley Authority

CHEMISTRY
Animal and Plant Health Inspect
Service **(Agriculture)**
Agricultural Research Service
(Agriculture)
Bureau of Engraving and Printing
(Treasury)
Drug Enforcement Administration
(Justice)
Environmental Protection Agency
Federal Bureau of Investigation
(Justice)
Food Safety and Inspection Service
(Agriculture)
Government Printing Office
International Trade Commission
National Archives and Records
Administration
National Institute of Standards and
Technology **(Commerce)**
National Technical Information
Service **(Commerce)**
Navy **(Defense)**
Patent and Trademark Office
(Commerce)
Research and Special Programs
Administration **(Transportation)**
U.S. Geological Survey **(Interior)**

CHINESE
Drug Enforcement Administration
(Justice)

CIVIL ENGINEERING
Army Corps of Engineers (**Defense**)
Bureau of Reclamation (**Interior**)
Defense Mapping Agency (**Defense**)
Environmental Protection Agency
Farmers Home Administration
  (**Agriculture**)
Federal Aviation Administration
  (**Transportation**)
Federal Emergency Management
  Agency
Federal Highway Administration
  (**Transportation**)
Forest Service (**Agriculture**)
General Services Administration
National Institute of Standards and
  Technology (**Commerce**)
Navy (**Defense**)
State, Department of
Tennessee Valley Authority
Urban Mass Transportation
  Administration (**Transportation**)
U.S. Geological Survey (**Interior**)

CLINICAL PSYCHOLOGY
Bureau of Prisons (**Justice**)

COMMERCE
Navy (**Defense**)

COMMERCIAL LAW
Office of the Comptroller of the
  Currency (**Treasury**)

COMMUNICATIONS
Federal Retirement Thrift
  Investment Board
Labor, Department of
National Archives and Records
  Administration
National Park Service (**Interior**)
National Telecommunications and
  Information Administration
  (**Commerce**)
Small Business Administration

U.S. Information Agency
Voice of America (**U.S.
  Information Agency**)

COMMUNICATIONS (VISUAL)
Defense Mapping Agency (**Defense**)

COMMUNITY PLANNING
Economic Development
  Administration (**Commerce**)
Environmental Protection Agency
Housing and Urban Development,
  Department of

COMPARATIVE RELIGION
National Endowment for the
  Humanities

COMPUTER AND
INFORMATION SYSTEMS
Navy (**Defense**)

COMPUTER ENGINEERING
Federal Bureau of Investigation
  (**Justice**)
Navy (**Defense**)

COMPUTER SCIENCE
Administrative Office of the U.S.
  Courts
Agriculture, Department of
Agricultural Stabilization and
  Conservation Service
  (**Agriculture**)
Army Corps of Engineers (**Defense**)
Army Finance and Accounting
  Center (**Defense**)
Army Military District of
  Washington (**Defense**)
Board of Governors of the Federal
  Reserve System
Bureau of the Census (**Commerce**)
Bureau of Engraving and Printing
  (**Treasury**)

Bureau of Economic Analysis
 (**Commerce**)
Bureau of Export Administration
 (**Commerce**)
Bureau of Indian Affairs (**Interior**)
Bureau of Labor Statistics (**Labor**)
Bureau of Land Management
 (**Interior**)
Bureau of the Public Debt
 (**Treasury**)
Commodity Futures Trading
 Commission
Consumer Product Safety
 Commission
Defense Communications Agency
 (**Defense**)
Defense Intelligence Agency
 (**Defense**)
Defense Logistics Agency (**Defense**)
Defense Mapping Agency (**Defense**)
Departmental Offices (**Treasury**)
Drug Enforcement Administration
 (**Justice**)
Employment and Training
 Administration (**Labor**)
Energy, Department of
Executive Office for U.S. Attorneys
 (**Justice**)
Executive Office of the President
Export-Import Bank of the United
 States
Federal Bureau of Investigation
 (**Justice**)
Federal Emergency Management
 Agency
Federal Highway Administration
 (**Transportation**)
Federal Retirement Thrift
 Investment Board
Federal Trade Commission
Financial Management Services
 (**Treasury**)
General Accounting Office
Government Printing Office

Health Care Financing
 Administration (**Health and
 Human Services**)
Housing and Urban Development,
 Department of
Immigration and Naturalization
 Service (**Justice**)
Internal Revenue Service
 (**Treasury**)
International Trade Commission
Justice, Department of
Labor, Department of
Library of Congress
Merit Systems Protection Board
National Aeronautics and Space
 Administration
National Institute of Standards and
 Technology (**Commerce**)
National Oceanic and Atmospheric
 Administration (**Commerce**)
National Security Agency (**Defense**)
National Technical Information
 Service (**Commerce**)
National Telecommunications and
 Information Administration
 (**Commerce**)
Navy (**Defense**)
Office of Justice Programs (**Justice**)
Office of the Secretary (**Commerce**)
Patent and Trademark Office
 (**Commerce**)
St. Lawrence Seaway Development
 Corporation (**Transportation**)
Securities and Exchange
 Commission
Selective Service System
Small Business Administration
Social Security Administration
 (**Health and Human Services**)
State, Department of
Tennessee Valley Authority
U.S. Customs Service (**Treasury**)
U.S. Marshals Service (**Justice**)
Veterans Affairs, Department of

CONSERVATION
Smithsonian Institution

CONTRACTING
Energy, Department of

CORRECTIONS
Secret Service (**Treasury**)

CORRECTIVE THERAPY
Veterans Affairs, Department of

COUNSELING PSYCHOLOGY
Veterans Affairs, Department of

CREATIVE ARTS THERAPY
Veterans Affairs, Department of

CREATIVE WRITING
Labor, Department of

CREDIT
Farm Credit Administration
   (**Agriculture**)
Small Business Administration

CRIMINAL INVESTIGATION
Housing and Urban Development,
   Department of

CRIMINAL JUSTICE
   (**CRIMINOLOGY**)
Bureau of Land Management
   (**Interior**)
Bureau of Prisons (**Justice**)
Developmental Offices (**Treasury**)
Drug Enforcement Administration
   (**Justice**)
Federal Emergency Management
   Agency
Federal Law Enforcement Training
   Center (**Treasury**)
General Services Administration
Government Printing Office

Immigration and Naturalization
   Service (**Justice**)
Interior, Department of the
Justice, Department of
Office of Inspector General
   (**Agriculture**) (**Health and
   Human Services**)
   (**Transportation**)
Railroad Retirement Board
Secret Service (**Treasury**)
U.S. Customs Service (**Treasury**)
U.S. Marshals Service (**Justice**)

CRYPTOGRAPHY
State, Department of

CRYPTOLOGY
Federal Bureau of Investigation
   (**Justice**)

CULTURAL ANTHROPOLOGY
U.S. Information Agency

CYTOTECHNOLOGY
Navy (**Defense**)

DATA MANAGEMENT
Financial Management Service
   (**Treasury**)

DATA PROCESSING
Defense Mapping Agency (**Defense**)
U.S. Marshals Service (**Justice**)

DENTAL HYGIENE
Navy (**Defense**)
Veterans Affairs, Department of

DENTISTRY
Bureau of Prisons (**Justice**)
Indian Health Service (**Health and
   Human Services**)
National Institute of Health (**Health
   and Human Services**)

DIETETICS
Indian Health Service **(Health and Human Services)**
Veterans Affairs, Department of

EARTH SCIENCE
Defense Intelligence Agency **(Defense)**
Defense Mapping Agency **(Defense)**

ECONOMICS
Agency for International Development
Army Finance and Accounting Center **(Defense)**
Board of Governors of the Federal Reserve System
Bureau of the Census **(Commerce)**
Bureau of Economic Analysis **(Commerce)**
Bureau of Labor Statistics **(Labor)**
Bureau of Land Management **(Interior)**
Bureau of Mines **(Interior)**
Commission on Civil Rights
Commodity Futures Trading Commission
Defense Logistics Agency **(Defense)**
Departmental Offices **(Treasury)**
Drug Enforcement Administration **(Justice)**
Economic Affairs **(Commerce)**
Economics Management Staff **(Agriculture)**
Employment and Training Administration **(Labor)**
Environmental Protection Agency
Executive Office of the President
Export-Import Bank of the United States
Federal Deposit Insurance Corporation
Federal Maritime Commission
Federal Railroad Administration **(Transportation)**

Federal Retirement Thrift Investment Board
Federal Trade Commission
Food and Nutrition Service **(Agriculture)**
Foreign Agricultural Service **(Agriculture)**
General Accounting Office
General Services Administration
Health Care Financing Administration **(Health and Human Services)**
International Trade Administration **(Commerce)**
International Trade Commission
Library of Congress
Maritime Administration **(Transportation)**
Minority Business Development Agency **(Commerce)**
National Archives and Records Administration
National Labor Relations Board
National Oceanic and Atmospheric Administration **(Commerce)**
National Science Foundation
Navy **(Defense)**
Office of the Comptroller of the Currency **(Treasury)**
Office of Thrift Supervisors **(Treasury)**
Securities Exchange Commission
Small Business Administration
U.S. Customs Service **(Treasury)**
U.S. Information Agency
U.S. Marshals Service **(Justice)**
U.S. Postal Service

EDUCATION
Army Finance and Accounting Center **(Defense)**
Bureau of Indian Affairs **(Interior)**
Bureau of Prisons **(Justice)**
Education, Department of
Forest Service **(Agriculture)**

Navy **(Defense)**
Small Business Administration
Smithsonian Institution
U.S. Coast Guard **(Transportation)**
U.S. Customs Service **(Treasury)**

EDUCATIONAL THERAPY
Veterans Affairs, Department of

ELECTRICAL ENGINEERING
Army Corps of Engineers **(Defense)**
Army Material Command **(Defense)**
Bureau of Export Administration
   (Commerce)
Bureau of Reclamation **(Interior)**
Defense Mapping Agency **(Defense)**
Energy, Department of
Federal Aviation Administration
   (Transportation)
General Services Administration
International Trade Commission
National Aeronautics and Space
   Administration
National Institute of Standards and
   Technology **(Commerce)**
National Security Agency
Navy **(Defense)**
Nuclear Regulatory Commission
Patent and Trademark Office
   (Commerce)
Rural Electrification Administration
   (Agriculture)
State, Department of
Tennessee Valley Authority
U.S. Postal Service
Voice of America **(U.S.
   Information Agency)**

ELECTRONICS
Bureau of Reclamation **(Interior)**
Federal Aviation Administration
   (Transportation)
Forest Service **(Agriculture)**

ELECTRONICS ENGINEERING
Army Materiel Command **(Defense)**
Bureau of Export Administration
   (Commerce)
Defense Communications Agency
   (Defense)
Drug Enforcement Administration
   (Justice)
Federal Aviation Administration
   (Transportation)
Federal Emergency Management
   Agency
General Services Administration
International Trade Commission
Justice, Department of
National Institute of Standards and
   Technology **(Commerce)**
National Telecommunications and
   Information Administration
   (Commerce)
Navy **(Defense)**
Rural Electrification Administration
   (Agriculture)
State, Department of

ELECTRONICS TECHNOLOGY
Voice of America **(U.S.
   Information Agency)**

ENGINEERING (GENERAL)
Bureau of Indian Affairs **(Interior)**
Bureau of Land Management
   (Interior)
Bureau of Mines **(Interior)**
Consumer Product Safety
   Commission
Defense Logistics Agency **(Defense)**
Defense Mapping Agency **(Defense)**
Drug Enforcement Administration
   (Justice)
Energy, Department of
Federal Communications
   Commission
Government Printing Office

Housing and Urban Development,
Department of
Internal Revenue Service
(Treasury)
Library of Congress
Maritime Administration
(Transportation)
Military Traffic Management
Command **(Defense)**
Minerals Management Service
(Interior)
National Highway Traffic Safety
Administration **(Transportation)**
National Institute of Standards and
Technology **(Commerce)**
National Oceanic and Atmospheric
Administration **(Commerce)**
Navy **(Defense)**
Office of Surface Mining
Reclamation and Enforcement
(Interior)
Patent and Trademark Office
(Commerce)
Research and Special Programs
Administration **(Transportation)**
Smithsonian Institution
Soil Conservation Service
(Agriculture)
State, Department of
Urban Mass Transportation
Administration **(Transportation)**
U.S. Coast Guard **(Transportation)**
U.S. Customs Service **(Treasury)**
Veterans Affairs, Department of

**ENGINEERING
MANAGEMENT**
Navy **(Defense)**

ENGINEERING PSYCHOLOGY
Consumer Product Safety
Commission

ENGINEERING TECHNOLOGY
Army Corps of Engineers **(Defense)**
Navy **(Defense)**

ENGLISH
Federal Trade Commission
Labor, Department of
National Archives and Records
Administration
Navy **(Defense)**
Research and Special Programs
Administration **(Transportation)**
U.S. Information Agency

ENTOMOLOGY
Animal and Plant Health Inspection
Service **(Agriculture)**
Forest Service **(Agriculture)**

**ENVIRONMENTAL
ENGINEERING**
Environmental Protection Agency
Navy **(Defense)**
Nuclear Regulatory Commission

**ENVIRONMENTAL SCIENCE
(ENVIRONMENTAL
STUDIES)**
Bureau of Land Management
(Interior)
Environmental Protection Agency

ETHICS
National Endowment for the
Humanities

FILM AND DRAMA
U.S. Information Agency

FINANCE
Administrative Office of the U.S.
Courts
Army Finance and Accounting
Center **(Defense)**
Board of Governors of the Federal
Reserve System
Defense Logistics Agency **(Defense)**
Departmental Offices **(Treasury)**
Economic Affairs **(Commerce)**

Export-Import Bank of the United
  States
Farm Credit Administration
  (**Agriculture**)
Federal Deposit Insurance
  Corporation
Government Emergency
  Management Agency
Government Retirement Thrift
  Investment Board
Financial Management Service
  (**Treasury**)
General Accounting Office
International Trade Administration
  (**Commerce**)
National Credit Union
  Administration
Office of the Comptroller of the
  Currency (**Treasury**)
Office of the Secretary (**Commerce**)
Office of Thrift Supervision
  (**Treasury**)
Rural Electrification Administration
  (**Agriculture**)
Securities and Exchange
  Commission
Small Business Administration
State, Department of
Travel and Tourism Administration
  (**Commerce**)
U.S. Postal Service

FINANCIAL MANAGEMENT
Economic Development
  Administration (**Commerce**)
Minority Business Development
  Agency (**Commerce**)
Navy (**Defense**)
St. Lawrence Seaway Development
  (**Transportation**)

FINE ARTS
Smithsonian Institution

FIRE PREVENTION ENGINEERING
National Institute of Standards and
  Technology (**Commerce**)

FIRE SCIENCE
Navy (**Defense**)

FISHERY BIOLOGY
Forest Service (**Agriculture**)
National Oceanic and Atmospheric
  Administration (**Commerce**)

FOOD ENGINEERING
Agricultural Research Service
  (**Agriculture**)

FOOD TECHNOLOGY (FOOD SCIENCE)
Agricultural Marketing Service
  (**Agriculture**)
Agricultural Research Service
  (**Agriculture**)
Food Safety and Inspection Service
  (**Agriculture**)

FOREIGN AFFAIRS (FOREIGN POLICY)
Bureau of Export Administration
  (**Commerce**)
U.S. Information Agency

FOREIGN AREA STUDIES
Defense Intelligence Agency
  (**Defense**)

FORESTRY
Bureau of Land Management
  (**Interior**)
Defense Mapping Agency (**Defense**)
Forest Service (**Agriculture**)
National Park Service (**Interior**)
U.S. Customs Service (**Treasury**)

GENERAL ADMINISTRATION
Energy, Department of
Navy (Defense)

GENETICS
Agricultural Research Service
(**Agriculture**)

**GEOCHEMICAL
ENGINEERING**
Nuclear Regulatory Commission

GEODESY
Defense Mapping Agency (**Defense**)
National Oceanic and Atmospheric
Administration (**Commerce**)

**GEOGRAPHY (GENERAL
GEOGRAPHY, PHYSICAL
GEOGRAPHY)**
Bureau of the Census (**Commerce**)
Bureau of Land Management
(**Interior**)
Defense Intelligence Agency
(**Defense**)
Defense Mapping Agency (**Defense**)
Environmental Protection Agency
U.S. Customs Service (**Treasury**)
U.S. Information Agency

**GEOLOGY (GEOLOGY
SCIENCES)**
Bureau of Land Management
(**Interior**)
Bureau of Reclamation (**Interior**)
Defense Mapping Agency (**Defense**)
Environmental Protection Agency
Forest Service (**Agriculture**)
Minerals Management Service
(**Interior**)
U.S. Customs Service (**Treasury**)
U.S. Geological Survey (**Interior**)

GEOPHYSICS
Defense Mapping Agency (**Defense**)

Mineral Management Service
(**Interior**)

GEOPHYSIOLOGY
U.S. Geological Survey (**Interior**)

GOVERNMENT
National Archives and Records
Administration
Navy (**Defense**)

HEALTH PHYSICS
Nuclear Regulatory Commission

HEALTH SCIENCES
Consumer Product Safety
Commission

**HEALTH SERVICES
MANAGEMENT**
Health Care Financing
Administration (**Health and
Human Services**)

HISTOPATHOLOGY
Navy (**Defense**)

HISTORY
Drug Enforcement Administration
(**Justice**)
National Endowment for the
Humanities
National Park Service (**Interior**)
Smithsonian Institution
U.S. Customs Service (**Treasury**)
U.S. Information Agency

**HISTORY AND CRITICISM OF
THE ARTS**
National Endowment for the
Humanities

HOME ECONOMICS
Food and Nutrition Service
(**Agriculture**)

HORTICULTURE
Agricultural Marketing Service
  (Agriculture)

HOSPITAL ADMINISTRATION
Veterans Affairs, Department of

HYDROLOGY
Bureau of Land Management
  (Interior)
Bureau of Reclamation **(Interior)**
Environmental Protection Agency
Forest Service **(Agriculture)**
National Oceanic and Atmospheric
  Administration **(Commerce)**
Office of Surface Mining
Reclamation and Enforcement
  (Interior)

**HYDROGEOLOGICAL
  ENGINEERING
  GEOMORPHOLOGICAL,
  GEOTECHNICAL)**
Nuclear Regulatory Commission

ILLUSTRATION
Veterans, Affairs, Department of

INDUSTRIAL ARTS
State, Department of

INDUSTRIAL ECONOMICS
International Trade Administration
  (Commerce)

INDUSTRIAL ENGINEERING
Bureau of Engraving and Printing
  (Treasury)
Defense Mapping Agency **(Defense)**
International Trade Commission
National Aeronautics and Space
  Administration
National Institute of Standards and
  Technology **(Commerce)**
Navy **(Defense)**

Small Business Administration
U.S. Postal Service

INDUSTRIAL HYGIENE
Navy **(Defense)**
Occupational Safety and Health
  Administration **(Labor)**

INDUSTRIAL MANAGEMENT
Navy **(Defense)**
Small Business Administration

INDUSTRIAL RELATIONS
Army Finance and Accounting
  Center **(Defense)**
International Trade Administration
  (Commerce)
National Labor Relations Board
Small Business Administration
U.S. Customs Service **(Treasury)**

INDUSTRIAL TECHNOLOGY
Defense Logistics Agency **(Defense)**

**INFORMATION
  MANAGEMENT**
Savings Bonds Division **(Treasury)**

INFORMATION SCIENCE
Library of Congress

INTERIOR DESIGN
Veterans Affairs, Department of

INTERNATIONAL BUSINESS
Bureau of Export Administration
  (Commerce)
International Trade Administration
  (Commerce)

**INTERNATIONAL
  ECONOMICS**
International Trade Administration
  (Commerce)
International Trade Commission

INTERNATIONAL RELATIONS (INTERNATIONAL AFFAIRS)

Bureau of Export Administration
(**Commerce**)
Library of Congress
U.S. Information Agency
Voice of America (**U.S. Information Agency**)

INTERNATIONAL TRADE

Bureau of Export Administration
(**Commerce**)
International Trade Administration
(**Commerce**)

JURISPRUDENCE

National Endowment for the
Humanities

JOURNALISM

Agriculture, Department of
Federal Trade Commission
Labor, Department of
National Archives and Records Administration
Navy (Defense)
Savings Bonds Division (**Treasury**)
Small Business Administration
U.S. Information Agency
Voice of America (**U.S. Information Agency**)

LABOR RELATIONS

National Labor Relations Board
Small Business Administration
U.S. Customs Service (**Treasury**)

LANDSCAPE ARCHITECTURE

Forest Service (**Agriculture**)

LAND SURVEYING

Bureau of Land Management
(**Interior**)

LANGUAGE STUDIES

Voice of America (**U.S. Information Agency**)

LANGUAGES (GENERAL)

Drug Enforcement Administration
(**Justice**)
National Endowment for the
Humanities

LAW

Administrative Office of the U.S.
Courts
Agency for International
Development
Board of Governors of the Federal
Reserve System
Bureau of Land Management
(**Interior**)
Commission on Civil Rights
Commodity Futures Trading
Commission
Drug Enforcement Administration
(**Justice**)
Equal Employment Opportunity
Commission
Executive Office of the President
Federal Aviation Administration
(**Transportation**)
Federal Communications
Commission
Federal Deposit Insurance
Corporation
Federal Emergency Management
Agency
Federal Maritime Commission
Federal Railroad Administration
(**Transportation**)
Federal Retirement Thrift
Investment Board
Federal Trade Commission
General Services Administration
Interior, Department of the
International Trade Commission
Labor, Department of

Library of Congress
Maritime Administration
   (Transportation)
Merit Systems Protection Board
National Highway Traffic Safety
   Administration **(Transportation)**
National Labor Relations Board
Navy **(Defense)**
Office of Attorney Personnel
   Management **(Justice)**
Office of the Secretary **(Commerce)**
   (Health and Human Services)
Office of the Solicitor **(Labor)**
Office of Thrift Supervision
   (Treasury)
Patent and Trademark Office
   (Commerce)
Securities and Exchange
   Commission
Small Business Administration
State, Department of
Transportation, Department of
Commission on Civil Rights
U.S. Postal Service
Veterans Affairs, Department of

LAW ENFORCEMENT
Bureau of Export Administration
   (Commerce)
Bureau of Prisons **(Justice)**
Federal Law Enforcement Training
   Center **(Treasury)**
Justice, Department of
Navy **(Defense)**
Office of Inspector General
   **(Commerce) (Health and
   Human Services) (Labor)**
Secret Service **(Treasury)**
U.S. Customs Service **(Treasury)**

LIBERAL ARTS
Administrative Office of the U.S.
   Courts
Agriculture, Department of
Bureau of Indian Affairs **(Interior)**

Bureau of Land Management
   (Interior)
Consumer Product Safety
   Commission
Education, Department of
Federal Retirement Thrift
   Investment Board
General Services Administration
Health Care Financing
   Administration **(Health and
   Human Services)**
Interior, Department of the
Justice, Department of
National Highway Traffic Safety
   Administration **(Transportation)**
National Park Service **(Interior)**
National Science Foundation
Navy **(Defense)**
Office of the Secretary **(Commerce)**
Patent and Trademark Office
   (Commerce)
Research and Special Programs
   Administration **(Transportation)**
Savings Bonds Division **(Treasury)**
Transportation, Department of
U.S. Customs Service **(Treasury)**
U.S. Fish and Wildlife Service
   (Interior)

LIBRARY SCIENCE
Army Material Command **(Defense)**
Executive Office of the President
Government Printing Office
International Trade Commission
Library of Congress
National Technical Information
   Service **(Commerce)**
Navy **(Defense)**
Patent and Trademark Office
   (Commerce)
Smithsonian Institution
Veterans Affairs, Department of

LIFE SCIENCES
Drug Enforcement Administration
   (Justice)

LINGUISTICS
National Endowment for the
    Humanities

LITERATURE
Labor, Department of
National Endowment for the
    Humanities

LOGISTICS MANAGEMENT
Defense Mapping Agency **(Defense)**
Navy **(Defense)**
U.S. Customs Service **(Treasury)**

MANAGEMENT
Bureau of Export Administration
    (Commerce)
Economic Affairs **(Commerce)**
Federal Trade Commission
State, Department of

**MANAGEMENT
    INFORMATION SYSTEMS**
Board of Governors of the Federal
    Reserve System
Defense Intelligence Agency
    (Defense)
Defense Mapping Agency **(Defense)**
Financial Management Service
    (Treasury)
General Accounting Office
Health Care Financing
    Administration **(Health and
    Human Services)**
Office of Personnel Management
Office of Thrift Supervision
    (Treasury)

MANUAL ARTS THERAPY
Veterans Affairs, Department of

MARITIME STUDIES
Drug Enforcement Administration
    (Justice)

MARKETING
Bureau of Export Administration
    (Commerce)
Federal Deposit Insurance
    Corporation
Federal Retirement Thrift
    Investment Board
International Trade Administration
    (Commerce)
International Trade Commission
Minority Business Development
    Agency **(Commerce)**
National Technical Information
    Service **(Commerce)**
Navy **(Defense)**
Savings Bonds Division **(Treasury)**
Travel and Tourism Administration
    (Commerce)
U.S. Mint **(Treasury)**

MATERIALS ENGINEERING
National Institute of Standards and
    Technology **(Commerce)**
Navy **(Defense)**
Nuclear Regulatory Commission

MATHEMATICS
Army Military District of
    Washington **(Defense)**
Bureau of Labor Statistics **(Labor)**
Defense Logistics Agency **(Defense)**
Defense Mapping Agency **(Defense)**
Drug Enforcement Administration
    (Justice)
Economics Management Staff
    (Agriculture)
Employment and Training
    Administration **(Labor)**
Health Care Financing
    Administration **(Health and
    Human Services)**
Justice, Department of
Library of Congress
National Aeronautics and Space
    Administration

National Highway Traffic Safety
Administration (**Transportation**)
National Institute of Standards and
Technology (**Commerce**)
National Oceanic and Atmospheric
Administration (**Commerce**)
National Security Agency
National Technical Information
Service (**Commerce**)
Navy (**Defense**)
U.S. Customs Service (**Treasury**)

MECHANICAL ENGINEERING
Army Corps of Engineers (**Defense**)
Army Material Command (**Defense**)
Bureau of Engraving and Printing
(**Treasury**)
Drug Enforcement Administration
(**Justice**)
Energy, Department of
Federal Aviation Administration
General Services Administration
International Trade Commission
National Aeronautics and Space
Administration
National Institute of Standards and
Technology (**Commerce**)
Navy (**Defense**)
Nuclear Regulatory Commission
Patent and Trademark Office
(**Commerce**)
Tennessee Valley Authority
U.S. Postal Service

**MEDICAL RECORDS
TECHNOLOGY**
Navy (**Defense**)

MEDICAL TECHNOLOGY
Navy (**Defense**)
Veterans Affairs, Department of

MEDICINE
Agency for Toxic Substances and
Disease Registry (**Health and
Human Services**)

Alcohol, Drug Abuse and Mental
Health Administration (**Health
and Human Services**)
Bureau of Prisons (**Justice**)
Food and Drug Administration
(**Health and Human Services**)
Indian Health Service (**Health and
Human Services**)
National Institutes of Health (**Health
and Human Services**)
Navy (**Defense**)

METALLURGY
International Trade Commission
National Institute of Standards and
Technology (**Commerce**)
Navy (**Defense**)
Nuclear Regulatory Commission

METEOROLOGY
Defense Mapping Agency (**Defense**)
National Oceanic and Atmospheric
Administration (**Commerce**)

MICROBIAL GENETICS
Agricultural Research Service
(**Agriculture**)

MICROBIOLOGY
Animal and Plant Health Inspection
Service (**Agriculture**)
Agricultural Research Service
(**Agriculture**)
Food Safety and Inspection Service
(**Agriculture**)
Navy (**Defense**)
Patent and Trademark Office
(**Commerce**)
Veterans Affairs, Department of

MILITARY SCIENCE
Drug Enforcement Administration
(**Justice**)
Federal Emergency Management
Agency

Navy (**Defense**)
U.S. Customs Service (**Treasury**)

MINERAL ECONOMICS
International Trade Commission

MOLECULAR BIOLOGY
Agricultural Research Service
   (**Agriculture**)

**NATURAL RESOURCE
   MANAGEMENT**
Army Corps of Engineers (**Defense**)

NAUTICAL SCIENCE
Defense Mapping Agency (**Defense**)

NAVAL ARCHITECTURE
Maritime Administration
   (**Transportation**)

NAVAL ENGINEERING
Navy (**Defense**)

NAVIGATION
Defense Mapping Agency (**Defense**)

NEAR EASTERN LANGUAGES
National Security Agency

NUCLEAR ENGINEERING
Energy, Department of
Navy (**Defense**)
Nuclear Regulatory Commission
Tennessee Valley Authority

**NURSING (PRACTICAL,
   VOCATIONAL)**
Navy (**Defense**)

NURSING (PROFESSIONAL)
Bureau of Prisons (**Justice**)
Government Printing Office
Indian Health Service (**Health and
   Human Services**)

National Institutes of Health (**Health
   and Human Services**)
Navy (**Defense**)
Veterans Affairs, Department of

NUTRITION
Food and Nutrition Service
   (**Agriculture**)
Veterans Affairs, Department of

**OCCUPATIONAL HEALTH
   MANAGEMENT**
Navy (**Defense**)

OCCUPATIONAL THERAPY
Veterans Affairs, Department of

OCEAN ENGINEERING
Navy (**Defense**)
OCEANOGRAPHY (GENERAL,
   GEOLOGICAL, PHYSICAL)
Defense Mapping Agency (**Defense**)
National Oceanic and Atmospheric
   Administration (**Commerce**)
Navy (**Defense**)

OPERATIONS RESEARCH
Energy, Department of

ORTHOTICS
Veterans Affairs, Department of

PAPER CONSERVATION
National Archives and Records
   Administration

PARALEGAL STUDIES
Executive Office for U.S. Attorneys
   (**Justice**)
Federal Trade Commission
Justice, Department of

**PARK AND RECREATION
   MANAGEMENT**
Army Corps of Engineers

PERSONNEL (HUMAN RESOURCES MANAGEMENT, PERSONNEL ADMINISTRATION, PERSONNEL MANAGEMENT)
Army Finance and Accounting Center (**Justice**)
Financial Management Service (**Treasury**)
National Labor Relations Board
Navy (**Defense**)
Office of Personnel Management
Small Business Administration
U.S. Customs Service (**Treasury**)
U.S. Marshals Service (**Justice**)

PHARMACOLOGY
Drug Enforcement Administration (**Justice**)
Environmental Protection Agency

PHARMACY
Drug Enforcement Administration (**Justice**)
Navy (**Defense**)
Veterans Affairs, Department of

PHILOSOPHY
National Endowment for the Humanities

PHOTO GRAMMETRY
Defense Mapping Agency (**Defense**)

PHOTO INTERPRETATION
Defense Mapping Agency (**Defense**)

PHOTOGRAPHY
Drug Enforcement Administration (**Justice**)
Federal Bureau of Investigation (**Justice**)

PHYSICAL EDUCATION
Veterans Affairs, Department of

PHYSICAL SCIENCES
Bureau of Land Management (**Interior**)
Bureau of Mines (**Interior**)
Bureau of Reclamation (**Interior**)
Defense Logistics Agency (**Defense**)
Drug Enforcement Administration (**Justice**)
Environmental Protection Agency
Library of Congress
National Institute of Standards and Technology (**Commerce**)
National Park Service (**Interior**)
Navy (**Defense**)
U.S. Customs Service (**Treasury**)
U.S. Geological Survey (**Interior**)

PHYSICAL THERAPY
Veterans Affairs, Department of

PHYSICS
Defense Mapping Agency (**Defense**)
Federal Bureau of Investigation (**Justice**)
National Aeronautics and Space Administration
National Archives and Records Administration
National Institute of Standards and Technology (**Commerce**)
National Oceanic and Atmospheric Administration (**Commerce**)
Navy (**Defense**)
Patent and Trademark Office (**Commerce**)
State, Department of

PLANT PATHOLOGY
Animal and Plant Health Inspection Service (**Agriculture**)
Forest Service (**Agriculture**)

PLANT PHYSIOLOGY
Agricultural Research Service
  (**Agriculture**)

POLICE SCIENCE (POLICE ADMINISTRATION)
Federal Law Enforcement Training
  Center (**Treasury**)
Navy (**Defense**)
U.S. Customs Service (**Treasury**)
U.S. Marshals Service (**Justice**)

POLISH
Federal Bureau of Investigation
  (**Justice**)

POLITICAL SCIENCE
Agriculture, Department of
Defense Logistics Agency (**Defense**)
Drug Enforcement Administration
  (**Justice**)
Education, Department of
Environmental Protection Agency
Federal Trade Commission
General Accounting Office
Justice, Department of
Library of Congress
National Archives and Records
  Administration
National Labor Relations Board
Navy (**Defense**)
Small Business Administration
U.S. Customs Service (**Treasury**)
U.S. Information Agency

PORTUGUESE
Drug Enforcement Agency (**Justice**)

POULTRY SCIENCE
Agricultural Marketing Service
  (**Agriculture**)

PRINTING MANAGEMENT
Government Printing Office

PROCUREMENT
Financial Management Service
  (**Treasury**)

PRODUCTION MANAGEMENT
Navy (**Defense**)

PSYCHIATRY
Bureau of Prisons (**Justice**)

PROGRAM ANALYSIS
Energy, Department of

PROSTHETICS
Veterans Affairs, Department of

PSYCHOLOGY
Alcohol, Drug Abuse and Mental
  Health Administration (**Health
  and Human Services**)
Army Finance and Accounting
  Center (**Defense**)
Navy (**Defense**)
Small Business Administration
U.S. Customs Service (**Treasury**)
U.S. Postal Service
Veterans Affairs, Department of

PUBLIC ADMINISTRATION
Army Finance and Accounting
  Center (**Defense**)
Bureau of Export Administration
  (**Commerce**)
Defense Logistics Agency (**Defense**)
Environmental Protection Agency
Executive Office of the President
Federal Emergency Management
  Agency
Federal Trade Commission
General Accounting Office
General Services Administration
Health Care Financing
  Administration (**Health and
  Human Services**)

Housing and Urban Development,
    Department of
National Labor Relations Board
National Science Foundation
Navy **(Defense)**
Office of Inspector General
    (Transportation)
Office of Personnel Management
Research and Special Programs
    Administration **(Transportation)**
Selective Service System
Small Business Administration
Transportation, Department of
Urban Mass Transportation
    Administration **(Transportation)**
U.S. Customs Service **(Treasury)**
U.S. Marshals Service **(Justice)**

PUBLIC AFFAIRS
Agriculture, Department of

PUBLIC HEALTH
Health Care Financing
    Administration **(Health and
    Human Services)**
U.S. Customs Service **(Treasury)**

PUBLIC POLICY
Executive Office of the President
Library of Congress
Minority Business Development
    Agency **(Commerce)**

PUSHTU
Drug Enforcement Administration
    (Justice)

PUBLIC UTILITIES
Energy, Department of

PURCHASING
Navy **(Defense)**

RADIO AND TELEVISION
Voice of America **(U.S.
    Information Agency)**

RADIO TELEPHONY
State, Department of

**RANGE CONSERVATION
    (RANGE MANAGEMENT)**
Forest Service **(Agriculture)**
Soil Conservation Service
    (Agriculture)

RECREATION THERAPY
Veterans Affairs, Department of

REMOTE SENSING
Defense Intelligence Agency
    (Defense)
Defense Mapping Agency **(Defense)**

RESPIRATORY THERAPY
Navy **(Defense)**
Veterans Affairs, Department of

RUSSIAN
Federal Bureau of Investigation
    (Justice)

SAFETY ENGINEERING
Navy **(Defense)**

**SCIENCE (ANY SCIENCE,
    GENERAL SCIENCE)**
Agency for Toxic Substances and
    Disease Registry **(Health and
    Human Services)**
Agriculture, Department of
Centers for Disease Control **(Health
    and Human Services)**
Food and Drug Administration
    (Health and Human Services)
Minerals Management Service
    (Interior)
National Institutes of Health **(Health
    and Human Services)**
National Science Foundation
Smithsonian Institution
State, Department of

SECRETARIAL STUDIES (SECRETARIAL SCIENCE)

Federal Emergency Management Agency

Federal Trade Commission

Navy **(Defense)**

SECURITY ADMINISTRATION

Defense Mapping Agency **(Defense)**

Energy, Department of

SLAVIC LANGUAGES

National Security Agency **(Defense)**

SOCIAL SCIENCE

Commission on Civil Rights

Employment and Training Administration **(Labor)**

General Accounting Office

Health Care Financing Administration **(Health and Human Services)**

Library of Congress

National Endowment for the Humanities

Office of Human Development Services **(Health and Human Services)**

Office of Justice Programs **(Justice)**

SOCIAL WORK

Alcohol, Drug Abuse and Mental Health Administration **(Health and Human Services)**

Bureau of Indian Affairs **(Interior)**

Bureau of Prisons **(Justice)**

Navy **(Defense)**

Veterans Affairs, Department of

SOCIOLOGY

Agriculture, Department of

Alcohol, Drug Abuse and Mental Health Administration **(Health and Human Services)**

Drug Enforcement Administration **(Justice)**

Environmental Protection Agency

U.S. Customs Service **(Treasury)**

U.S. Information Agency

SOIL SCIENCE (SOIL CONSERVATION)

Defense Mapping Agency **(Defense)**

Forest Service **(Agriculture)**

Soil Conservation Service **(Agriculture)**

SPACE SCIENCE

Navy **(Defense)**

SPANISH

Drug Enforcement Administration **(Justice)**

Federal Bureau of Investigation **(Justice)**

SPEECH PATHOLOGY

Veterans Affairs, Department of

STATISTICS

Army Military District of Washington **(Defense)**

Bureau of the Census **(Commerce)**

Bureau of Economic Analysis **(Commerce)**

Bureau of Labor Statistics **(Labor)**

Commission on Civil Rights

Defense Logistics Agency **(Defense)**

Economics Management Staff **(Agriculture)**

Executive Office of the President

Office of Justice Programs **(Justice)**

Travel and Tourism Administration **(Commerce)**

U.S. Customs Service **(Treasury)**

Veterans Affairs, Department of

SYSTEMS MANAGEMENT

State, Department of

SURVEYING
Defense Mapping Agency **(Defense)**

TECHNICAL WRITING
Navy **(Defense)**

TELECOMMUNICATIONS
U.S. Customs Service **(Treasury)**

TEXTILE TECHNOLOGY
International Trade Commission

TOXICOLOGY
Drug Enforcement Administration
  (Justice)

TRANSPORTATION
Military Traffic Management
  Command **(Defense)**
Urban Mass Transportation
  Administration **(Transportation)**

**TRANSPORTATION
  ENGINEERING**
Federal Highway Administration
  (Transportation)

TV PRODUCTION
U.S. Information Agency

URBAN PLANNING
Federal Emergency Management
  Agency

URDU
Drug Enforcement Administration
  (Justice)

VETERINARY MEDICINE
Food and Drug Administration
  (Health and Human Services)
Food Safety and Inspection Service
  (Agriculture)

VETERINARY SCIENCE
Animal and Plant Health Inspection
  Service **(Agriculture)**

WILDLIFE BIOLOGY
Forest Service **(Agriculture)**

GLOSSARY

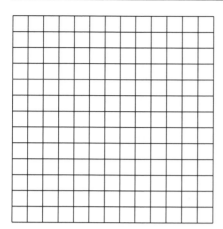

College Placement Annual: A book, published by the College Placement Council, that gives current information about government and nongovernment hiring plans. It is available through college placement offices.

Dictionary of Occupational Titles: Published by the government, it provides information on hundreds of jobs. It assigns each occupation a number, which classifies the job by the type of work, required training, physical demands, and working conditions.

Federal Employees Retirement System: The government retirement program, which has three parts—a Basic Benefit Plan, Social Security, and a Thrift Saving Plan.

Federal Job Information Centers: The regional and local offices of the Office of Personnel Management. They have all federal job announcements and application forms.

Federal Yellow Book: A directory to government offices, arranged by agency; published by the Washington Monitor Inc.

General Schedule: The federal government's General Schedule pay system has 15 grade levels, encompassing about 450 white-collar occupations. See also Wage Board Schedule.

Job Banks: Run by the Job Service Offices, they usually list state and local job announcements as well as other openings.

Job Service Office: The state equivalent of the Federal Job Information Center.

Merit Systems Protection Board: Fired government workers may appeal to this body.

Occupational Group: The Personnel Classification System divides white-collar federal jobs into 22 Occupational Groups. Each group has a code indicating the pay system, Occupational Group number, and title.

Occupational Outlook Handbook: Published by the government, it describes about 250 occupations, both government- and nongovernment-related, in detail.

Office of Personnel Management: The OPM manages employment policy for more than half the civil service. It defines the qualifications required for different occupations, develops, gives, and grades written exams, refers applicants to agencies with openings, and publicizes job openings.

Qualification Standards for White-Collar Positions Under the General Schedule: Also known as Handbook X-118, it is published by the Office of Personnel Management. It gives the name of the occupation, its series number, and the requirements for entering jobs at different salary levels. There is a companion manual, X-118A, for blue-collar jobs.

SF-171: The Application for Federal Employment, Standard Form 171, is required for every federal employees's personnel file. The four-page form is available at Federal Job Information Centers and many federal agencies' personnel offices, post offices, libraries and Job Service Offices.

U.S. Government Manual: Published annually by the General Services Administration, Office of the Federal Register, it contains names, addresses, telephone numbers, and descriptions of every federal agency.

Wage Board Schedule: The federal government's pay system for blue-collar workers. The 15 degrees of the pay scale are adjusted for local costs of living.

Washington Information Directory: Published by Congressional Quarterly, its information on government offices is arranged by subject.

X-118: See Qualification Standards for White-Collar Positions Under the General Schedule.